# All Media Are Social

From TV to smartphone apps to movies to newspapers, mass media are nearly omnipresent in contemporary life and act as a powerful social institution. In this introduction to media sociology, Lindner and Barnard encourage readers to think critically about the power of big media companies, state-media relations, new developments in journalism, representations of race, class, gender, and sexuality in media, and what social media may or may not be doing to our brains, among other topics. Each chapter explores pressing questions about media by carefully excavating the results of classic and contemporary social scientific studies. The authors bring these findings to life with anecdotes and examples ripped from headlines and social media newsfeeds. By synthesizing research on new media and traditional media, entertainment media and news, quantitative and qualitative studies, *All Media Are Social* offers a succinct and accessibly-written analysis of both enduring patterns and some of the newest developments in mass media. With strong emphases on theory and methods, Lindner and Barnard provide students and general readers alike with the tools to better understand the ever-changing media landscape.

**Andrew M. Lindner** is Associate Professor of Sociology at Skidmore College in Saratoga Springs, NY. He studies the intersection of culture, mass media, and politics. His research has appeared in publications including New Media & Society, Social Problems, and Information, Communication, & Society.

**Stephen R. Barnard** is Associate Professor at St. Lawrence University in Canton, NY. His research and teaching focus on the role media and communication technologies play in relations of power, practice, and democracy. He is author of *Citizens at the Gates: Twitter, Networked Publics, and the Transformation of American Journalism*.

# Sociology Re-Wired

Edited by Jodi O'Brien and Marcus Hunter
*Seattle University and University of California, Los Angeles*

Sociology Re-Wired captures this combustible moment in American and global societies with new books that innovate and re-configure social and political issues. This hybrid series publishes timely, relevant, original research and textbooks that address significant social issues informed by critical race theory, Black feminism and Queer Studies traditions. Series books are written in a publicly accessible, multi-vocal style broadening the reach and impact of significant scholarly contributions beyond traditional academic audiences.

Some titles published in this series were published under an earlier series name and a different editorship.

**Published:**

*Social Statistics: Managing Data, Conducting Analyses, Presenting Results, Third Edition* by Thomas J. Linneman

*Who Lives, Who Dies, Who Decides?: Abortion, Assisted Dying, Capital Punishment, and Torture, Third Edition* by Sheldon Ekland-Olson

*Caged Women: Incarceration, Representation, & Media* edited by Shirley A. Jackson and Laurie L. Gordy

*The New Black Sociologists: Historical and Contemporary Perspectives* edited by Marcus A. Hunter

*The Black Circuit: Race, Performance, and Spectatorship in Black Popular Theatre,* by Rashida Z. Shaw McMahon

*All Media Are Social: Sociological Perspectives on Mass Media* by Andrew M. Lindner and Stephen R. Barnard

# All Media Are Social

## Sociological Perspectives on Mass Media

Andrew M. Lindner and
Stephen R. Barnard

Routledge
Taylor & Francis Group

NEW YORK AND LONDON

First published 2020
by Routledge
52 Vanderbilt Avenue, New York, NY 10017

and by Routledge
2 Park Square, Milton Park, Abingdon, Oxon, OX14 4RN

*Routledge is an imprint of the Taylor & Francis Group, an Informa business*

*Library of Congress Cataloging-in-Publication Data*
A catalog record for this title has been requested

ISBN: 978-0-415-74953-4 (hbk)
ISBN: 978-0-415-74954-1 (pbk)
ISBN: 978-1-315-79605-5 (ebk)

Typeset in Bembo
by Swales & Willis, Exeter, Devon, UK

For Beth
     -A.L.

For Grumps
     -S.B.

# Contents

*Illustrations*                                                    ix
*Acknowledgements*                                                 xi

**SECTION 1**
**Overview**                                                        1

1  All Media Are Social                                             3
2  Theorizing the Media                                            11

**SECTION 2**
**Production**                                                     27

3  Who Pays for It?                                                29
4  In the Hands of a Few                                           43
5  Big Brother Knows You're Watching                               61
6  The Makers and the Breakers                                     76

**SECTION 3**
**Content**                                                       91

7  Fear and Loathing on Cable News                                93
8  Doing Gender and Sexuality in Media                           113
9  Unequal Images in an Unequal Age                              126

**SECTION 4**
## Audiences 143

10  Are We Robots? 145

11  Or Are We Rebels? 158

*Recommended Resources for All Media Are Social* 178
*Index* 185

# Illustrations

## Figures

| | | |
|---|---|---|
| 1.1 | Average Media Use by U.S. Adults, 2017 | 3 |
| 2.1 | The Cultural Diamond | 13 |
| 2.2 | Bourdieu's Journalistic Field | 18 |
| 2.3 | Culture Industry System | 19 |
| 3.1 | Top Newspapers by Circulation | 30 |
| 3.2 | Online Advertising Revenues, 2003–2016 | 34 |
| 3.3 | Federal Appropriations for the CPB, 1969–2018 | 39 |
| 4.1 | Vertical vs. Horizontal Integration | 45 |
| 5.1 | FCC Offices in Washington, D.C. | 64 |
| 5.2 | Public Opinion Regarding Net Neutrality, 2017 | 67 |
| 6.1 | *The New York Times* Newsroom in September 1942 | 83 |
| 6.2 | *CNN* Newsroom in November 2011 | 83 |
| 7.1 | Ideological Consistency by Party, 2017 | 96 |
| 7.2 | Americans' Confidence in Mass Media | 97 |
| 8.1 | Numerical Representations of Women in Media Content | 115 |
| 8.2 | Numerical Representations of Women as Media Workers | 115 |
| 9.1 | Director's Race for Films by Top Hollywood Film Distributors | 128 |
| 9.2 | Dev (Aziz Ansari) Auditioning for the Role of a Cab Driver in *Master of None* | 129 |
| 9.3 | #IfTheyGunnedMeDown Image by @CapriSun_Rell | 133 |
| 10.1 | John F. Kennedy and Richard Nixon after Their First Televised Debate | 148 |
| 10.2a & b | Public Perception vs. Reality of Crime, 1993–2017 | 150 |
| 11.1 | The Yes Men's Satirical Version of *The New York Times* | 159 |

11.2   Google Searches for "Media Bias," 2004–2019          160
11.3   Screenshot of Wikipedia during the Stop SOPA
       Blackout                                             169
11.4   Transparency Rankings of Companies by Category       172

## Table

4.1   Concentration within Mass Media Industries           49

# Acknowledgements

In July of 1964, Paul McCartney strummed out the chords for an uptempo new tune on a jangly acoustic guitar. With its warm sound in D major and the optimistic chorus of "we can work it out," the song exemplifies McCartney's sunny disposition and pop sensibility. When McCartney brought his early draft to the studio, John Lennon proposed adding a darker section in B minor with the bleak lyric, "life is very short." The resulting song, "We Can Work It Out," presents a study of contrasts between Vaudeville versions of cheery Paul and cynical John. But, somehow, the song comes across not as disjointed, but as a cohesive whole that is greater than the sum of its parts.

Neither of the two authors of this book is a lyrical visionary like Lennon nor has the melodic genius of McCartney. Still, like many pairs of collaborators, we brought different abilities and perspectives to the task of writing this book – a qualitative researcher's attention to meaning, a quantoid's obsession with measurement. It is our hope that the book strikes the reader as a harmonious text, but what is certainly true is that it is a better book than either of us could have written alone. For this reason, we first want to acknowledge our appreciation of each other's contributions in researching, writing, and re-writing this book.

There is another Beatles song that is so frequently mentioned in book acknowledgments sections as to be a cliché. We won't mention it. However, this book came to be with an extraordinary amount of support from our colleagues, family, and friends. Sociologist, champion of public sociology, and professional good guy, Doug Hartmann, initiated the conversations that led to this project. Steve Rutter, Social Sciences Publisher for Routledge, supported the book in its early days, even when it ended up taking much longer than expected. Finally, Dean Birkenkamp, senior editor at Routledge, has shepherded the book to publication. Together, we thank Doug, Steve, and Dean for supporting this project. Additionally, we extend our deep appreciation to the many academic colleagues whose intellectual contributions are reflected in the pages of this book. Lend us your ears and we'll try not to sing out of key.

If the insight of stratification is sociology's primary contribution to the world, as some have argued, I'd have to be a real ingrate to spend my days teaching sociology and not recognize the immense advantages I have had in this life. That starts with my parents, Eileen and John Lindner, who have supported me in innumerable ways, but who also passed on to me their love of learning and passion for justice. I have also been the beneficiary of the love and support of my brother, Peter Lindner, and his family, as well as the extended Van Velsor family. For all of this, I am deeply and forever grateful. I also feel lucky to have a stupendous group of friends and colleagues who have shown an ongoing solidarity and at least a partial willingness to hear out the bad first version of my ideas. Thank you to Dan Hawkins, Jason Houle, Matthew Marlay, Ed Walker, Ryan Larson, Jenni Mueller, Amon Emeka, Dominique Vuvan, Susan Walzer, and many others. In writing this book, I have been grateful for thoughtful and critical feedback on the proposal and chapter drafts from John Brueggemann, Matthew Lindholm, Andreas Rekdal, and Brianna Cochran. At the risk of sounding terribly maudlin, the next round's on me. Finally, and most importantly, I thank my wife and best friend, Beth Van Velsor, for your support, encouragement, and love across nearly two decades, six states, and two continents.

                                                          - Andrew M. Lindner


I am grateful for my family and friends who have, each in their own way, made my life better and more enjoyable. First and foremost, thanks to my partner Anna, and our children, Ryan and Everett, who bring me joy and a sense of purpose every day. My parents, grandparents, and many aunts and uncles have done so much to foster my intellectual curiosity and compassion over the years, and I am eternally thankful. So too have my friends and colleagues, albeit a bit later. My dear friend Nathan Morehouse has, in his unique way, helped me grapple with many of life's great questions while also making sure I remember to laugh. David Criger has played a remarkably similar role in my life, yet has also given generously of his time to this book by reading and offering detailed comments on early drafts of multiple chapters. As the aphorism goes, I hope to give as good as I get. Thanks, also, to my longtime mentor, Victoria Johnson, for introducing me to media sociology and inspiring me to make a contribution to the field. I will never forget how I felt when she told me—then a young graduate student lamenting the lack of sociological commitment to the study of media—that I might help re-awaken it. I hope I won't forget how I feel at the time of this writing—inspired by the flurry of exciting scholarship and humbled that, with this book and a slew of others, we appear to be on our way.

                                                          - Stephen R. Barnard

# Section 1

# Overview

# Chapter 1

# All Media Are Social

These days, we encounter media in the form of our Facebook feed on smartphones while we eat breakfast, on our laptops throughout the day, and on podcasts as we fall asleep. American adults spend an average of 12 hours per day using various forms of media (see Figure 1.1). As sociologist Todd Gitlin has noted, "In a society that fancies itself the freest ever, spending time with communications machinery is the main use to which we have put our freedom."[1] Media are the primary means by which we learn the decisions our politicians make, but mass media play a role in socializing us about how we ought to dress, what we ought to

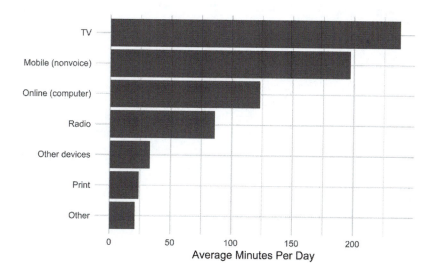

*Figure 1.1* Average Media Use by U.S. Adults, 2017
[Source: Statista]

eat, and how we see ourselves in relation to others. In other words, the media—the sum total of the organizations and the people who work for them, the users, and creators, the technology undergirding it all—are an incredibly important social institution in contemporary society. Media are essential to socialization, identity-construction, but also the dissemination of news in democratic societies. This book explores the landscape of the diverse field of media sociology. In this chapter, we will attempt to better understand both of those terms ("media" and "sociology") and what it means to think about media in a sociological way.

## All Media

Given how central a role media play in our lives, it is not surprising that the term, "media," has taken on a variety of different meanings. Technically speaking, "media" is the plural of the word "medium" (i.e., "mediums"). According to the Oxford English Dictionary, "media" is defined as "the main means of mass communication, *esp.* newspapers, radio, and television, regarded collectively; the reporters, journalists, etc. working for organizations engaged in such communication."[2] By this definition, "media" include technological platforms like books, social media web sites, TV, computers, and smartphones, but also specific TV shows, apps, and movies as well as the people who contribute to making these things.

*Black Panther* is an example of media. So are *The Washington Post* and Reddit.com. So are all the books in your local library and your favorite fitness tracking app. Journalists, coders working for Google, and the Hollywood movie stars are all members of the media. This one word means all of those different things. As the mildly pedantic title of this book suggests, the grammatically correct way of conjugating the word "media" is "the media are" because media are plural.

Nonetheless, language has a sneaky way of changing when the grammatical purists and dictionary writers aren't looking. Occasionally, students will think of media as referring to just the digital tools that facilitate social interaction like text messaging apps, Snapchat, Instagram, Facebook, and Twitter. Since the late-2000s, we have tended to refer to these web sites and apps as "social media" because they allow us to engage in some forms of mediated social interaction. But the truth is that social media are just one type of media and all forms of media, including ones that feel solitary, have profoundly social dimensions. For example, reading a book can connect you with the experiences of people in very different places and points in time, deepening empathy and understanding, even if you are sitting in a room by yourself. Hence, the title of this book and this chapter, *All Media Are Social.*

Another more narrow use of the term comes from the realm of politics, in which "the media" is sometimes used to refer to mainstream news outlets, journalists, and other members of the press. Ironically, in this usage, the definite article ("the") in front of the word "media" seems to imply a singular entity—not just any media, it's *the* media. It may be obvious to point out, but news organizations like CNN and *The Wall Street Journal* (*WSJ*), reporters like Maggie Haberman and Bob Woodward, and pundits like Sean Hannity and Chris Matthews are most certainly not a single entity. But, perhaps, this shortcut reflects a sense that "the media" are a sort of chatty, homogeneous social club with shared cultural and ideological assumptions. Therefore, it is not uncommon to see grammatically incorrect claims that "the media is" one thing or another.

Todd Gitlin also sees the grammatical error ("the media is") as linked to the view that media are monolithic, but argues that it extends far beyond just politics. Gitlin claims that our sense of "the media" as a singular entity stems from a deep homogeneity across entertainment media, news media, the Internet, TV, etc. As he writes, "something feels uniform—a relentless pace, a pattern of interruption, a pressure toward unseriousness, a readiness for sensation, and anticipation of the next new thing."[3] While Gitlin's interpretation is both critical and expansive, the underlying point is that part of the reason that people sense a unity across all the various types of media is because they tend to share cultural and aesthetic qualities and often links of ownership and shared financial incentive.

This observation should not come as a surprise. The media *are* many things, but the media *is* a social institution. Just as the family is an institution, but individual families are different from each other in many ways, so, too, the media are an institution with norms that constrain the action of individual actors and organizations, but there are also real differences across various types of media. Media sociologists are interested in all the different component parts that make up "the media," including different technologies, organizations, media workers, ownership models, cultures, and the ways that audiences respond to and are affected by media.

## Are Social

What does it mean to study media sociologically? Many different disciplines, including communications, media studies, technology studies, law, historians, and literary studies, are interested in examining media. Some of these disciplines, like literary studies, are fundamentally humanistic in nature. They tend to approach a given media artifact, say, Jordan Peele's 2017 horror movie *Get Out* and interpret the various meanings in this "text." For example, one fairly apparent reading of that movie is that it acts as an allegory for race relations in the contemporary U.S. However, scholars with differing emphases might read the text for its innovation in the horror genre, its gender politics, and so on.

Unlike these humanist disciplines, sociology is a social science, meaning we use systematic methods to collect various forms of data. In sociology, these data could be quantitative (e.g., surveys, experiments, count-based content analyses, etc.) or qualitative (e.g., interviews, ethnography, observation, etc.). While some sociologists specialize in developing social theory that informs and is reinforced by empirical findings, one characteristic that separates sociologists from some disciplines studying media is that we rely on social scientific methods to answer questions.

Substantively, sociology attempts to understand the dynamic relationship between individuals and society.[4] How do *social structures*, or stable patterns of routines and relationships organized through institutions and individuals within a society, enable or constrain individual behavior? How do individuals use their *agency* or free will to reinforce or change features of society? Media sociology tries to ask these questions within the context of the social institution of mass media. For example, an important question in media sociology involves the underrepresentation of women and people of color in Hollywood movies (more on that in chapters 8 and 9). Many people see underrepresentation as a problem, but who actually has power over deciding who stars in movies? Many casting agents and even studio executives, who seem pretty powerful, claim they would like to have more diverse casts, but feel constrained by the structure of a capitalist marketplace and audience preferences.[5] But if it is the system to blame, where did that system come from? What continues to hold it in place? And how can things change?

The deeper questions undergirding this example are about power. Who has it? When do they get to use it? Sociologists, in general, tend to be interested in how power works both through social structures, but also through *culture*. It's not just laws, job titles, access to resources, and other structures that constrain behavior. It also happens through social norms, cultural tastes and preferences, and *ideology*, or a system of beliefs people hold. For example, relatively few people even in a wealthy society like the U.S. earn most of their money from the stock market, so why does the nightly TV news broadcast give us a daily stock market report? There's no law saying they have to. Rather, it is reflective of an ideology that the overall well-being of major companies is important. For that reason, most journalists and producers working on these broadcasts probably feel unempowered to change it because there is a strong social norm to report what the Dow Jones did today. The point is that culture and structure are often linked and both exercise great power over how media work.

Even though structure and culture shape behavior in powerful ways, there is such a thing as taking an idea too far. In 2017, *The Atlantic* ran a story with the headline, "Have Smartphones Destroyed a Generation?"[6] This headline is a perfect example of *technological determinism* or the view that social outcomes stem directly from the introduction of new technologies. Smartphones are invented and, BOOM, a generation is destroyed. Media sociologists tend to be critical of such arguments for a few reasons. While new technologies can shape behavior, people also have agency. More importantly, as sociologists Jennifer Earl and Katrina Kimport argue, "[I]t is people's usage of technology—not technology itself—that can change social processes."[7] Rather than thinking of technology as determining some outcome, media sociologists increasingly think of technologies in terms of technological *affordances* or "the range of functions and constraints that an object provides."[8] For example, compared to a printed book, one affordance of e-reader devices is that the user can search for a particular word or phrase. We need not make the assumption that any outcome must occur simply because a technology offers particular affordances. Researchers have elaborated their theorizing of affordances by observing that people must perceive that an affordance exists in order to make use of it, and that technology's affordances may not be equally available to all users. For example, people with physical disabilities may lack the dexterity to make use of all affordances of touch-screen devices.[9] Viewed from this perspective, it is obvious that to the extent that young people's behavior is changing, it is probably not caused by the devices themselves, but by some of the ways that young people use them.

Media sociologists are not alone in asking questions about power, structure and agency, culture, and technological affordances. Many researchers in communications and media studies are interested in the same questions. Some of the most fruitful collaborations have come from researchers who collaborate across disciplinary lines. Moreover, many communications departments have incorporated more courses with a sociological perspective into their curriculum. But what makes a question about media inherently sociological is if it considers how structure, culture, and agency interact to place limits or create new opportunities for people.

Despite this shared focus, let's be clear about something: media sociology, like sociology in general, is a low-consensus field. Sociologists have ongoing debates about preferred methods, whether scientific objectivity is possible, whether scholar-activism is desirable, and how much evidence there is to support various claims. We, as the two authors of this book, have frequently disagreed about any number of questions within media sociology.

But this is a big tent book. In the coming chapters, we incorporate theoretical and empirical studies, qualitative and quantitative research, studies with a range of orientations regarding questions about objectivity and activism, and findings regarding both the U.S. and the wider global media system. We believe that one of sociology's great strengths as a discipline is the diversity of perspectives and methods we bring to bear on questions about society. None of which is to say that we ought to hold back on critique. Constructive critique, too, is an essential part of any healthy discipline. In this book, we aim to offer a broad overview of some of the most crucial sociological insights on media as well as some of the remaining unanswered questions and ongoing debates within media sociology.

## What this Book—Or any Other Book—Cannot Do Well

Books are a slow medium. That's partially for technological reasons. Compared to a tweet, which publishes instantly, it takes a lot of time to typeset the manuscript, print on paper, glue on the binding, and ship the physical book to a bookstore. But to avoid a purely technologically deterministic outlook, books are also slow for cultural reasons. Rarely do publishers print a 280 character or even a 500-word book. Rather, a book like this one contains about 70,000 words and it takes time to do the necessary research, write up drafts, and edit them. Our socially constructed expectations of what a book should be like make it a plodding process.

Because books are slow, there are some things they cannot do well. They cannot stay on top of the latest breaking news stories, technological innovations, or changes of policy. In Chapter 5, we describe the pendulum swing of policy over Net Neutrality. In the course of writing this book, we observed that swing happening in real time and we have no idea what the current policy will be by the time you are reading this. Similarly, the most popular media platforms and technologies are changing at an extraordinary pace. Just as blogging and early social media platforms like MySpace declined in the 2010s and gave way to Facebook and Twitter, so, too, it is quite possible that by the time you read this, the current forms of social media may have been replaced by augmented reality glasses (or something that we lack the foresight and creativity to imagine).

Still, books have some special affordances that have continued to make them valuable even as new technologies have emerged. Books are particularly well-suited for extended arguments and explaining big ideas. Books allow for the kind of complexity and nuance that requires a few hundred pages. They also encourage the reader to engage in a type of sustained attention that is not as easily achieved on a device that pops notifications up every 30 seconds.

With these affordances of the medium in mind, what we attempt to do in this book is to offer frameworks that conceptualize how the institution of mass media works. Readers can then use these frameworks to make sense of new developments in media as they occur. It is also true that there are some enduring conditions of mass media that have stayed constant since at least the mid-20th century and seem likely to continue. In such cases, the challenge for the reader is not to apply a well-established insight to the moment, but, instead, to stretch one's imagination to consider how things might change for the better.

## Organization of the Book

This book is organized into four sections. The first section, which includes this chapter and Chapter 2, offers an overview of media sociology and the prevailing theories in the field. The next three sections roughly match up with three broad levels of analysis in media sociology: production, content, and audiences.

In the Production section (chapters 3–6), we explore how economic and political structures as well as the cultural context affect media production. In Chapter 3, we consider how the various sources of funding for media (e.g., subscriptions, advertising, public-funding, etc.) shape the types of incentives media organizations have to produce certain types of content. In Chapter 4, we evaluate the debates over how concentrated media ownership grants extraordinary power to relatively few people and may serve to create less diverse media content. Then, in Chapter 5, we turn to exploring the role of governments in regulating and managing media. Lastly, Chapter 6 maps out the culture of media workers with a particular emphasis on the field of journalism.

The Content section (chapters 7–9) highlights research examining which topics and types of people are either represented or left out in various forms of mass media. Chapter 7 explores how news organizations cover politics and considers debates over issues like liberal bias in the news, the growth of partisan news outlets, and the role of new forms of media in politics like citizen journalism and social media. In Chapter 8, we explore representations of gender and sexuality in mass media, giving particular attention to entertainment media and rising concerns about gendertrollling online. Similarly, Chapter 9 covers representations of race and social class in media and how they often intersect.

Finally, in the Audiences section (chapters 10 and 11), we ask how media content affects people and how people push back against it. Chapter 10 examines the expansive body of research on how people use media and how media can shape what people think about and how they think about it. But lest we conclude that people are helpless in the face of mass media, Chapter 11 returns to the concept of agency and describes forms of resistance and activism to challenge media messages and systems of representation.

Every book involves choices. As the authors of this book, we attempt to offer an overview of the field that represents all three levels of analysis, rather than doing a deep dive on just one. The thought of how many important areas of research, intriguing sociological questions, and cool studies we have had to leave out of *All Media Are Social* weighs heavily on us. But we see this book as a starting point and as an invitation to media sociology. We hope that what you learn here will spark an interest that will lead you to read more in the field and conduct some research of your own.

## Notes

1 Gitlin, Todd. 2007. *Media Unlimited*. New York: Macmillan. P. 1.
2 Anon. 2018. "media, *n.*" *OED Online*. Oxford University Press. Retrieved December 10, 2018. Available at: http://dictionary.oed.com.
3 Ibid. p. 7.
4 For a review of core sociological concepts, see: Bruce, Steve. 2018. *Sociology: A Very Short Introduction*. Oxford, UK: Oxford University Press.
5 Bielby, William T. and Denise D. Bielby. 1994. "'All Hits Are Flukes': Institutionalized Decision Making and the Rhetoric of Network Prime-Time Program Development." *American Journal of Sociology* 99(5):1287–1313.
6 Twenge, Jean M. 2017. "Have Smartphones Destroyed a Generation?" *The Atlantic*, Sept. (www.theatlantic.com/magazine/archive/2017/09/has-the-smartphone-destroyed-a-generation/534198/).
7 Earl, Jennifer, and Katrina Kimport. 2011. *Digitally Enabled Social Change: Activism in the Internet age*. Cambridge, MA: MIT Press. p. 14.
8 Davis, Jenny L. and James B. Chouinard. 2016. "Theorizing Affordances: From Request to Refuse." *Bulletin of Science, Technology & Society* 36(4):241.
9 Ibid.

# Chapter 2

# Theorizing the Media

In this chapter, we will explore several important theories for understanding contemporary mass media. We will begin by learning about the "cultural diamond," a valuable analytical tool for organizing the theories we will encounter. Then, we will examine theories of media creation, theories of media representation, and theories of media reception—all of which will be essential in later chapters.

## The Trouble with Theory

What does it mean to theorize contemporary mass media? What are the prevailing theories of mass media? Those are difficult questions to answer for two reasons. First, sociologists in general mean very different things when we say "theory." In an important article, Gabriel Abend argues that there are nine different meanings to the word "theory" that sociologists use.[1] Here, we describe three types of "theory" that are important for understanding media. One type of theory is simply a generalized proposition about the relationship between two or more variables. For example, we might develop a theory of why TV reporters are less likely to challenge political authorities than newspaper reporters. It's not just a story about a few reporters in one town; it's generalized to reporters more widely. But it's not a particularly grand theory about society as a whole. Theories of the first type stick close to empirical observations.

Researchers offering generalized propositions rarely call themselves "theorists." People who do call themselves "theorists" or who "do theory" are usually engaged in a type of thinking more removed from concrete observations. As Abend argues, theorists like Karl Marx, Emile Durkheim, Max Weber, and more recent thinkers like Jurgen Habermas and Pierre Bourdieu are engaged in "'interpretations,' 'analyses,' 'critiques' … [that] involve the study of 'meaning.'" Such theorists are very concerned with laying out the precise logic of their theory and deal with larger ideas about how society works. Some elements of these theories may be testable, but they often contain broad historical or social claims that cannot be proven or disproven by one (or even many) studies.

A final type of theory is "an overall perspective from which one sees and interprets the world." Post-modernist theory, feminist theory, Marxist theory, and rational choice theory are all examples of guiding systems of ideas with embedded assumptions about the relationship between the individual and society, our capacity to know "truth," and the extent of conflict in society.[2] These assumptions run so deep that they are rarely overturned by the results of an empirical study.

Because thinkers writing about media are referring to different things when we say "theory," sometimes we end up talking past each other. At the same time, often scholars will tip their hat to each of these types of theory within a single study. As we consider various theories, we need to be attuned to the scope, assumptions, and connection to empirical observations of each.

The second reason it is difficult to draw up a list of media theories is that unlike, say, urban sociology or sociology of education, media sociology lacks a clear-cut canon and a prevailing theoretical tradition (or, even more fun, two dominant dueling theories). Instead, as Silvio Waisbord has noted, "media sociology remains an archipelago in the academic world," informed by thinkers, ideas, and studies in disciplines like communications, cultural studies, political science, and race and gender studies.[3] In part, that is because the topic of mass media isn't owned by sociology alone. A number of scholars have argued that sociology has the bad habit of parceling off our best ideas to other disciplines[4] and that sociology handed over mass media as a topic to communications. Another way of looking at it is that mass media is too big and important an institution to belong to just one field.

In addition to people outside the discipline, scholars from many subfields of sociology also study media. A scholar of race, for example, might examine the overrepresentation of black men in crime news on television. In most cases, the researcher's intention is to tell us something about another institution or pattern in society (here, racism) rather than how media works. While it might seem like a fussy semantic distinction, we might distinguish between a "sociology of media," in which sociologists find out about another pattern or institution (e.g., social movements) through media, and "media sociology" where researchers focus on explaining the institution of mass media itself.[5] Though many scholars doing "sociology of media" have made important contributions to our understanding of society in general and the sociological canon on media, we will focus primarily on theories of "media sociology."

Given these divides of theory, between disciplines, and even within the discipline of sociology, it is not surprising that our big ideas about media are scattered. Recently, several scholars are making efforts to develop a stronger, more unified subfield of media sociology by writing books and essays that help organize the field and by renaming a section of the American Sociological Association to better incorporate media sociology.[6] Still, there is no singular tradition of theorizing and research in mass media. While that diversity of thought may be a strength for the field in the future, we now turn to a concept called the "cultural diamond" to try and make sense of this complicated field.

## The Cultural Diamond

In 1994, Wendy Griswold introduced the cultural diamond (see Figure 2.1), a tool for understanding culture. The diamond has four points: *creators, receivers, the cultural object,* and the *wider social world.* A *cultural object* does not need to be a physical thing and can be almost anything constructed within a culture. A TV show, an Internet meme, an IKEA table, a slice of pizza, and the concept of the "mom jeans" are all *cultural objects. Creators* produce *cultural objects* and *receivers* use, interpret, and experience them. People, institutions, and social constructs within the *wider social world* affect how *cultural objects* are created, perceived, and distributed.

Think of a Hollywood movie. The creators include a whole system of movie studios, production companies, a director, actors, cinematographers, grips, and editing teams. The cultural object—the movie—is reviewed by movie critics in the social world and, ultimately, viewed by moviegoers. All of the pieces of the diamond are interconnected.

However, Griswold wants us to think of culture not as a straight line from creators to receivers, but as a system where each point in the diamond affects the others. Receivers don't just robotically accept cultural objects. They interpret and repurpose them in various ways. Likewise, creators don't exist in a vacuum. They respond to receivers

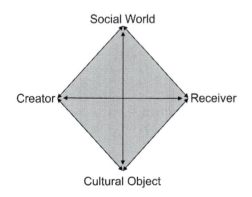

Social World

Creator

Receiver

Cultural Object

*Figure 2.1* The Cultural Diamond

and ideas in the social world. Cultural objects are affected by the social world, but can also change it. Each line in the cultural diamond is a two-way street.

The various theories of media can be organized into the cultural diamond. Some theories center on the creators and the processes behind media *production*. A second group of theories focus on the cultural objects themselves or social *representations*. The third group focus on *reception* in the link between cultural objects and receivers.

The social world runs through all of these theories. A classic sociological puzzle is the entangled relationship between culture and structure. Within the social world on the cultural diamond live many features of the social structure of global society. Making sense of a cultural object, creators, or receivers is impossible without knowing whether a society is a democracy or an authoritarian state, a capitalist market economy, or a collectivist tribal village society with greater or less degrees of inequality between women and men, etc. To gain a stronger understanding of mass media, we must move through the cultural diamond, theorizing each point and each link.

## The Creators

Let's begin with the left side of the cultural diamond with its links to the cultural object and the wider social world. Arguably, it is here that sociologists have made the most significant contributions to the study of mass media. At multiple levels, scholars have developed theories that help us understand the circumstances and conditions surrounding the creation of media objects, whether they be movies, tweets, or newspaper articles.

### Political Economy

Among the most influential macro-level theories is the work of a group of thinkers based at the Institute for Social Research in Frankfurt, Germany and widely known as The Frankfurt School. Influenced by Karl Marx, the first generation of Frankfurt School theorists, including Max Horkheimer, Theodor Adorno, and Herbert Marcuse, attempted to apply Marx's critique of capitalism to more recent developments in politics, economics, and culture. Critical of both Soviet communism and western capitalism, they sought not to offer a blueprint for social change, but to offer a critique that would provide some indication of what might be right or better.

Adorno, in particular, focused his critique on the capitalist "culture industry" that produced obedient consumers rather than open-minded, critical thinkers. As he wrote in 1944, "Movies and radio need no longer pretend to be art. The truth that they are just business is made into an ideology in order to justify the rubbish they deliberately produce."[7] In Adorno's conception, cultural creators are little more than businessmen, trying to reap the largest profits. In doing so, they turn out music and movies with little room for imagination. The consequence is "the stunting of the mass-media consumer's powers of imagination" and "the breaking down of all individual resistance."

Some of Adorno's work, like his absolute contempt for the "stylized barbarity" of jazz, reads as simply resistant to the modern world. Still, his critique of the communication technologies and the capitalist nature of mass media in contemporary society remains valuable today. As we analyze the left side of the cultural diamond, Adorno's theorizing prompts us to consider how the economic and ideological framework of a society shapes the work of cultural creators, how public and private media may differ, and how an "authoritarian" medium like movies may differ from a medium like books. We will return to these questions in Chapter 3.

Adorno's once graduate student and very important theorist in his own right, Jurgen Habermas, has similarly raised questions about how we communicate in democratic societies that have important implications for media sociology. For Habermas, just having voting booths isn't enough to make a society a true democracy. At the heart of a truly democratic society is a robust "public sphere" where individual citizens come together to discuss important issues. The ideal public sphere has four characteristics: 1) it is *inclusive* of people of different social classes, ages, races, etc., 2) has a *disregard of status*, judging people's ideas on their own merit, not on the social status of the speaker, 3) engages in *rational-critical discourse*, and 4) addresses issues of *common concern*.[8]

While Habermas believes that such a public sphere thrived in 18th century London coffeehouses and Parisian salons, in modern capitalist society, the possibility for public sphere is undercut by a for-profit media that has little incentive to help build understanding, welcome the excluded, and offer rational discussion of important issues. Instead, Habermas argues that the capitalist news media is a "platform for advertising" that "prestructures" nearly all debate in ways that preserve established social hierarchies. How we carry out political discourse today will be an important question in Chapter 7.

Habermas' critique of current democratic discourse continues to be influential, but his outline for what a healthy public sphere might look like has also inspired more recent researchers. Many scholars, such as Manuel Castells, have theorized about the potential of the digital communications and online communities to create more equitable "media spaces" where the public sphere might be renewed.[9] Those researchers applying Habermas' ideas about the public sphere to the web are essentially analyzing the way that new technology can shape who can be a creator and what kind of cultural objects they produce. In other words, within the cultural diamond, they are conceptualizing the links among the creators, the social world, and cultural objects.

The most important media theorist for understanding the role technology plays in structuring what is possible for creators is philosopher and literary scholar Marshall McLuhan. McLuhan is most famous for his pithy turn-of-phrase, "the medium is the message"—or maybe his cameo in Woody Allen's *Annie Hall* where he tells a loudmouthed intellectual, "you know nothing of my work." McLuhan's argument was that various media, say, print vs. television, awaken or shut off different senses. Forget about worrying about what's on TV; it's the TV itself that is worth noting. Unlike Adorno, who had a sharp critique of new technology, McLuhan saw great promise in electronic media, with its use of images and sounds, to connect people around the world into a "global village."[10] More recent media scholars like Yochai Benkler have expanded on that reasoning, seeing the technology of the Internet as ushering in a society with the potential for collaborative peer production across global social networks.[11] For that reason, McLuhan is sometimes accused of being a "technological optimist" or of being insufficiently critical of the effects of electronic media on our senses.

What Adorno, Habermas, and McLuhan would all agree on is that the organization of the state and the economy matter for the type and amount of cultural objects available to us. According to sociologist Paul Starr, all societies make *constitutive choices*, choices that "create the material and institutional framework" of mass media within their society. In his Pulitzer Prize-winning book, *Creation of the Media*, Starr argues that several constitutive choices were made in the early U.S. that helped make it a worldwide communications leader.[12]

In particular, Starr attributes the especially rapid growth of mass media in the U.S. primarily to a unique blend of free-market capitalism and government intervention. In writing the Constitution, the founding fathers guaranteed free speech, rights to intellectual property, and a Post Office. The protection of intellectual property rights provided great incentive for creators in a capitalist marketplace to make cultural objects like movies, music, and smartphones because they had exclusive rights to profit on what they made. The Post Office subsidized media like magazines and newspapers by offering low cost bulk mail rates, which allowed them to sell to subscribers at a cheaper price.

When given the constitutive choice of whether to privatize the telegraph in the 1840s, England decided to keep it government-run, while the U.S. decided to privatize it, allowing companies with the financial incentive to grow to build larger networks and develop innovative technology. Later, a robust regulatory and anti-trust system used the government to protect the market from its natural tendency toward monopoly control by a powerful single company. The early Internet had no bigger backer than the U.S. government, but the web was also opened up to private enterprise for companies like Google to create. In all of these cases, the choices made in the U.S. used the government to unleash the power of members of the public and the market to produce mass media content.

In any society, the constitutive choices that are made structure the context in which creators produce cultural objects. Do they have the freedom to produce what they imagine? Do they have financial resources and incentives to bring it to fruition? Does society aide in the development of new technologies or restrict it? These choices can lead to mass media that inhibit imagination as Adorno argued or help us bridge global divides as McLuhan imagined. But in understanding the creator's point in the cultural diamond, we must be attentive to the constitutive choices that various societies make.

## Cultural Fields and Systems

Between the macro-level theorizing of political economy and the micro-level theories of meaning within a particular context, there is what is sometimes known as the "mezzo" level of theorizing that examines media as a field or a type of system.[13] Notable among mezzo level theorists is sociologist Pierre Bourdieu, who developed *field theory*. Bourdieu argues that there are many different fields including the fields of politics, of sports, of fashion, of journalism, and so on. Fields are social spaces structured by external forces (e.g., the market) and internal features of culture like norms and values where organizations and individual actors struggle to define and maintain the field.[14]

Within any field, there is both homogeneity and heterogeneity. Fields are held together by shared "systems of presuppositions" known as *doxa*. Within the journalistic field, for example, *doxa* might include what counts as newsworthy, which publications are most prestigious, and how many sources are necessary to confirm a story. But Bourdieu also argues that fields are "sites of struggle" defined by two poles: the autonomous pole and the heteronomous pole (see Figure 2.2). The "heteronomous pole" represents forces that structure the field like the market, while the "autonomous" pole represents forms that are culturally elite within the field (e.g., the type of serious investigative reporting that wins awards). In any field, these two poles are at odds. Individual journalists and media outlets occupy positions between the two poles with intellectual publications, like *The New Yorker*, hewing towards the autonomous pole. Meanwhile, market-driven, "if it bleeds, it leads" television news cluster close to the heteronomous pole. Or in the field of film, we could imagine Hollywood blockbusters near the heteronomous pole and quiet indie movies near the autonomous pole.

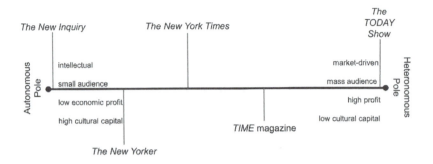

*Figure 2.2* Bourdieu's Journalistic Field

More recently, several media sociologists have tried to connect Bourdieu's field theory with a school of thought called the *new institutionalism*.[15] New institutionalists see great uncertainty or risk within fields as organizations fight to survive. In the face of such risk, organizations—think news outlets or movie studios or record labels—come to adopt similar practices, systems, and products in a process called *isomorphism*.[16] By combining these theories of media fields, we can better understand why organizations and actors in a field create similar cultural objects, but also why they often differ. Bourdieu's field theory will be particularly important in Chapter 6 when we discuss the work of people within media industries.

Another model for understanding media at the organizational level is Paul Hirsch's *culture industry system*.[17] It's easy for us to romanticize a single creator for any cultural object: the brilliant but tortured novelist, the visionary filmmaker, a nerd coding away at the next world-changing app. But Hirsch argues that a more elaborate system exists to turn out mass culture products that are predictable in quality and likely to succeed in the marketplace.

As we see in Figure 2.3, there is an oversupply of potential actors, novelists, directors, etc. within the *technical subsystem* just waiting for the chance to create. They encounter a filter (#1) in the form of casting directors or acquisitions editors who select from the vast supply of talent. Once a creative artist has passed that filter, he or she joins up with an organization like a record label in the *managerial subsystem* to create the cultural object.

The object then passes through a second filter (#2) where gatekeepers like movie critics, DJs, and late night talk show hosts within the *institutional subsystem* decide whether it is worthy of attention. At the third filter (#3), consumers decide whether or not to read the book or watch the movie. But the system doesn't stop there. Consumers then provide feedback to the managerial subsystem and the institutional subsystem both by

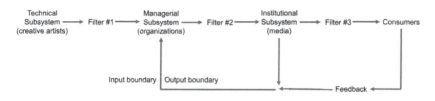

*Figure 2.3* Culture Industry System

purchasing the product and saying whether they liked it. As Griswold points out, Hirsch's system maps onto the cultural diamond neatly.[18]

Finally, sociologist Richard A. Peterson was essential in developing a research tradition known as the *production of culture*.[19] Researchers working in this area investigate the forces that shape the work of creators as they make and distribute cultural objects. According to the theory, there are six key facets that shape the production of culture: technology, law and regulation, industry structure, organization structure, occupational careers, and market. For example, Peterson showed how major changes in these six features of the music industry allowed rock music to displace swing bands as the most popular form of music in just three years starting in 1954.[20]

If macro-level theories offer a sense of how the structure of society as a whole affects mass media, theories of cultural fields and systems help us understand some of the forces that enable and constrain the work of cultural creators. These theories of cultural fields and systems will become particularly important in Chapter 6 when we examine the labor of workers within media industries.

## The Cultural Object

What do we know about the cultural object? In one sense, mass media images reflect their society. Journalists try to represent important world events to their audiences each day. Lady Gaga's "Born This Way" reflected changing attitudes towards gays and lesbians in the U.S. And even fantasy movies like the *Harry Potter* series adopt forms of language, dress, and hierarchies that are recognizable as part of our culture. On the other hand, if media reflects society, it is a "fun house mirror" at best, often distorting the truth.[21] Moreover, unlike an inanimate mirror, media representations are constructed by people and, therefore, reflect the creator's perceptions of the world. As Denis McQuail once argued, "Perhaps the single most important issue in the sociology of mass communications is … does the mass media content mirror social values and the prevailing social structure or does it independently originate change?"[22]

The school of thought that argues that media representations mirror society is known as *reflection theory*. Of course, the crassest version of reflection theory is obviously silly. Thousands of high schools perform a production of Shakespeare's "Romeo and Juliet" each year, but when was the last time you said, "O, I am fortune's fool!"? Likewise, as the #OscarsSoWhite protests in 2016 pointed out, movies and the award shows that celebrate them do not come close to reflecting the racial diversity in American society (a point we will return to in chapters 9 and 11).

Even if media do not often mirror society itself, media representations often represent some part of the prevailing social structure. Karl Marx's famous quote that "the ideas of the ruling class are in every epoch the ruling ideas" is a form of reflection theory. For many Marxists, TV shows reflect capitalist interests and offer the rest of us illusory relief from the brutality of capitalism.

While the orthodox Marxist view is too totalizing, Antonio Gramsci, an Italian Marxist theorist imprisoned by Mussolini's fascist regime in the 1920s, developed the concept of *hegemony*. Hegemony occurs when a dominant group presents their view of the world in such a way that the masses accept it completely and "consent" to their own domination. In our society, most of our cultural objects reflect the values of free-market capitalism, liberal individualism, and white privilege (among others).

To say that cultural objects simply reflect social structure imagines culture as a one-way street and lets the creators off the hook. In fact, other scholars, especially in the fields of semiotics and cultural studies, emphasize that all media representations are, in fact, *social constructions*. As preeminent cultural theorist Stuart Hall wrote, "we give things meaning by how we represent them."[23] Social theorist Michel Foucault writing about "discourses" made a similar argument. Any given discourse is neither true nor false, he argued, but still constructs "truth effects" in which some discourses and ideas become legitimate and viewed as the truth. A TV commercial of a mom picking kids up in a shiny new minivan isn't true ("the family" are actors playing roles) and isn't false (some moms do pick kids up and drive a minivan). What's important for Foucault is how that commercial reaffirms ideas about gender, motherhood, the value placed on consumer purchases, and so on.

Current media sociologists tend to think of media representations as "cultural resources produced by and for society, and as symbolic sites where issues, problems, tensions, and dilemmas are negotiated and contested."[24] Media representations often clash with each other and are often leveraged by creators to present competing visions of society to receivers. Think of dueling political campaign ads. Each is embedded with different stories about how society works, who is to blame, and what qualifies someone to hold elected office. Many media representations are not constructed with that level of consciousness—NFL producers probably aren't thinking about their role in constructing masculinity and nationalism when they plan the game day show—but images still construct reality rather than merely reflecting it.

Many scholars have paid particular attention to representations of identities in media, particularly gender and race. *Feminist media studies* is a large and robust field of research that has paid particular attention to the underrepresentation and often patriarchal representation of women across a range of media. This field sits between the humanities and the social sciences, using both empirical methods and forms of critical analysis. While feminism is internally diverse, like the Frankfurt School, researchers within feminist media studies tend to have a critical orientation towards the ways women are represented in mass media. However, an emergent literature in the field aligns itself with *postfeminism*, a perspective that breaks with the long-stigmatized label of "feminist," sees some sexist representations as relatively harmless, and attempts to encourage forms of femininity, sexuality, and "girl power."[25]

The cross-disciplinary field of feminist media studies continues to thrive and, within sociology, the Sex and Gender section is one of the discipline's biggest. However, Laura Grindstaff and Andrea Press argue that gender scholars in sociology have largely ignored media, focusing instead on issues related to work and family. The result is that feminist media studies is inadequately sociological, often failing to take advantage of our best methods. At the same time, gender representations are not a part of the mainstream conversation in sociology. We explore these issues more in Chapter 8.

Media research on representations of race have often focused on political communications. Stuart Hall, for example, explored how the term "mugging" adopted by crime reporters in Britain stoked racialized fears of a threat posed by black men concentrated in ghettoes. These images created a fissure between the black community and the white working class who might have otherwise been political partners in demanding the government address issues of unemployment.[26] Similarly, researchers have examined "dog whistle politics" in mass media, encoded language that builds on white antagonism toward blacks to create opposition to social welfare state policies. These studies conceptualize media representations as a powerful tool for maintaining white opposition to policies that would address structural racism.

To a great extent, media studies of race have focused on the particular case of African-Americans. In recent years, there have been a small but growing number of studies on depictions of Hispanics. After the events of September 11, 2001, with intense expressions of hostility towards Muslims, there has been some initial research examining media depictions of the "Islamic threat." Still, these new important areas for media representation studies have not been theoretically conceptualized and empirically documented in the way studies of blacks have been. We return to the subject of media representations of class and race in Chapter 9.

Whether we see cultural objects as mirroring society or simply reflecting the institutions, hierarchies, and social norms that organize society, these theories of media representations help us understand the tidal wave of images we encounter every day.

### The Receivers

Finally, we turn to the receivers. Concerns about the effects of media on people are as old as media. In Ancient Greece, Socrates worried about the consequences of the written word on our ability to remember. In the 1950s, psychiatrist Fredric Wertham's book, *Seduction of the Innocent*, argued that comic books corrupt the minds of children by exposing them to violence, criminality, and sex. He even thought Batman and Robin were a gay couple, promoting homosexuality among kids.[27] Today, people with a range of ideological beliefs worry about violent video games, political propaganda on Fox News, and the effect of smartphones on social interactions.

Much of the best research on these subjects is part of the media effects tradition within the discipline of communications. The studies tend to be lab experiments with random assignment and carefully controlled conditions. The earliest work in this area imagined mass media to be like a hypodermic needle, injecting beliefs directly into receivers. Researchers today have a far more nuanced view, questioning the magnitude of such effects and how long they last. One important branch of media effects, the *minimal effects* tradition, points to statuses like race, class, and gender as greatly affecting how much and in what direction media affect us. We will discuss the various strands of media effects research in Chapter 10. The theories within media effects research tend to be relatively grounded theories drawn from psychology. For example, *exemplification theory* argues that examples presented in mass media are particularly powerful heuristics or mental shortcuts that are more likely to stick in the mental schemata (or clusters of ideas) in our brains.[28]

Even though media effects theories differ in how strong or weak they see mass media images as being, for the most part, they see the link between the cultural object and receivers as being a one-way street. But people aren't robots, obediently taking commands. We have agency and are active meaning makers.

For one, people are able to have different interpretations of the same text. What does the Bible say? What does the Constitution say? Reasonable people, looking at the same exact text in those two documents, arrive at very different conclusions about what they mean. This capacity for books, Facebook posts, movies, and songs to have different meanings to different people is known as *polysemy*. So, the link between receivers and the cultural object is two-way. Cultural objects can affect us, but we also construct the meaning of the objects.

But people don't construct meaning in a vacuum. We are affected by our friends, family members, and other people around us. Sociologists have documented the way that cultural tastes flow through social networks and that people make sense of cultural objects in groups. Saying, "I like all music except for country," is not simply a critical assessment of country music. It is also a way of marking a social boundary between groups you identify with and "the other."[29] The subtext of the comment is "I'm not the *type of person* who likes country music." We learn lessons about media from our friends and family and communicate about our relationships through our tastes.

Similarly, we often consume media together. While movie theaters in the U.S. have a norm against talking, Americans visiting the cinema in India are sometimes surprised by how interactive and social the experience is. Indian filmgoers openly chitchat during the movie, sing along with songs, and talk back to the screen. If that seems strange, consider families and friends gathering together to watch the Oscars or the Super Bowl and do much of the same. On most days, both of the co-authors of this book swap emails and texts with friends and family, linking to articles and sharing some of our own comments. In all of these ways, groups help define the meaning of the cultural object for individuals.[30]

## Theorizing the Media

These theories are only a small sample of the sociological ways that people have and are theorizing mass media. Some of the theories, like the *production of culture* tradition, are making what Abend sees as generalized propositions. Others, like Habermas and Bourdieu, are developing interpretative theories, while still others, like *feminist media studies*, document the world empirically with a theoretical perspective. As we move through the cultural diamond over the course of this book, we will consider and challenge all of these theories. But it is important to remember that there is no one great theory to rule them all.

## Notes

1   Abend, Gabriel. 2008. "The Meaning of 'Theory'." *Sociological Theory* 26:173–199.
2   Alexander, Jeffrey C. 1987. "What is Theory?" In Alexander, Jeffrey C. *Twenty Lectures: Sociological Theory Since World War II.* New York: Columbia University Press, pp. 1–21.

3  Waisbord, Silvio. 2014. "Introduction: Reappraising Media Sociology." In Silvio Waisbord (ed.), *Media Sociology: A Reappraisal.* Cambridge, UK: Polity Press, pp. 19.

4  Szelenyi, Ivan. 2015. "The Triple Crisis of Sociology." *Contexts Blog,* April 20. Available at: https://contexts.org/blog/the-triple-crisis-of-soci ology/; Pooley, Jefferson and Elihu Katz. 2008. "Further Notes on Why American Sociology Abandoned Mass Communication Research." *Journal of Communication* 58:767–786.

5  First used by Griswold applied to cultural sociology and sociology of culture in *Cultures and Societies in a Changing World* (1994). At media sociology pre-conference to the ASA in 2014, Ronald Jacobs applied it to media sociology and sociology of media.

6  Benson, Rodney. 2004. "Bringing the Sociology of Media Back in." *Political Communication* 21:275–292; Waisbord, Silvio. 2014. *Media Sociology: A Reappraisal.* New York: John Wiley & Sons; Earl, Jennifer. 2015. "CITASA: Intellectual Past and Future." *Information, Communication & Society* 18:478–491; Revers, Matthias and Casey Brienza. 2017. "How Not to Establish a Subfield: Media Sociology in the United States." *The American Sociologist.* 1–17.

7  Adorno, Theodor W. 1946. "The Culture Industry: Enlightenment as Mass Deception" In Horkheimer, Max and Theodor W. Adorno (eds.), *Dialectic of the Enlightenment.* Stanford, CA: Stanford University Press, pp. 121.

8  Habermas, Jurgen. 1991. *The Structural Transformation of the Public Sphere: An Inquiry into a Category of Bourgeois Society.* Cambridge, MA: MIT press.

9  Castells, Manuel. 1997. *The Power of Identity; Volume Ii: The Information Age: Economy, Society, and Culture.* Oxford, England: Blackwell.

10 McLuhan, Marshall. 1994. *Understanding Media: The Extensions of Man.* Cambridge, MA: MIT press.

11 Benkler, Yochai. 2006. *The Wealth of Networks: How Social Production Transforms Markets and Freedom.* New Haven, CT: Yale University Press.

12 Starr, Paul. 2005. *The Creation of the Media: Political Origins of Modern Communications.* New York: Basic Books.

13 Benson 2004.

14 Bourdieu, Pierre. 1993. *The Field of Cultural Production: Essays on Art and Literature.* New York: Columbia University Press; Bourdieu, Pierre. 1998. *On Television.* New York: New Press.

15 Benson, Rodney. 2006. "News Media as a 'Journalistic Field': What Bourdieu Adds to New Institutionalism, and Vice Versa." *Political Communication* 23:187–202; Fligstein, Neil and Doug McAdam. 2012. *A Theory of Fields.* New York: Oxford University Press; Rohlinger, Deana A. 2007. "American Media and Deliberative Democratic Processes." *Sociological Theory* 25:122–148.

16 See discussion in Benson (2006).

17 Hirsch, Paul M. 1972. "Processing Fads and Fashions: An Organization-Set Analysis of Cultural Industry Systems." *American Journal of Sociology* 639–659.

18 Griswold, Wendy. 2012. *Cultures and Societies in a Changing World.* Thousand Oaks, CA:Sage.

19 Peterson, Richard A. and N. Anand. 2004. "The Production of Culture Perspective." *Annual Review of Sociology* 30(1): 311–334.

20 Peterson, Richard A. 1990. "Why 1955? Explaining the Advent of Rock Music." *Popular Music* 9: 97–116.

21 Moy, Patricia and Michael Pfau. 2000. *With Malice Toward All? The Media and Public Confidence in Democratic Institutions: The Media and Public Confidence in Democratic Institutions.* Santa Barbara, CA: ABC-CLIO.

22  McQuail, Denis. 1969. *Towards a Sociology of Mass Communications.* New York, NY: Collier-Macmillan. p. 68.

23  Hall, Stuart (ed.) 1997. *Representation: Cultural Representations and Signifying Practices.* Thousand Oaks, CA: Sage.

24  Orgad, Shani. 2014. "When sociology meets media representation." In Waisbord (2014).

25  Grindstaff, Laura and Andrea Press. 2014. "Too Little But Not Too Late: Sociological Contributions to Feminist Media Studies." In Waisbord (2014).

26  Hall, Stuart, Chas Critcher, Tony Jefferson, John Clarke, and Brian Roberts. 1978. *Policing the Crisis: Mugging, the State and Law and Order.* London: Palgrave Macmillan.

27  Beaty, Bart. 2005. *Fredric Wertham and the Critique of Mass Culture.* Jackson, MS: University Press of Mississippi.

28  Zillmann, Dolf and Brosius, Hans-Bernd. 2012. *Exemplification in Communication: The Influence of Case Reports on the Perception of Issues.* New York: Routledge.

29  Bryson, Bethany. 1996. "'Anything But Heavy Metal': Symbolic Exclusion and Musical Dislikes." *American Sociological Review.* 61: 884–899.

30  Griswold 2012.

# Section 2

# Production

# Chapter 3

# Who Pays for It?

In late 2015, news outlets were rife with stories about "cord-cutting," people dropping their expensive cable packages and getting the TV and movies they wanted through Roku, iTunes, Amazon, or elsewhere on the web. To customers, $50–$100 a month for cable TV (above and beyond Internet service) seemed like a ridiculous expense, despite the fact that they were getting access to thousands of hours of programming each month. In fact, the average American pays only about 75 cents per hour for cable TV.[1] Nonetheless, many people felt like they were getting ripped off when they could get most of the content for cheaper or even for free. But, as we shall see, media content is never actually free.

## Who's Paying for It?

There are three ideal typical models for paying for media content: a) fee-based, b) advertising-supported, and c) publicly-funded. These models are ideal types in the sense that most media outlets earn revenue from a combination of fees (e.g., buying a newspaper or paying Netflix a monthly fee) and advertising (e.g., sponsored tweets on Twitter), not just a single source. Moreover, mass media organizations have found new types of revenue streams. The enormous financial success of the *Star Wars* franchise for LucasFilms was due at least as much to selling Han Solo and Darth Vader action figures as from selling movie tickets.[2] Still, historically and across a range of media today, fee-based, advertising-supported, and publicly-funded models have been and are the primary ways of funding the media content. In this chapter, we will explore each of these models and what existing research has shown about what the adoption of one over another means for the kind of programming outlets produce.

### Fee-based

Who pays for mass media? In one sense, we all do. Whether it's by paying $2.50 for a copy of *The New York Times* at the newsstand, clicking on an ad on Google, or paying our taxes, we, as consumers and citizens, foot the bill. But the historically dominant and, perhaps, most straightforward way of paying for media is the fee-based model. In Shakespeare's day, "groundlings," as commoners were known, would pay one penny to stand in the Globe Theatre Yard and watch a play (even at that time, the Theatre made additional revenue by selling food and beer during the play).[3] The first modern newspapers, which began to be printed in the early 1600s, consisted mostly of lists of prices of goods at the market or of accounts of military proceedings.[4] The merchants and aristocratic types who read these newsletters would pay a fee that covered the labor costs of gathering the information, the cost of ink, paper, and running a printing press, as well as the postage to distribute them.

Today, newspapers, premium cable TV stations like HBO, and bands selling their latest album continue to use fee-based models. Online, examples of fee-based models include web sites selling monthly subscriptions to exclusive content hidden behind "paywalls," web-based movie rental services like Apple's iTunes, and premium memberships like higher sound quality music on services like Spotify.

In 2007, the English band, Radiohead, conducted a radical experiment in fee-based models when they let Internet users pay whatever amount they wanted for the band's seventh studio album, *In Rainbows*. The album

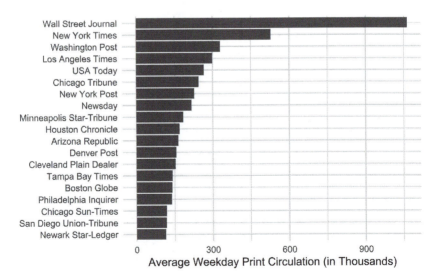

*Figure 3.1* Top Newspapers by Circulation
[Source: Statista]

was downloaded over 2 million times. While lead singer Thom Yorke told *Time* magazine that the experiment was a "'Fuck you' to [a] decaying business model," it's worth noting that the band also sold 1.75 million physical copies using traditional distribution networks. Since then, a number of musicians have adopted the web-based "pay-what-you-want" model.[5]

In one sense, for purely fee-based media, like Radiohead and most other bands, all customers are created equal. Rich or poor, young or old, male or female, anyone willing to pay $9.99 for an album is the same in the eyes of the seller. The main objective is to collect as many fees as possible, whether we're talking concert tickets, magazines, or episodes of TV shows on iTunes.

Because of the need to attract the biggest audiences possible, media outlets using fee-based models need to be highly attentive to *market demand* or the aggregate desires of potential customers in a given industry or organizational field. An old newsroom mantra is "if it bleeds, it leads." In other words, editors give prominent placement to stories about crime and scandals not because of their inherent news value, but because they sell papers. Similarly, movie studios do not make films like *Alvin and the Chipmunks: The Squeakquel* because of a deep artistic impetus to challenge current public discourse on rodents. Studios make movies like *The Chipmunks* because they perceive market demand for child-friendly, light fare.[6] The danger of responding to market demand is that media producers fall victim to the "tyranny of the consumer," choosing customer preferences over a concern for quality.

Still, perhaps contrary to popular belief, particularly within the domain of news, editors tend to be very wary about letting perceived market demand supersede editorial judgment about what is newsworthy (we'll discuss this more in Chapter 6). In one classic qualitative study of a newsroom, Herbert Gans found that journalists deliberately disregard both Letters to the Editor and audience research statistics (both indicators of market demand) and, instead, produce the type of news they and editors prefer.[7]

In the same way, every edgy rock band wants to avoid the damning label of being "sell outs." In some sectors of the culture industry, being seen as resisting market demand is essential to being viewed "authentic" and respected.[8] Indeed, in some fields, there is substantial market demand for being seen as resisting market demand. Auteur filmmakers sometimes succeed precisely because their movies seem to defy the rules of the marketplace.

Regardless of how they present themselves, cultural producers working within a fee-based model simply must be conscious of market demand. One recent quantitative study of three New York-based online news web sites examined how the instant feedback of web page clicks by readers affected journalists' decision-making about the placement of future news stories. Their results showed that "audience preferences [play] an intricate and dynamic role in influencing whether and how online newsroom editors decide to feature certain news stories over others at multiple time points a day."[9] There are any number of niche audiences with preferences for media content more sophisticated than *Sharknado*, but the primary incentive in for-profit, fee-based models is to attract as large an audience as possible in order to maximize profit.

But that's not the full story. Media content producers with a regularly reoccurring or ongoing product, like newspapers and magazines or like Netflix and Spotify, want to attract the *type* of customer who has the disposable income to keep buying their product. Why do newspapers go to all the trouble of delivering their product to people's homes at the crack of dawn while charging them less than the newsstand price? Because they know home subscribers end up spending more per year than the occasional newsstand purchaser.

Likewise, movie theater chains know that young people spend a much higher proportion of their disposable income on entertainment.[10] So, it is not quite true that fee-based media are apathetic to the demographics of their customers. Newspapers want to produce content that attracts higher income customers, and movie theaters want to appeal to young people.

More importantly, most media outlets today do not rely on a single source of income. The Food Network earns money from cable television fees, but also from advertising and merchandise like cookbooks and kitchen utensils. These various revenue streams complicate media content producers' calculus about which customers to target. One constant is that higher income consumers are almost always more desirable. As a consequence, there is an enormous amount of media content reflecting the concerns, interests, and tastes of affluent people, while the preferences of lower income consumers and coverage of problems that matter to them are often largely excluded.

### Advertising-supported

For a long time, people wondered how Google, Facebook, and Twitter— Internet behemoths who seem to give away their products for free—would make money. In Aaron Sorkin's 2010 movie, *The Social Network*, a fictionalized version of Facebook founder Mark Zuckerberg says of his site, "We don't know what it is, what it can be, what it will be. All we know is that it's cool; that's a priceless asset." For some observers, the Internet entrepreneurs of the 2000s had too much vision and not enough business plan. However, by one estimate, social media sites took in $8.4 billion in ad revenues in 2014. In the same year, Google alone made more than $45 billion in ad revenue.[11] There's clearly money to be made giving your product away for "free."

These companies have merely perfected a business model that broadcast radio and TV have been using for decades. Unlike newspapers, CDs, or DVDs, radio stations have no physical product to sell. Their primary service is broadcast free to anyone with an antenna. Radio and TV stations make money by selling ad time to companies that want to sell their goods and services to the station's audiences.

Like fee-based models, broadcast stations' earning potential lies with being able to attract substantial audiences. As we've seen, not all customers are equal even in fee-based models. But advertisers are even more motivated to target particular demographics. A diaper company like Pampers doesn't want to run ads that will only be seen by teenagers, and Mercedes doesn't want to market to low-income listeners. For that reason, firms like Nielsen track not only TV and radio stations' audience size, but also audience demographics like income, education, age, gender, and race.

In tracking audience characteristics, sites like Facebook and Google have a leg up on radio and TV. The local Top 40 pop radio station may know *in the aggregate* that their listeners are young people with a fair amount of disposable income. But Google knows about their users at the *individual level*. In other words, Google knows you. Web sites collect enormous amount of information on their user's demographic characteristics, tastes, and political views from users' patterns of usage. Using advanced algorithms, sites can accurately estimate other facts about the user.

Though you may have never reported your income on Facebook, web analytics tools have shown that Facebook is able to guess many of their users' annual incomes and political views almost perfectly. This information allows them to tailor advertisements to appeal directly to users. Google and Facebook know whether you're more likely to like clothes from J. Crew or JC Penny's. They know whether campaign ads from Democrats or Republicans are more likely to persuade you. They know if you might be in the market for a new car and whether you're likely to be shopping for a Mustang or a mini-van.

Maybe we need to change our perspective here. We often assume that Google's product is their search engine and that their customer is you, the searcher. But what if the product is you? In 2014, Ello, a privacy-oriented Facebook competitor, posted a manifesto to its site, reading,

> Your social network is owned by advertisers. Every post you share, every friend you make and every link you follow is tracked, recorded and converted into data. Advertisers buy your data so they can show you more ads. You are the product that's bought and sold.[12]

If online companies collect most of their revenue from advertisers, then the advertisers are their primary customer. The most successful online media companies are those that sell the best—some would say the most invasive—data.

Companies like Facebook, Google, and Twitter say that they disclose all their practices in the Terms of Service (TOS) agreement that all users accept when they create an account. However, though it may be hard to believe, not every user reads all 20,000 words of each TOS agreement or has the law degree necessary to understand all the technical jargon. Consequently, many users are unaware of just how much personal information they are turning over to a private company.

However, the tides may slowly be turning since companies' handling of digital data began receiving greater media attention following the 2016 U.S. presidential election. Because of this reporting, we've learned that it isn't just Google and Facebook who have access to deeply personal information—including search and browsing histories, photos, friends' contact information, and the text from (even deleted) messages—but countless other companies who Facebook "partners" with. Technology giants like Amazon, Microsoft, Netflix, Spotify, Yahoo, and many others received Facebook data about "hundreds of millions of people a month," and often without user consent because "Facebook considered the partners extensions of itself."[13] Furthermore, not only does Facebook encourage these companies to

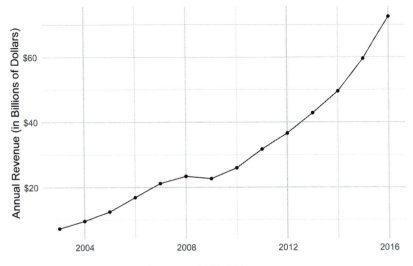

*Figure 3.2* Online Advertising Revenues, 2003–2016
[Source: Interactive Advertising Bureau.]

reciprocate their own data sharing, but they have also built tools for web developers so Facebook can receive personally identifiable data on users of other digital services—even if they do not login with Facebook, and even if they don't have a Facebook account at all.[14] Moreover, as the revelations about Facebook's handling of user data grew more shocking, the company's strategy, according to *The New York Times*, was to "Delay, deny and deflect," even going as far as to fund a smear campaign against one of its most prominent critics.[15]

Let that sink in for a minute. The infrastructure of the Internet is increasingly built to facilitate the collection of user data, and companies are sharing this data—and in some cases purchasing it—in order to produce the most detailed profiles possible of Internet users. What they do with that data, which includes information about most if not all likely readers of this book, is hard to know since transparency is not their strong suit. We do know that this data infrastructure, along with the tools they have created to help potential advertisers work within it, are the real secret to Facebook's financial success. The better Facebook's system can understand and target you, the user, the more attractive it will be to advertisers, and the more profitable Facebook's product will be. It isn't too hard to see that this system incentivizes a set of data practices that appear to be at odds with its publicly stated mission to "Give people the power to build community and bring the world closer together."[16]

These examples make clear that tech companies that rely on advertising revenue do not have any incentive to truly satisfy users, make their lives better, or enrich them in some ways. Rather, their primary incentive is to keep their attention and redirect it to a set of merchants.[17] For this reason, the goal is to make social media as addictive as possible to users, rather than as rewarding as possible. If Facebook charged users $10 a month, they would need to be much more concerned about customer satisfaction instead of mere user retention.

Advertising brings with it a set of incentives that don't exist in fee-based models. In his book, *Sociology of the News*, media sociologist Michael Schudson tells the story of how the leadership of *The New York Times* in the early 1980s hoped that struggling competitor, *New York Daily News*, wouldn't go out of business, even though they stood to gain a new set of readers. The reason being that former *Daily News* readers tend to be working class and less educated, a demographic much less desirable to advertisers than the average reader of *The New York Times*.[18] If the *Times* earned all of its income from newsstand sales and subscriptions (i.e., had an entirely fee-based model), the paper's leadership might have thought about how to tailor more of their content to welcome working class readers and sell more newspapers. But the substantial advertising revenues gave the paper incentive to keep ad rates high by maintaining an elite readership.

*The New York Times* is far from unusual in its concern with ensuring a desirable audience for advertisers. In fact, the *Times* is less affected than most outlets, having always earned a substantial share of its revenue from circulation.[19] By contrast, television networks earn the vast majority of their revenue from advertising, both in the form of commercials and product placements.

Broadly speaking, the most highly-prized target demographic on television are affluent, white adults between the ages of 18 and 49. Certainly, different shows and networks target different groups. Black Entertainment Television (BET) has a largely African-American audience. The CW skews younger. Sports programming has a disproportionately male audience. However, less desirable target demographics mean lower advertising rates.

Even more so than in fee-based models, ad-supported media outlets have significant incentives to tailor their content to attract audiences with higher ad rates. In a 1991 study, social scientist Phyllis Kaniss found that Philadelphia newspapers, eager to increase ad revenue, began to cover news that would appeal to high-income suburbanites rather than inner-city residents.[20]

That does not mean that BET will give up on programming that features black performers in order to garner white audiences. As we'll see in Chapter 4, big media conglomerates, like Viacom, which owns BET, tend to have a range of media properties that aim to reach nearly all demographics groups. But BET does strive to appeal to younger and more affluent black viewers, who have more disposable income, in particular in order to maintain their ad rates.

In sum, while media outlets relying on fee-based models have relatively more incentive to respond to market demand of the wider paying public, media organizations reliant on advertising revenue tend to be more attentive to tailoring their content to a desirable demographic. In practice, most for-profit media outlets draw revenue from a mixture of these two ideal typical forms. Moreover, revenue source is far from the only factor that affects the type of content we encounter. Crime news is not only popular because of market demand. It is also an easy type of story to cover and is usually viewed as newsworthy by editors and producers.[21] The AMC executives who greenlighted *Breaking Bad* certainly wanted to attract the kind of demographics that would increase the channel's ad revenue, but they probably also wanted to produce a good show.

### The Public Option

Academics, activists, and cultural critics alike have long been concerned with the role that profit motive plays in media. As Frankfurt School theorist Theodor Adorno wrote in a famous essay in 1944, "Movies and radio need no longer pretend to be art. The truth that they are just business is made into an ideology in order to justify the rubbish they deliberately produce."[22] In the 1980s, sociologist Todd Gitlin conducted qualitative interviews with literally hundreds of network executives, producers, writers, and actors for his book *Inside Prime Time*. His research showed that television network executives' key criterion for selecting new programming was the likelihood that the show would attract big audiences in order to secure the highest advertising rates.[23] This "television-industrial complex," as Gitlin calls it, values neither quality nor use to the public, just profitability. If reality TV sells, they make more reality TV shows. For Adorno and thinkers who have followed, the impulse to earn a profit leads movies, music, television, journalism, and the rest to become trivial, crude, and ruthlessly homogenous. In other words, this perspective holds that for-profit media inherently produce homogenous and simplistic content.

For radical critics like Adorno, there is simply little hope for media (or what he calls "the culture industry") without fundamentally overturning capitalism. However, politically liberal commentators often see non-profit media offering a legitimate alternative without the pressures of market demand or advertiser preferences. In the U.S., for-profit media, organized and produced by companies in the private sector, has always been the predominant model. But especially in the second half of the 20th century, in most developed nations, the predominant producer of mass media was the government. The *publicly-funded* model is one in which a significant proportion of the media outlet's budget is supported through designated taxes or government allocations. Many public broadcasting entities also rely on audience contributions, donations from charitable foundations, commercial financing, and merchandising. What is common to all public media is their non-profit status.

To American ears, government-funded media often raises fears about the potential for propagandistic state-run programming. There are certainly troubling examples of state-sponsored media pushing the official message of the regime and even engaging in gross distortions. Rossiya 24, for example, is a Russian state-owned television news channel founded in 2007 and funded by VGTRK, the All-Russia State Television and Radio Broadcasting Company. Though the station makes claims to offer objective reporting, its news coverage consistently paints President Vladmir Putin's policies in a favorable light and, at times, veers into outright lies. In 2014, the *New York Times* reported that Rossiya 24, covering the conflict in the Ukraine, had claimed between four and eleven pro-Russian civilians had been killed by militants in a helicopter with automatic weapons. In reality, local civilians threw rocks at a Ukrainian commander, causing no fatalities.[24]

In a far less extreme example, Japan's NHK news network, a public media system based on Britain's BBC, has been accused on a few occasions of self-censoring content. According to sociologist Rodney Benson, in 2001, bending to "political pressure," NHK allegedly edited a documentary claiming

Emperor Hirohito played a role in the sexual enslavement of women during WWII. Because Japanese law explicitly prohibits "political interference in programming content," NHK has vigorously denied these allegations.[25]

Though private ownership may, at times, provide freedom from state interference, there are also plenty of examples of private, for-profit media supporting political administrations. Silvio Berlusconi, prime minister of Italy for three terms during the 1990s and 2000s, was also the controlling shareholder of Mediaset, a for-profit mass media conglomerate that owned three of the seven national TV channels. Because of Berlusconi's ability to exert "undue influence" over Italy's national media, the *Freedom of the Press 2004 Global Survey* downgraded Italy's ranking from "Free" to "Partly Free."[26] In the U.S., private, for-profit news outlets like Fox News and MSNBC have frequently been accused of acting as propaganda wings of the Republican and Democratic parties respectively.

Neither public nor private media are immune from public influence. However, most developed countries have created independent organizations and funding structures for their public media that significantly reduce the risk of state influence. In Norway, for instance, where the Norwegian Broadcasting Company (NRK) operates three national and ten regional channels, the NRK's founding documents guarantee that the stations "operate free and independently [of] persons or groups that, for political, ideological, economic, or other reasons, wish to exert influence on its editorial content." The Norwegian Media Authority (NMA) is an independent organization charged with overseeing NRK, collecting taxes in the form of TV licensing fees that support their work, and serving "as a buffer between government and all Norwegian broadcasters."[27]

In the U.S., the Public Broadcasting Service (PBS), the producer and distributor of *Sesame Street* and *This Old House*, is overseen by an organization comparable to Norway's NMA called the Corporation for Public Broadcasting (CPB). However, unlike the NHK and the BBC and most other international public media, which can independently collect taxes to fund their work, the CPB has no independent funding mechanism. The U.S. Congress allocates funds for the CPB each year in the federal budget. That means that the CPB has to actively lobby Congress for funding each year and is under constant threat of having its funding cut. The fights are often so bad that NPR, which began as our national public radio network, became a private non-profit organization in the 1980s.[28]

Public media systems like Norway's and Britain's allow for the greatest degree of immunity from market demand and preferences of advertisers. Sometimes that's not so great for entertainment value. Saturday Night Live once parodied the BBC as featuring "a ten hour documentary on British top soil." However, many public media organizations throughout

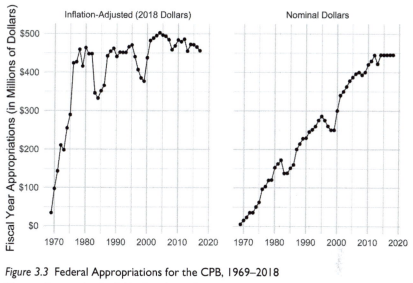

*Figure 3.3* Federal Appropriations for the CPB, 1969–2018
[Source: Corporation for Public Broadcasting]

the world produce some of the most trusted news as well as successful entertainment programming (in all fairness to the BBC, it has also produced hits like *Downton Abbey, Doctor Who,* and *The Office*).

## How Do Models Differ by Media?

Sometimes the medium dictates the form of revenue. For broadcast technologies, like radio and television, advertising has always been their primary source of revenue simply because they had no way of charging fees. The introduction of cable television in the 1980s and the growth of satellite radio since the 1990s allowed these media to charge fees by signing up subscribers.

Conversely, movies historically made their money by selling tickets. However, the 1982 film, *ET,* was not only a box office hit, it also proved innovative with a prominent product placement for Reese's Pieces. The candies, which the main character, Elliott, uses to lure the title extra-terrestrial out of hiding, saw a 65% spike in their sales in the weeks following the movie's opening.[29] Since that time, movie studios have often supported their fee-based ticket sales with additional advertising revenue for product placement. For now, print books have largely avoided advertising, though that prohibition has more to do with norms and values of the book publishing industry than any technological limitation.

Both because of technological possibility and culture, other media, including the web and periodicals, allow for multiple forms of revenue. Online, even companies selling similar content make different strategic decisions about whether to adopt a fee-based or advertising-based model. YouTube and Netflix are both fundamentally video providers. However, YouTube, which is owned by Google, earns almost all its revenue from advertising, while Netflix operates on a primarily fee-based model.

As a medium that employs multiple sources of revenue, newspapers offer a particularly instructive case. Europe, where many late 19th and early 20th century newspapers were subsidized by political parties,[30] has long had an approximately 50/50 split of revenue from advertising and circulation. By contrast, American newspapers, until very recently, have tended to earn about 80% of their revenue from advertising rather than from circulation.[31]

As content has become readily available online, print ad rates have declined and digital advertising has not been great enough to make up the difference. Unfortunately, circulation in both the U.S. and Europe is also down—it just hasn't declined quite as much. As a consequence, newspapers are drawing a higher proportion of their revenue from fee-based sources than advertising. In the 1990s, American newspapers earned about four times the revenue from advertising as circulation; in 2013, that was down to only two times as much.[32]

Worldwide, 2014 was the first year where circulation revenue ($92 billion) surpassed advertising revenue ($87 billion), mostly due to big increases in newspaper readership in India, the Middle East, and Latin America. Moreover, 93% of the circulation revenue came from print circulation.[33] Taken together, these trends tend to suggest that the fee-based model is ascendant in newspapers even if we hear a lot about advertising online.

## Conclusion

To return to the growing number of cord-cutters, they may be paying the cable company less, but most of them continue to pay for their media content in various ways. First, they continue to pay the cable company for their Internet connections and may have had to pay more for a faster Internet connection to support all of their streaming video. They have also purchased the sleek little boxes from Roku and Apple that allow them to stream video. Most of these cord-cutters also pay fees to services like Hulu, Netflix, and Amazon Prime. When they stream video on the web or use some of these fee-based services, many of them still watch advertisements. And, finally, we all pay for PBS's *Sesame Street* with our tax dollars. Many Americans have shaved a few dollars off their monthly media budget by cord-cutting, but media content is never free and we all end up paying for it one way or another.

# Notes

1 The average American pays $64.41 a month on basic cable television (FCC Report On Average Rates For Cable Programming Service And Equipment, 2013) and spends 84 hours a month watching TV (Bureau of Labor Statistics, American Time Use Survey, 2014).

2 Lawrence, John Shelton. 2006. "Spectacle, Merchandise, and Influence." In Matthew Wilhelm Kapell and John Shelton Lawrence (eds.), *Finding the Force of the Star Wars Franchise*. New York: Peter Lang, pp. 1-20.

3 Gitlin, Todd. 2002. *Media Unlimited*. New York: Henry Holt.

4 Starr, Paul. 2004. *Creation of the Media*. New York: Basic Books.

5 Tyrangiel, Josh. 2007. "Radiohead Says: Pay What You Want." *Time Magazine*, October 1, 2007.

6 Zeitchik, Steven. 2015. "'Minions': Should Hollywood make More PG Movies?" *Los Angeles Times*, July 14.

7 Gans, Herbert. 1979. *Deciding What's News*. New York: Random House.

8 Lena, Jennifer. 2012. *Banding Together: How Communities Create Genres in Popular Music*. Princeton, NJ: Princeton University Press.

9 Lee, Angela, Seth C. Lewis, and Matthew Powers. 2014. "Audience Clicks and NewsPlacement: A Study of Time-Lagged Influence in Online Journalism." *Communication Research* 41:505–530.

10 For a vivid account, see the documentary, *Merchants of Cool* (2001).

11 Manjoo, Farhad. 2015. "Google, Might Now, but Not Forever." *The New York Times*, Feb. 11.

12 Manifesto available at https://web.archive.org/web/20141001022505/http:// ello.co/request-an-invitation

13 Dance, Gabriel J. X., Michael LaForgia, and Nicholas Confessore. 2018. "As Facebook Raised a Privacy Wall, It Carved an Opening for Tech Giants." *The New York Times*, December 18. www.nytimes.com/2018/12/18/technol ogy/facebook-privacy.html

14 Privacy International. 2018. "How Apps on Android Share Data with Facebook —Report." *Privacy International*. Retrieved January 14, 2019 (http://privacyinter national.org/report/2647/how-apps-android-share-data-facebook-report).

15 Frenkel, Sheera, Nicholas Confessore, Cecilia Kang, Matthew Rosenberg, and Jack Nicas. 2018. "Delay, Deny and Deflect: How Facebook's Leaders Fought Through Crisis." *The New York Times*, November 30.

16 Anon. n.d. "Facebook—About." Retrieved January 14, 2019 (https://www. facebook.com/notes/mark-zuckerberg/bringing-the-world-closer-together/ 10154944663901634/).

17 Wu, Tim. 2016. *The Attention Merchants*. New York: Alfred A. Knopf.

18 Schudson, Michael. 2011. *The Sociology of News*. New York: W.W. Norton.

19 Chittum, Ryan. 2009. "NYT Now Gets As Much Money from Circulation as from Ads." *Columbia Journalism Review*, July 23, 2009.

20 Kaniss, Phyllis. 1991. *Making Local News*. Chicago: University of Chicago Press.

21 Schudson. 2011.

22 Adorno, Theodor. 1944 (trans. 1977). "The Culture Industry: Enlightenment as Mass Deception." In Max Horkheimer and Theodor Adorno (eds.), *Dialectic of the Enlightenment*. New York: Herder and Herder, p. 121.

23 Gitlin, Todd. 2000. *Inside Prime Time*. Berkeley, CA: University of California Press.

24 Herszenhorn, David M. 2014. "Russia Is Quick to Bend Truth About Ukraine." *The New York Times*, April 15.

25  Benson, Rodney and Matthew Powers. 2011. *Public Media and Political Independence*. New York: Free Press. Available at: https://freedomhouse.org/art icle/global-press-freedom-deteriorates

26  Freedom House Report, "Global Press Freedom Deteriorates," April 28, 2004. Available at: https://freedomhouse.org/article/global-press-freedom-deteriorates.

27  Benson and Powers. 2011.

28  Lindner, Andrew. 2012. *When Public Radio Goes Private*. PhD Dissertation. The Pennsylvania State University.

29  Babin, Laurie A. 1996. "Advertising via the Box Office: Is Product Placement Effective?" *Journal of Promotion Management* 3:31–52.

30  Schudson, Michael. 2001. "The Objectivity Norm in American Journalism." *Journalism* 2:149–170.

31  Edmonds, Rick. 2015. "Worldwide Newspaper Circulation Revenues Pass Advertising for the First Time." *Poytner Online*, June 1. Available at: https://www.poynter.org/reporting-editing/2015/worldwide-newspaper-circulation-revenues-pass-advertising-for-the-first-time/.

32  Analysis of data from Newspaper Association of America.

33  Edmonds. 2014.

# Chapter 4

# In the Hands of a Few

As the previous chapter demonstrated, there is plenty of good reason to believe that for-profit models—whether fee- or advertising-based—shape the content of the media they fund. But does the size of the media company that produces an album, a film, or a web site matter? Some media critics argue that the reason we have 500 channels and nothing good on TV is neither inherent in capitalism nor is it fundamentally due to the corrupting influence of advertising or market demand.

Instead, some commentators, most notably journalist Ben Bagdikian, have argued that, in the past 50 years, already big media companies have become simply massive by gobbling up smaller newspapers, television and radio stations, book publishers, music labels, and so on. As the number of media conglomerates has declined, there are fewer voices in the room and great incentive to cross-promote media products. The upshot of this extreme concentration in ownership is ever-increasing "homogenization" in our media landscape.

For advocates of the so-called "Homogenization Hypothesis," the growing concentration in ownership doesn't just mean that all of our sit-coms are the same. Bagdikian and others see the squelching of diversity by media giants as a fundamental threat to democracy. But are they right? Does concentration in ownership reduce diversity? Or are there other entangled factors at work? In this chapter, we will explore competing theories about media ownership and the empirical evidence on each side.

## A Day in the Life of a Concentrated Media System

If you wake up in the morning and turn on "The Today Show" on NBC, you're likely to see an interview with an actor or actress starring in the latest Universal Studios movie, maybe the newest *Jurassic Park* sequel or the latest in the Jason Bourne series or the newest Oscar-bait biopic like *Steve Jobs*. Maybe they will catch you up on the latest season of *Top Chef* on Bravo, Al Roker's cameo appearances in the *Sharknado* movies on Syfy, or a great goal from English Premier League soccer on NBCSN. Maybe you'll hear about something happening on Telemundo, MSNBC, E!, USA, or Oxygen. Every one of those media properties is owned by the same media conglomerate, Comcast. And, if you get your Internet and/or television service through Comcast, you're paying that conglomerate's parent company directly. Comcast also owns the Universal theme parks, the Philadelphia Flyers and 76ers, and a venture capital company, which partially owns fantasy sports site FanDuel and digital news site VoxMedia.[1]

This example might seem like we are picking on Comcast, which was the world's biggest media company as of 2015, but that kind of concentrated ownership is the norm, not the exception. We see it in the newspaper industry where Gannett alone owns 17 daily newspapers and more than 200 weekly newspapers reaching more than 4.8 million people a day. In local TV news, as of 2015, the five biggest companies (News Corp, CBS, Univision, Tribune Co., and Walt Disney Co.) each reaches into the homes of more than 20% of the American public on a daily basis. Even more astonishing, for four of those companies, local TV news is essentially a side project, bringing in less than 5% of the media company's total revenue.[2]

Media conglomerates have grown in three different ways. First, some large media companies simply buy a large number of the same type of media properties. Gannett, for example, essentially specializes in newspapers. They may own a whole lot of newspapers, but that's all they do. Another form of media concentration is *vertical integration* where media companies attempt to buy up more of the parts within a single industry. For example, CBS is a studio, which produces its own shows. They are also a distributor, selling those shows to stations. And they own many stations. In effect, they own media properties at each step of the process from creation to you. A third process is called *horizontal integration*, which involves buying media properties across several industries. We see this process at work with Comcast, which owns properties in the film industry, in television, and online.

The net effect of all of these forms of conglomeration, according to one accounting, is that in 1983, 90% of American media was owned by 50 companies and, by 2011, 90% was controlled by only six companies.[3] Ben Bagdikian, the most prominent voice opposing media concentration and author of *The New Media Monopoly*, goes further and says it's not just six corporations, but, "five men [who control] all the media once run by fifty corporations of twenty years earlier."[4]

## The Homogenization Hypothesis

Concentration in ownership reduces diversity in media in ways that can be downright deadly, proponents of the Homogenization Hypothesis tell us. Sociologist Eric Klinenberg's 2007 book, *Fighting for Air*, tells us the tragic story of how concentrated media led to multiple deaths after train

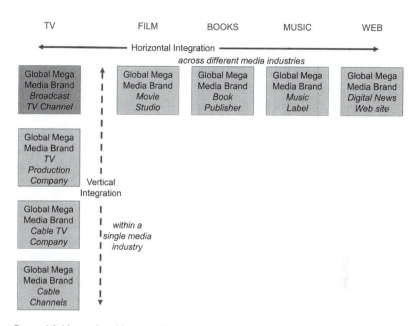

*Figure 4.1* Vertical vs. Horizontal Integration

derailment near Minot, North Dakota. In the middle of the night on January 18, 2002, a Canadian Pacific Railway train jumped the rails, spilling 240,000 gallons of anhydrous ammonia, a hazardous chemical, which, when airborne, can burn the eyes and skin and shut down a person's respiratory system. Local officials had to warn the public to stay indoors at all costs. With local television off the air for the night and local power outages, the radio was the only choice to broadcast emergency information to the public.

But there was no emergency information on the local radio stations. Instead, as Klinenberg writes, "all six of Minot's name-brand stations… continued playing a standard menu of canned music served up by smooth-talking DJs trading in light banter and off-color jokes while the giant toxic cloud floated into town." Why? Because all of the local stations, like so many across the country, had been bought up by Clear Channel, which centralized its programming to a single studio in San Antonio, Texas. Unable to broadcast the emergency information in a timely fashion, ultimately, one person died, 330 had to be treated for injuries from exposure, and many in the town have had lingering respiratory issues.

The case in Minot is unusual in the sense that concentrated ownership rarely leads to fatalities. On the other hand, the loss of local programming is all too common. With the exception of your local public radio or college station, few communities are lucky enough to have programming that isn't beamed from some distant studio. Prior to the Telecommunications Act of 1996, which expanded the upward limit on the number of stations a media company could own, the ten biggest companies together owned just 290 stations. Within a decade, by 2005, they owned 2,504 stations.[5] By 2012, Clear Channel alone owned 828 stations, reaching 160 million people (almost half the country!) daily.[6]

Corporate mergers in every media sector mean that companies have cut costs by concentrating the production of content—finding "efficiencies" or "synergies" in corporate-speak. In newspapers, that means a greater reliance on national wire services, centralized production processes, and content-sharing agreements with local television stations.[7] In the six years between 2006 and 2012, newspapers cut 30% of newsroom positions or about 14,000 jobs.[8] On TV, an increasing number of local news segments are pre-packaged by their parent company. In their 2011 report on the "Information Needs of Communities," even the Federal Communications Commission concluded that "The independent watchdog function that the Founding Fathers envisioned for journalism…is in some cases at risk at the local level."[9]

All of that means that local communities have less of the civic information they need to judge their local politicians, less investigative reporting into local social and environmental problems, and less exposure for local arts of all sorts. How do corrupt politicians get busted? How do social injustices get uncovered? How can a great local band in Manchester, New Hampshire break out onto the national scene if most of the country's playlists are selected in San Antonio?

Klinenberg's primary concern is the loss of diversity in the form of localism, but looking around entertainment media, we're also struck by the overwhelming sameness of national programming. From the endless parade of superhero movies and cooking competition TV shows to the predictable hit songs by the same three artists (or, sometimes, it seems like just Taylor Swift). According to the logic of the Homogenization Hypothesis, when fewer companies own nearly all of the media ecosystem, there is a less competitive and diverse marketplace because they are essentially able to air or print whatever content they prefer.[10] If there were more media companies, so the logic goes, they would need to be more attuned to public preferences as they competed for audience share. Furthermore, with a wider range of media companies, there might be more diversity of content as some companies choose to produce content for niche audiences.

For Bagdikian, the most troubling trend of media concentration is the loss of diversity in ideas within journalism. He argues that news outlets systematically underreport the sins of their parent company and provide favorable coverage to the political ideas preferred by the company leader-ship. Bagdikian argues that the major news outlets failed to report the Bush administration's misrepresentations during the build-up to the 2003 Iraq War because the owners of the mega-media companies were hesitant to critique the Bush administration during a time of war. While he does acknowledge "truthful" reporting from outlets like *The New Yorker* (owned by major media company Condé Nast, by the way), such pockets of truth lack the influence of major news outlets like CBS, NBC, and ABC. Others have pointed to the way that media mogul Rupert Mur-doch has used his vast media empire, including Fox News channel, the *New York Post*, and the *WSJ*, to advance his conservative economic views.[11] There is also some evidence that news outlets have sheltered their parent companies from criticism. On multiple occasions, for example, NBC News did not report that their parent company at the time, General Electric, was fined by the government for persistent pollu-tion in the Hudson River.[12]

In sum, for proponents of the Homogenization Hypothesis, media owner-ship has become increasingly concentrated and that trend has produced a media system where a small number of voices dominate the conversation. On the face of it, the argument sounds compelling and seems to match our intuitive sense of how power is concentrated. However, as we shall see, not only is the concentration of media ownership overstated, there is very little support for the idea that concentration in ownership reduces diversity—and, under some circumstances, the opposite may be true.

### How Concentrated Are Media?

One important point of contention is the seemingly simple question of just how concentrated mass media industries are in the U.S. The famous claim mentioned above that 90% of mass media are owned by six corpor-ations is widely repeated online, has been mentioned in Congressional testimony, and is cited by Bagdikian and many of his followers. In fact, after an extensive search, we have not been able to uncover the origin of this statistic, but what is clear is that it is almost certainly not true. It is true that the four largest mass media companies control about 53% of what we read and watch. But, compared to other industries, it's only moderately concentrated. It is also not in the range of industry concentra-tion that would trigger anti-trust laws. And it most certainly cannot be accurately described as a "media monopoly."

The real story of media concentration is a complicated one and requires both breaking down the various industries of the mass media sector and then considering integration across the various industries. Economists who study concentration in industries use two different met-rics of concentration. First, they use what's referred to as C4 or the total market share owned by the top four companies within the industry. The problem with that measure is that it could be that C4 is 90%, but that 89% of that is owned by the top firm. Moreover, it doesn't tell us anything about the distribution outside of the top four companies.

A better measure is the Herfindahl-Hirschman Index (HHI for short). The U.S. Department of Justice (DOJ) and the Federal Trade Commission (FTC) use HHI as a way of assessing how concentrated an industry is and in deciding whether they need to enforce anti-trust laws. As the DOJ web site explains:

> The HHI is calculated by squaring the market share of each firm competing in the market and then summing the resulting numbers. For example, for a market consisting of four firms with shares of 30, 30, 20, and 20 percent, the HHI is 2,600 ($30^2 + 30^2 + 20^2 + 20^2 = 2,600$). An industry with very highly diffused ownership would have an HHI close to 0 and an industry with only one firm would have an HHI of 10,000. The DOJ suggests the following guidelines for interpreting HHI:

> Less than 1,500: low concentration
> 1,500–2,500: moderately concentrated
> More than 2,500: highly concentrated

Back to mass media. The researcher who has done the best job of pulling together media ownership data is economist Noam Eli. In 2009, Eli examined in great detail ownership patterns over time across four important sectors: mass media, information technology, telecommunications, and Internet media. Table 4.1 summarizes some of his findings within the mass media sector. Across these various industries of the mass media sector, we find different degrees of concentration. Quite to the contrary of popular rhetoric, daily newspapers have very low concentration. On the other hand, in radio production networks, the top four firms (including the top company, Clear Channel) own 73.6% of the market. Still, none of these industries even approach the HHI of 2,500 necessary to qualify as highly concentrated. Recall that Clear Channel owns more than 800 stations. But to put that figure in context, there are more than 30,000 radio stations in the country.[13]

In the last row of the table, we can see that the average across all mass media industries (weighted for their relative size) is 52.9% and the HHI is only 1,209. That's lower than the concentration in the retail coffee industry where the giants of Dunkin' Donuts and Starbucks combined represent more than 60% of the market (HHI of 1,901). Then again, media isn't coffee. News media, in particular, play a central role in supporting a functioning democracy. Even entertainment media like movies, music, and novels can challenge the

*Table 4.1* Concentration within Mass Media Industries

| Industry | C4 (Market Share of Top 4 Firms) | HHI in 2009 (Measure of Industry Concentration) | HHI in 1984 | HHI in 1996 |
|---|---|---|---|---|
| Radio Stations | 13.1% | 72 | 0.1 | 6.4 |
| Radio Production Networks | 73.6% | 1,736 | 1,380 | 2,309 |
| TV Stations | 27.7% | 253 | 73 | 110 |
| TV Shows for Network Prime Time | 62.4% | 1,223 | 681 | 1,119 |
| Film Production and Distribution | 65.9% | 1,419 | 1,262 | 1,245 |
| Movie Theater Chains | 45.4% | 653 | 182 | 249 |
| Music Publishers | 55.1% | 920 | 541 | 1,081 |
| Book Publishers | 31.6% | 337 | 139 | 203 |
| Daily Newspapers | 21.9% | 172 | 155 | 230 |
| Weighted Mass Media Sector Average | 52.9% | 1,209 | 564 | 693 |

HHI: Less than 1,500: low concentration; 1,500–2,500: moderately concentrated; More than 2,500: highly concentrated
Source: Eli, 2009

way we see the world, offer representations that inform self-identity, and enrich the wider marketplace of ideas. It is worth considering whether we need a different standard of concentrated ownership for media than for other consumer goods.

By the same token, examining HHI over the years, we do see that in most industries concentration has grown. Since the 1980s, prime time TV, for example, has almost doubled in its HHI. That pattern holds up for the sector as a whole, growing from an HHI of 564 in 1984 to 693 in 1996 to 1,209 in 2009. Still, in some industries like radio networks and music publishers, concentration has eased a bit from a peak in the 1990s.

If the "media monopoly" is overstated at the national level, there are certainly many cities with only one daily newspaper (or none) and, therefore, few sources of local journalism and programming. But, in many cases, local newspapers aren't being driven out of business by mega-media competitors, but by declining pools of readers willing to pay for the product.

None of this discussion denies that the mass media sector is moderately concentrated and, therefore, perhaps a source of concern. However, it does show that some of the rhetoric about concentration in ownership is hyperbolic and, in some cases, just plain wrong. With this in mind, let's turn to the second part of the Homogenization Hypothesis, which argues that the current media system lacks diversity.

### How Much Diversity?

The Homogenization Hypothesis argues that we have witnessed a decline in the diversity of content as concentration in ownership has grown. But what do we mean when we say diversity? Sociologists Joshua Gamson and Pearl Latteier point to three types of diversity: format diversity, demographic diversity, and idea diversity.[14] *Format diversity* might be thought of as the different categories of programming available. National news, local news, cooking shows, cop shows, country songs, reggae songs, action movies, indie movies, etc. *Demographic diversity* refers to the variety of the types of people we read about or see in media. Is there diversity in terms of race, gender, social class, sexual orientation, ability or disability, or geography? *Idea diversity* means the variety of political, social, or religious ideas we encounter.

In the age of a thousand television channels, video, music, and news on the web, and books shipped overnight, it's hard to argue that we have a lack of format diversity. There are so many good TV shows that, in a sketch at the 2015 Emmys, host Andy Samberg imagined having to live in a bunker for a year to be able to watch it all. The extreme diversity in music has led some music critics to worry about "balkanization" of tastes and the loss of a "rock canon."[15] Noting the vast number of new ventures in journalism online, including FiveThirtyEight, Vox.com, ProPublica, and Gimlet Media, Ira Glass, longtime host of public radio show *This American Life*, argued that "We're living through a new golden age of journalism."[16] Even in places, like Minot, North Dakota, where local media has disappeared, social media sites like Facebook and Twitter, community web sites, and online radio streams allow for dissemination of local news and arts. High levels of format diversity also make possible more idea diversity. The Internet offers an ever-expanding marketplace of ideas where outside the mainstream can flourish. There is no shortage of format and idea diversity available.

Of these three forms of diversity, there is no question that demographic diversity is the most limited. As we will discuss in chapters 8 and 9, media are not a mirror that reflects society. Traditional forms of media dramatically overrepresent men, the affluent, whites, and people without any physical limitations. Unlike format and idea diversity, those patterns do not change as dramatically online. Web users are disproportionately white, affluent, and male; and producers of web content are even more so.[17]

Moreover, we need to be careful about assuming that the web has ush-ered in a utopia of format and idea diversity. There is a big difference between what's available to those who go looking for something good and what most people watch and read. The most popular TV shows are sports, police procedurals like *CSI*, and reality programs like *The Voice*. The movies with the biggest box office returns tend to feature super-heroes or teens facing a dystopian future. One of the most common sources of information about current events is local TV news, which offers few ideas outside the narrow dichotomy of Democrats and Repub-licans (we will address that more in Chapter 7). And an awful lot of what appears on Facebook consists of cute puppy photos and "What Harry Potter character are you?" quizzes. Diversity is out there, but most people aren't looking for it.

### Does Concentration Reduce Diversity?

If the picture on both concentrated ownership and diversity is mixed, what about the link between the two? Is the lack of diversity in the most widely available content caused by concentrated ownership? A popular theory in economics, the Hotelling-Steiner Effect, holds that concentration in ownership will lead to *more* format diversity. With many different media companies in a market, they will also compete for the "median consumer" and provide whatever kind of content the lar-gest number of people want. But as we move towards greater concen-tration in ownership, companies don't have to compete as much for the masses and can diversify their content to reach niche markets. For example, in a music radio market with many different owners, most will choose to play Top 50 music because that's what most customers want. But, if there are only one or two companies in the market, they already have the Top 50 market locked down and can expand into other genres. In short, the Hotelling-Steiner tradition argues the *exact opposite* of the Homogenization Hypothesis.[18]

While there is very sophisticated research supporting the Hotelling-Steiner Effect, it is not without its critics. As media sociologist Gabriel Rossman writes:

> what the economists are capturing [in studies of radio] is that, under oligopoly, Adult Contemporary stations are splitting into the narrow subformats of Hot AC and Soft AC, which is different from the true increase in diversity implied by the original theory[19]

What concentrated ownership supports, then, within a particular market is not truly risky or inventive programming, but slight diversifica-tion of formats.

If Rossman is critical of the Hotelling-Steiner Effect, his research on radio also rejects the Homogenization Hypothesis. In his book, *Climbing the Charts*, Rossman points out that if it was the case that the big chain owners, like Clear Channel, were simply pushing out a single playlist to all of their stations each day, any variation would be *between* chains, not *within* chains. In other words, a Clear Channel and a Cumulus station might be different, but all Clear Channel stations would be alike. But that's not what his findings showed. The similarity between stations in the same chain as compared to any other stations was not greater than what we would expect by random chance.

But the reason that Clear Channel stations are no more similar than any other station is not because there's a huge amount of diversity. Rather, it's because *all* of the stations, regardless of chain, were deeply homogenized. Rossman shows there is, in fact, homogenization, but it is not because of concentrated ownership. As he writes, "what gives a song an advantage in a competitive market is the backing of a major firm with the resources and connections to promote the song."[20] Rihanna's "Man Down" was an instant success in 2011 not because Clear Channel forced it upon stations, but because Def Jam records spent more than $1 million promoting it, while actually recording the album cost a mere $78,000.[21] Using a massive promotional blitz, artists like Rihanna can make sure their songs are playing on every station in the country.

Two decades earlier, media scholar Robert Entman studied 91 local newspapers and found no differences in news diversity between newspapers with monopolies, quasi-monopolies, or in competitive markets. As with Rossman's findings, the lack of differences was not because all were diverse, but because all the newspapers were so similar. Most of the newspapers ran wire stories, covered the same type of stories, and cited the same type of sources. The conclusion from both studies is that the sameness pervading our radio stations and newspapers is certainly linked to practices common in capitalistic, profit-driven industries—just not a particular effect of concentrated ownership.

## If Not Concentration, Then What?

The evidence for the Homogenization Hypothesis is limited at best. If it is not concentrated ownership, then what helps explain whether media content is highly diverse or not? For Rossman, the homogeneity in broadcast radio stems primarily from mega promotional campaigns that favor big name artists. Working across various media, other scholars have offered a range of explanations for the level of diversity in content.

Examining pop music, sociologists Richard Peterson and David Berger showed that it is not the number of firms in the industry that matters. It's the number of record labels that affects how much diversity there is. Until about 1960, almost all firms had only one record label. After 1960, through a series of mergers, the number of firms declined (i.e., ownership became more concentrated). However, firms acquired multiple labels to reach the growing number of niche audiences (e.g., rock n' roll, country, folk, etc.). By looking at the number of different songs in the top 10 and top 100 songs of the Billboard music charts, they showed that diversity was associated not with the number of firms, but with the number of labels.[22]

Building on that analysis, sociologist Paul Lopes has argued that *open systems*, with more labels, create opportunities for a wider range of songs, artists, and new genres to break onto the Billboard charts. *Closed systems*, with fewer labels, produce far less diversity. There may be a small number of companies that own most of the labels and, ultimately, collect the profits. But an open system allows for diversity even if there is concentration in ownership.[23] The same could be said of TV where a few companies own most of the channels, but the huge number of channels allows for experimentation and a show for every kind of viewer (even fans of televised bass fishing!).

But just because media industries may be increasingly open does not mean they are ideologically diverse. For example, scholarship on the "political economy" of media has illustrated the integral role mass media play in (re)producing political and economic power.[24] According to Edward Herman and Noam Chomsky's "propaganda model," American mass media effectively manipulate public opinion through five "filters," or channels of influence: a profit-driven ownership structure, a reliance on advertising revenue, a reliance on official sources, the production of "flak" or criticism of media, and a tacit fear of ideologies deemed un-American, such as communism.[25] While it is true, as we will discuss in later chapters, that most journalists maintain a sense of agency in their day-to-day work, their work is often limited by these filters "because of their socialisation in the newsroom as well as the internalisation of dominant values, norms, and ideologies" prominent in their workplace, profession, and nation.[26] Herman and Chomsky contend that this tendency, when viewed within the confines of a moderately concentrated media industry, systematically produces content that represent the interests of the ruling class rather than those of a diverse and democratically engaged public.

First, rather than being incentivized to promote a diverse and informed citizenry, the market's *profit-driven ownership structure* requires companies to give preference to media products that generate consumers. And while these companies compete for audiences, their shared interest in maintaining a populace of consumers means that they are incentivized to cooperate, intentionally or not, to uphold the (capitalist) economic order. Such cooperation can range from implicitly preferencing pro-market views to waging an organized propaganda campaign designed to combat labor unions, as associations of American corporations did in the aftermath of World War II.[27]

Second, because most media companies' *rely primarily on advertising revenue* instead of subscription fees, donations, or tax subsidies, media companies are encouraged to avoid highly controversial content that might turn away audiences, and by extension, advertisers. This is a central reason why companies have reacted to pressure from audiences by letting go of media stars, like Bill O'Reilly of Fox News[28] or Matt Lauer of NBC,[29] after they were accused of multiple accounts of sexual harassment as part of the #metoo movement. And, given the for-profit orientation of most media companies, the perceived pressure from audiences also extends to subscription-driven services, which would explain why Netflix swiftly distanced itself from Kevin Spacey after similar allegations.[30]

Third, news media *rely primarily on official and elite sources*, such as representatives of government agencies and corporations, who frequently provide information and perspectives on newsworthy events. By providing a platform for corporate elites and government officials, and not offering it to others without such position, news media further legitimate the authority of these institutions while systematically disadvantaging potential sources and perspectives that may challenge the dominant narrative on a given issue. These biases can even extend across national contexts, as many African newspapers have been shown to give preference to narratives constructed by journalists, and their respective sources, from prominent Western countries.[31]

Fourth, political and economic elites often generate media criticism, or *flak*, in an effort to discipline or discredit reporting they disagree with. U.S. President Donald Trump's dismissal of many media stories and outlets as "fake news"—a rhetorical strategy intended to deflect and delegitimize journalism he dislikes—is an infamous example. You might be surprised to learn that media participate in the production of flak, too, primarily through partisan media outlets like Fox News and MSNBC that blend news with opinion and have been known to battle back-and-forth over their coverage of a given issue. Because flak is so common, it can function indirectly as a "prior threat mechanism" because the potential for petitions, lawsuits, or smear campaigns can lead media makers toward self-censorship.[32]

Finally, Herman and Chomsky contend that media perpetuate a dominant ideology of *"anti-communism."* However, since the global decline of communism in the 1980s, the focus has broadened to a more general "fear" of other groups and ideologies considered by the elite to be un-American. For example, American media coverage of the global "war on terror" typically conforms to this frame by presenting information from a U.S. perspective. Whether by interviewing political elites, embedding reporters with American military forces, and even by employing a majority of staff members socialized in a culture accepting of

American hegemony, American media have long normalized an imperialist view of U.S. foreign relations. By producing coverage that is critical or ignorant of unorthodox perspectives, media implicitly give preference to those that are already in place in a given society.

We know what you may be thinking: "this sounds like a conspiracy theory." It is not. The general consensus among social scientists is that relations of power and domination are more often latent or unintended functions of social structures—in this case, a moderately concentrated, highly profitable, and loosely regulated media system—rather than malicious and convoluted conspiracies. From the perspective of these media companies and the elites whose interests they supposedly serve, it is understandable, perhaps even rational, to operate according to the principles outlined above.

It may come as little surprise that many have criticized Herman and Chomsky's propaganda model for being overly prescriptive and ideological. Nevertheless, few scholars have been able to refute its basic claim: that American media companies tend to produce content that aligns, more or less, with political and economic ideologies—like individualism, nationalism, capitalism, and consumerism—that, first and foremost, serve elite interests.

## Do Owners Matter?

There is no question that owners do, in fact, matter. History has given us examples of media moguls committed to operating muckraking newspapers that act to protect the public against abuses of power. It has also shown us examples of owners who abuse power themselves by using news outlets to advance their own interests. Most mass media industries may be only moderately concentrated in ownership, but it's quite possible to have a very unconcentrated industry with many owners all doing the same kinds of bad things. Additionally, anywhere there is concentrated ownership, there is also concentrated power, giving rise to the *potential* to exploit the power of media on a mass scale.

Several research findings have shown that ownership can, and often does, influence the content media outlets produce. For example, in their analysis of over a thousand local newspaper stories about a controversial right-to-die legal case from 139 U.S. newspapers, Deana Rohlinger and Jennifer Proffitt found that independently-owned newspapers were more likely to adopt partisan framings and to engage the politics surrounding the case, while chain newspapers adopted a risk minimization strategy of steering clear of politics. Rohlinger and Proffitt conclude that "audiences of independently owned outlets are more likely to be exposed to a more robust conversation about controversial issues than their corporately owned counterparts."[33]

Similarly, following the 1996 Telecommunications Act, which, as we describe above, loosened media industry restrictions on ownership, researchers found "substantial differences in how newspapers reported on these proposed regulatory changes depending on the financial interests of their corporate owners."[34] Other studies have identified similar differences between how newspapers owned by smaller and larger media conglomerates covered the Supreme Court's controversial *Citizens United* ruling, which allowed corporations to donate unlimited amounts of money to political campaigns.[35] The researchers reasoned that much of this added spending would go directly to media companies to purchase television advertising. It turns out, they were right. According to one estimate, political campaigns spent more than $9 billion in both the 2012 and 2016 elections,[36] compared to $2.6 billion in 2008,[37] the majority of which went to local television stations.

Other researchers claim that the question is not how big or small the company is, but *who* owns it. Political scientist James Hamilton writes, "When ownership is concentrated in an individual or family, then these people may take pleasure in sacrificing some profits for the sake of the public good (as they perceive it)."[38] For example, the Sulzberger family, which still owns a controlling share of *The New York Times*, has long shown an interest in supporting investigative journalism aimed at informing the public even though it is very expensive.

By contrast, many owners are not shy about the fact that they enjoy the political influence they get from owning a large media company. One of the most prominent examples is Rupert Murdoch, the conservative magnate behind News Corporation, which owns the most circulated American newspaper, the *WSJ*, as well as 21st Century Fox, which owns America's most popular cable news company, Fox News.[39] After Murdoch purchased the *WSJ* in 2007, researchers found that the newspaper's editorial pages were much more critical of Democrats, and much less critical of Republicans, than they were in the years prior.

In much the same manner, Sinclair Broadcast Group has aggressively purchased local TV news affiliates since its founding in the 1970s. It is now the largest television station operator in the country with 193 television stations in over 100 markets, reaching 40% of the U.S.viewing public. While they have pushed news segments with strong conservative slants for years, there was a public outcry in early 2018 when Sinclair imposed a "must-run" segment requiring all of their news anchors to give a scripted speech about the biased news media and so-called "fake news." The apparent goal of the segment was to discredit other news outlets that had criticized President Trump. In subsequent reporting, many journalists working for Sinclair stations described their own discomfort in being forced to read these statements imposed by their owner.[40] Even though Sinclair owns a small fraction of all television stations in the country, they were able to push a political message to such a broad audience precisely because of their concentrated ownership.

## Concentrated Ownership in an Age of Tech Behemoths

Though some of the most alarmist arguments are overblown, there are cases today where highly concentrated ownership threatens diversity in ways that might reasonably trouble citizens and consumers. The Sinclair Broadcasting story offers one. But, in a strange twist, among the most disturbing developments in concentrated media ownership is not a "media monopoly" where there is a single seller, but a "media monopsony" where there is a single buyer. Many commentators are increasingly concerned with Internet retailer Amazon. com's extreme influence over the book industry. In most respects, Amazon is horizontally integrated. It has a music service, streaming video, and a line of tablet computers. It also sells everything from couches to TVs to home-cleaning services. In fact, its efforts at vertical integration have been limited. It has a very small publishing service that has yet to produce anything that might be called a "hit" book. They don't print the physical books. They have very few storefronts. They don't deliver the books themselves (USPS and FedEx do that). Still, it is the company's power within the single industry of book retail that gives rise to concerns.

In 2014, *New York Times* columnist Paul Krugman wrote, "Amazon. com ... has too much power, and uses it in ways that hurt America."[41] The immediate impetus for Krugman's story was a dispute between Amazon and a book publisher Hachette that tried to refuse Amazon's insistence on a bigger cut of the revenue from book sales. After Hachette balked, Amazon dramatically raised the prices on their books and listed Hachette books as backordered, essentially coercing Hachette into agreeing to the new contract terms.

On the one hand, Amazon's pushy tactics keep prices lower for consumers. But Authors United, a group of writers campaigning against Amazon's "cultural monopoly," says that Amazon's power is bad for both writers and consumers. As journalist Vauhini Vara explained in *The New Yorker*, "Amazon has used its market power ... to influence which books get attention ... [and] these practices ... make [publishers] more risk-averse in deciding which books to publish."[42] Consequently, publishers are less likely to take chances on innovative books and writers, leading to a less diverse and vital literary culture.

Perhaps most disturbing is that there is little check on Amazon's monopsony. The DOJ and the FTC are unlikely to sue Amazon because they actually do lower consumer prices and most anti-trust laws are designed to make sure that monopolies are not engaged in price-gouging. The Federal Communications Commission (FCC), which does attempt to ensure diversity in media, has no claim over Amazon because they are not a broadcaster and only a limited content producer. No research to date has documented Amazon's dampening effects on the book industry. Still, the Amazon example illustrates how concentration in media ownership often leads to a concentration in power in ways that can be concerning.

Ultimately, no theory is deterministic of how much format, demographic, and idea diversity exist in our contemporary media ecosystem. There is substantial evidence that factors like profit-motive, revenue source, substantial promotional campaigns, and the openness of systems affect the type of content available to the public. While owners can and do matter, there is less support for the idea that concentrated ownership is the primary cause of our homogeneous media system.

## Notes

1  Le, Vanna. 2015. "The World's Largest Media Companies Of 2015." *Forbes Online*. May 22. Available at: www.forbes.com/sites/vannale/2015/05/22/the-worlds-largest-media-companies-of-2015/.
2  Pew Research Center. 2015. "Report: State of the News Media 2015." Available at: www.journalism.org/2015/04/29/state-of-the-news-media-2015/.
3  Shah, Anup. 2011. "Media Conglomerates, Mergers, Concentration of Ownership." *Global Issues*. Available at: www.globalissues.org/article/159/media-conglomerates-mergers-concentration-of-ownership.
4  Bagdikian, Ben H. 2004. *The New Media Monopoly*. Boston: Beacon Press.
5  Rossman, Gabriel. 2012. *Climbing the Charts*. Princeton, NJ: Princeton University Press.
6  Pew Research Center's Project for Excellence in Journalism. 2015. "Who Owns the News Media." Available at: https://web.archive.org/web/20130726133522/www.stateofthemedia.org/media-ownership/.
7  Hochberg, A. 2013. "The Challenges, Benefits Of Consolidated Editing & Design Centers." Retrieved December 5, 2014, from www.poynter.org/news/mediawire/223931/the-challenges-benefits-of-consolidated-editing-design-centers/; Potter, D., & Matsa, K. E. (2014). "Sharing With Other Media." Retrieved from https://www.poynter.org/newsletters/2013/the-challenges-benefits-of-consolidated-editing-design-centers/.
8  American Society of Newspaper Editors. 2013. "Newsroom Employment Census." Available at: http://asne.org/content.asp?pl=121&sl=284&contentid=284.
9  Federal Communications Commission. 2011. "Report: THE INFORMATION NEEDS OF COMMUNITIES." Available at: www.scribd.com/doc/57454752/FCC-Report-THE-INFORMATION-NEEDS-OF-COMMUNITIES
10  Signorielli, Nancy. 1989. "Television and Conceptions About Sex Roles: Maintaining Conventionality and the Status Quo." *Sex Roles* 21:341–360.
11  Wolff, Michael. 2008. *The Man Who Owns the News: Inside the Secret World of Rupert Murdoch*. New York: Broadway Books.
12  Lee, Martin A. 1991. "USA: Arms and the Media: Business as Usual." *Index on Censorship* 20:29–31.
13  Federal Communications Commission. 2015. "Broadcast Radio AM and FM Application Status Lists." Available at: www.fcc.gov/encyclopedia/broadcast-radio-am-and-fm-application-status-lists. Noam, Eli. 2009. *Media Ownership and Concentration in America*. New York: Oxford University Press.
14  Gamson, Joshua and Pearl Latteier. 2004. "Do Media Monsters Devour Diversity?" *Contexts* 3:26–32.

15  "Expert Forecast: Rock Music." 2000. "Wall Street Journal." Online. Available at: http://interactive.wsj.com/millennium/articles/flash-SB944517220243220711. htm.

16  Gillian, Reagan. 2011. "To make a Long Story … Long? Remnick, Glass and Friends see a Big Future in Long-Form Journalism." *Politico*. Available at: https://www.politico.com/states/new-york/albany/story/2011/03/to-make-a-long-story-long-remnick-glass-and-friends-see-a-big-future-in-long-form-journalism-000000.

17  Schradie, Jen. 2011. "The Digital Production Gap: The Digital Divide and Web 2.0 Collide." *Poetics* 39(2):145–168.

18  Sweeting, Andrew. 2010. "The Effects of Mergers on Product Positioning: Evidence from the Music Radio Industry." *The RAND Journal of Economics* 41:372–397.

19  Rossman, Gabriel. 2007. "if at first you don't succeed …"*OrgTheory*. Available at: https://orgtheory.wordpress.com/2007/10/19/if-at-first-you-dont-succeed/.

20  Rossman, Gabriel. 2011. "Gettin' Down on 'Friday.'" *Contexts* 10:68–69.

21  Chace, Zoe. 2011. "How Much Does It Cost To Make A Hit Song?" *Planet Money*, June 30. Available at: www.npr.org/sections/money/2011/07/05/137530847/how-much-does-it-cost-to-make-a-hit-song.

22  Peterson, Richard A. and David Berger. 1971. "Entrepreneurship in Organizations: Evidence from the Popular Music Industry." *Administrative Science Quarterly* 10:97–107.

23  Lopes, Paul D. 1992. "Innovation and Diversity in the Popular Music Industry, 1969 to 1990." *American Sociological Review* 57:56–71.

24  McChesney, Robert W. 2008. *The Political Economy of Media: Enduring Issues, Emerging Dilemmas*. New York: Monthly Review Press.

25  Herman, Edward S. and Noam Chomsky. 2002. *Manufacturing Consent: The Political Economy of the Mass Media*. New York: Pantheon.

26  Zollmann, Florian. 2017. "Bringing Propaganda Back into News Media Studies." *Critical Sociology* 0896920517731134.

27  Carey, Alex. 1996. *Taking the Risk Out of Democracy: Corporate Propaganda Versus Freedom and Liberty*. Urbana: University of Illinois Press.

28  Guo, Jeff. 2017. "Why Fox News Finally Dropped Bill O'Reilly." *Vox*. Retrieved July 19, 2018 (www.vox.com/policy-and-politics/2017/4/19/15361182/bill-oreilly-fox-harassment-allegations-fired).

29  Setoodeh, Ramin and Elizabeth Wagmeister. 2017. "Matt Lauer Accused of Sexual Harassment by Multiple Women (EXCLUSIVE)." *Variety*. Retrieved August 22, 2018. Available at: https://variety.com/2017/biz/news/matt-lauer-accused-sexual-harassment-multiple-women-1202625959/).

30  Fiegerman, Seth. 2018. "Kevin Spacey Cost Netflix $39 Million." *CNNMoney*. Retrieved August 21, 2018. Available at: https://money.cnn.com/2018/01/22/media/netflix-kevin-spacey-cost/index.html).

31  Wahutu, j Siguru. 2018. "What African Media? Rethinking Research on Africa's Press." *Global Media and Communication* 14(1):31–45.

32  Pedro, Joan. 2011. "The Propaganda Model in the Early 21st Century (Part I)." *International Journal of Communication* 5(0):41.

33  Rohlinger, Deana and Jennifer M. Proffitt. 2017. "How Much Does Ownership Matter? Deliberative Discourse in Local Media Coverage of the Terri Schiavo Case." *Journalism* 18(10):1274–91. Page 1283.

34  Gilens, Martin and Craig Hertzman. 2000. "Corporate Ownership and News Bias: Newspaper Coverage of the 1996 Telecommunications Act." *The Journal of Politics* 62(2):369–86. Page 369.

35 Bailard, Catie Snow. 2016. "Corporate Ownership and News Bias Revisited: Newspaper Coverage of the Supreme Court's Citizens United Ruling." *Political Communication* 33(4):583–604.

36 Kaye, Kate. 2017. "Data-Driven Targeting Creates Huge 2016 Political Ad Shift: Broadcast TV Down 20%, Cable and Digital Way Up." *Ad Age*. Retrieved January 25, 2018. Available at: http://adage.com/article/media/2016-political-broadcast-tv-spend-20-cable-52/307346/.

37 Seelye, Katharine Q. 2008. "About $2.6 Billion Spent on Political Ads in 2008." *The Caucus*. Retrieved January 25, 2018 Available at: http://thecaucus.blogs.nytimes.com/2008/12/02/about-26-billion-spent-on-political-ads-in-2008/.

38 Hamilton, James T. 2006. *All the News That's Fit to Sell*. Princeton, NJ: Princeton University Press.

39 Folkenflik, David. 2013. "Five Myths about Rupert Murdoch." *Washington Post*, November 8. Retrieved January 12, 2018. Available at: www.washingtonpost.com/opinions/five-myths-about-rupert-murdoch/2013/11/08/341837ea-47bf-11e3-b6f8-3782ff6cb769_story.html.

40 Fortin, Jacey and Jonah Engel Bromwich. 2018. "Sinclair Made Dozens of Local News Anchors Recite the Same Script." *The New York Times*, April 2. Available at: www.nytimes.com/2018/04/02/business/media/sinclair-news-anchors-script.html.

41 Krugman, Paul. 2014. "Amazon's Monopsony is Not O.K." *New York Times*, Oct. 19. Available at: www.nytimes.com/2014/10/20/opinion/paul-krugman-amazons-monopsony-is-not-ok.html.

42 Vara, Vauhini. 2015. "Is Amazon Creating a Cultural Monopoly?" *The New Yorker*, August 23. Available at: www.newyorker.com/business/currency/is-amazon-creating-a-cultural-monopoly.

## Chapter 5

# Big Brother Knows You're Watching

Apple's 1984 Super Bowl commercial has been called the most famous—and sometimes the greatest—advertisement of all time.[1] Directed by Ridley Scott for $650,000 and loosely riffing on George Orwell's novel *1984*, the ad depicts a dystopian future where people with mandatory uniforms and shaved heads obey an authoritarian Big Brother on a giant screen. A woman in bright red running shorts and sneakers disrupts the orderly proceedings and charges down a center aisle chased by the Thought Police. Big Brother is (presumably) defeated when the runner hurls a sledgehammer into the screen, shattering it.

Orwell wrote his novel wary of how governments might exploit mass media to control the public. With their Super Bowl ad, Apple was arguing implicitly that their computers would turn the power of media production over to the public, rescuing them from the tyranny of governments. This sort of libertarian vision of individual freedom provided via free market capitalism has always been an essential feature of the ideology of Silicon Valley. The contest between companies and the government for control of media was cast in dramatic relief in 2016, when the FBI took Apple to court, attempting to force the company to develop new technology that would unlock the iPhone 5c of one of the perpetrators in a mass shooting in San Bernardino, CA.

While Apple's Super Bowl commercial and 2016 court battle raise important questions about propaganda, privacy, and the state, the simple story that the government should keep its damn hands off mass media is too simple. All states and political actors play some role in structuring, regulating, and managing mass media in ways that can be both beneficial and troubling. In this chapter, we will explore forms of media regulation and management carried out by states around the world. We will also examine how digital media have created new possibilities for liberation from regimes as well as new means of state control.

## The State and the Media

When sociologists say "the state," they mean more than just the President and Congress. Social theorist Max Weber's well-known definition of the state was an organized authority with "a monopoly on the legitimate use of physical force within a given territory." According to his definition, the public sees the state's use of force as legitimate. We accept that the police, for example, can use forms of force if we violate laws. Because the public accepts this, the state has the power to create laws that can be enforced by people officially acting on its behalf. Most current sociologists see *the state* as including the government, all its departments and bureaucratic offices, the police and military, and the welfare state (including functions like education and the social safety net). In the U.S., power is spread across various branches of the state (e.g., Congress, the Supreme Court, and the President) and across different levels (municipal, county, state, and federal). It's all part of the state.

All states structure media, though various countries adopt different approaches. Throughout much of the world, state-funded public media entities, like the UK's BBC, produce a substantial portion of media content. In the U.S., we tend to think of media as originating with the individual members of the public (e.g., if I start a blog) or with private corporations like cable companies, movie studios, newspapers, and social media startups. Given that most media originate in the private sector, one might reasonably ask, why does the state get to interfere? For a few reasons.

First, in many cases, the infrastructure and R&D (research and development) costs necessary to develop and support media are just too massive for any one private company to make those investments. The state builds electrical grids, subsidizes the cost of laying fiber optic cables, and spent years funding the development of this kooky project called the Internet. It's not that the state is interfering in media, but rather the state is playing a role in creating the framework for media.

The state also protects the public interest. As we have seen, the U.S. Constitution guarantees freedom of the press and establishes a postal service which subsidizes the distribution of newspapers and other periodicals. These provisions act in the public interest by encouraging an independent press to serve as a watchdog. Just as the Department of Health inspects the sanitary conditions in restaurants, the FCC regulates media content in ways that are intended to promote the public interest. Similarly, Congress funds the government agency known as the Corporation for Public Broadcasting (CPB) to support public television and radio, which provides news and entertainment in the public interest.

Acting in the public interest, the state also regulates access to broadcast media, those media delivered over the airwaves like radio and TV. FM radio stations broadcast at frequencies from 87.9 to 107.9 and, in any given geographic market, there are only so many frequencies. Rather than having chaos where radio stations try to out-broadcast each other on the same frequency (as was the case in the 1920s), the state has a licensing process that grants exclusive permission to an organization to use a frequency in a market. In the same way that the state protects our scarce natural resources through the National Parks system and ensures public safety by licensing drivers to use our roads, the state protects the public interest by regulating access to the airwaves.

Of course, there are wide-ranging debates about what exactly is the "public interest." Some (libertarians in particular) favor *deregulation*, with the state imposing fewer restrictions on media companies. They argue that competition in an unregulated free market would produce the kind of media content that the public wants. By this logic, state regulation is simply unnecessary interference and runs contrary to the public interest. Advocates of greater regulation believe that there are "market failures" where customers and democracy are not well served by the natural tendencies of the market. Examples of market failures could be when businesses become monopolies or when the interests of vulnerable minorities (e.g. children) aren't adequately served by companies, with the free market working against public interest. As we will see, the U.S. may have more or less regulation in the future, but doing away with all media regulation is probably unlikely.

Finally, states regulate and manage media in ways that promote the ideology of the ruling regime. Authoritarian states, like North Korea, have strict limits on the media content that the public can access and tend to heavily fund propagandistic media praising the country's leaders. Though it's far less blatant, the U.S.'s approach to regulating media also promotes our values of democracy (e.g., by guaranteeing freedom of the press) and free market capitalism (by privatizing most media systems). Every ruling party throughout the world adopts a wide range of media management tactics to attempt to garner favorable coverage for their ideas.

## Regulation and the FCC

The responsibility for supporting and managing media is distributed throughout the state. The courts enforce copyright laws. The DOJ and the FTC bring anti-trust cases, which attempt to break up monopolies and oligopolies in media markets when necessary. Congress funds the CPB and the National Endowment for the Arts (NEA). However, the most important regulatory body when it comes to media is the FCC.

Founded in 1934 to regulate the radio, telephone, and telegraph systems, the FCC today regulates television, cable, satellite, wireless networks, and the Internet. The commission is led by five commissioners, appointed by the President and confirmed by the Senate for five-year terms. The commissioners tend to be communications lawyers, businesspeople, and legislators. In practice, three are from the President's political party and two from the other major party.

*Figure 5.1* FCC Offices in Washington, D.C. Source: www.flickr.com/photos/fccdot gov/4808818548

Broadly speaking, the FCC's current goals are to promote competition in media markets, promote "Internet openness," affordability, and access for consumers, to encourage localism and diversity in media content, and enhance the nation's cybersecurity.[2] These goals fall into three categories of regulation: access, ownership, and content.

### Access: Broadcasting Licenses

The earliest function of the FCC was to issue radio licenses. Who had access to the scarce public resources of the airwaves remained a hotly contested issue through the mid-2000s. In issuing licenses, the FCC tends to favor for-profit businesses, often those owned by major chains like ClearChannel, the conglomerate discussed in Chapter 4. There are good reasons for giving licenses to corporate radio companies. They tend to comply with regulations: they don't curse on the air, they file the right paperwork, their shows sound professional. But, for some, that's exactly the problem: they don't offer any real diversity.

In the late 1990s and early 2000s, pirate radio stations, like Pirate Cat Radio in San Francisco, Boulder Free Radio, and Knoxville First Amendment Radio, tested the FCC by breaking onto the airwaves without a license, usually broadcasting from someone's garage. Often expressing radical ideas, playing explicit, uncensored versions of songs, and lacking the slick professional DJs of corporate radio, pirate radio stations undoubtedly brought greater diversity to the airwaves.[3] Some cleverly claimed a right to air citing an obscure provision in the Code of Federal Regulations allowing for unlicensed broadcasting in a "time of emergency"—a phrase they interpreted very liberally.[4]

To a great extent, the FCC shut down pirate radio with a series of raids and fines starting at $10,000. But, in 2000, as a concession to those arguing for more open and local programming, the FCC also began to address the needs of non-commercial community radio stations by issuing two thousand low power (10 and 100 watt) licenses. (By way of comparison, WNYC, New York City's largest public radio station, transmits at 10,000 watts during daytime hours). It is also worth noting that the demand for licenses has been reduced by the emergence of streaming digital radio, on-demand music services, and podcasting. Still, balancing the demands of the business community with the need for localism and diversity in content remains a challenge for the FCC in the licensing process.

Access means two different things. On the one hand, it means which potential producers of content have access to the radio and television airwaves. On the other hand, it also means which citizens and consumers have access to media. Today, the FCC has shifted more of its focus to ensuring widespread, affordable broadband Internet access to the American public.

### Access: Digital Inequalities

Since the 1990s, the FCC has focused on addressing the so-called *digital divide*, or the gap between people who have access to information and communication technologies and those who don't. Of course, today, there are very few Americans who never have any access to the web, email, or social media. For this reason, media scholars now tend to think in terms of *digital inequalities*, a term that takes into account "[not] merely who is online ... [but also] differences in how those who are online access and use the medium."[5] If the initial focus in the late 1990s was principally on expanding physical access to computers and the Internet, scholars and activists have encouraged the FCC to consider a wider range of digital inequalities including gaps in who can afford technology, in the ability to use technologies to do important tasks, and in vulnerability to being hacked online.

Older, lower income, rural, and non-white Americans are less likely to have home broadband and tend to have more limited skills in using computers and the Internet. While the FCC, the Department of Education, states, and school districts across the country have made an enormous push to get computers into schools and libraries, fewer than half of households with annual incomes below $30,000 have broadband Internet at home. Sociologist Laura Robinson, in a qualitative study of disadvantaged youth in California's agricultural region, found that many of the teens she interviewed experience instability in access to the Internet. They couldn't depend on consistent broadband access at home, faced 30-minute time limits at the library, and had to negotiate with uncles for brief access to a smartphone.[6] With such instability, it is very difficult for disadvantaged teens, for example, to find the time to adequately research colleges and complete all the required online admissions and financial aid forms necessary to apply—an inequality that reinforces existing inequalities.

To address persistent digital inequalities, the FCC funds a range of projects to expand mobile and cable Internet in underserved areas, subsidize broadband service for low-income households, and supports a range of programs aimed at educating communities in using information and communication technologies. Even more important than the FCC's work in funding projects to address digital inequalities is their job as a regulator, setting rules for the corporations that provide access to all Americans.

### Access: Net Neutrality

In recent years, one of the most important debates involving the FCC has been how they would act to address Net Neutrality. The concept of Net Neutrality, coined by law professor Tim Wu, is one that mandates all Internet traffic to be treated equally by Internet Service Providers (ISPs), regardless of its origin. Under a "neutral" Internet, ISPs would not be allowed to block, slow down, or otherwise discriminate against online content. Some examples that sparked the debate over Net Neutrality include the blocking of certain websites by ISPs, such as Comcast's buffering of the streaming service, Netflix, beginning in December, 2013.[7] Done for financial reasons—Netflix's streaming service is a direct competitor with Comcast's Xfinity on-demand service—there were no provisions barring ISPs from engaging in censorship for other reasons, including political.

The regulatory question at the heart of Net Neutrality is whether or not the Internet should be regulated like public utilities, including other communication media (for example, electricity, telephone, and postal mail) where providers are required to offer basic services to all subscribers. Or should it be treated as a competitive commodity where providers can set their own terms like refusing service or tacking on additional fees for less profitable users/areas? The problem with treating Internet service like a competitive marketplace is that there is very little broadband competition in most markets.[8]

Under the Obama administration and after years of back and forth rulings, the FCC had moved to regulate broadband Internet as a public utility classifying Internet providers as "common carriers," meaning they would be regulated like other utilities. In 2017, Ajit Pai, the Trump-appointed chairman of

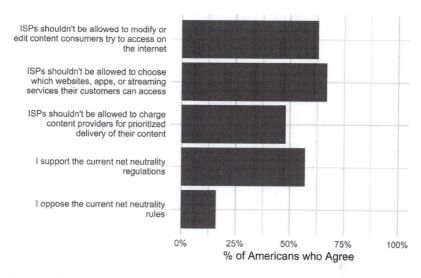

*Figure 5.2* Public Opinion Regarding Net Neutrality, 2017
[Source: Consumer Reports, 2017]

the FCC, moved forward with a proposal to repeal that classification, and by the end of the year voted to repeal Net Neutrality altogether.[9] While Net Neutrality officially ended on June 11, 2018, the issue is far from settled—there are legal challenges working their way through the courts, congressional lawmakers appear poised to introduce new legislation, and some states have even passed their own similar regulations.[10] Thus, the likely future of Internet regulation is a pendulum swinging back and forth between Republican administrations, which favor less regulation on corporations, and Democratic ones, which favor more regulation to protect the public interest.

## Ownership

"San Antonio is the seventh-largest city in the United States. … But the speed of its Internet service is no match for the Latvian capital, Riga, a city of 700,000 [which] is at least two-and-a-half times that of San Antonio's. … And the cost of Riga's service is about one-fourth. … The United States … is falling dangerously behind."— Edward Wyatt, *The New York Times*[11]

In the U.S., we have worse Internet service than most developed nations and an unsure future regarding Net Neutrality. The FCC can make regulatory rules about pricing and access that improve citizens' Internet access. But the underlying problem is that in most U.S. communities, there are few ISPs and, therefore, no real competition. The current state of affairs is reflective of the U.S. government's reluctance to impose strict rules in a second category of regulation: ownership.

As we have seen in Chapter 4, the FTC, DOJ, and FCC work together to limit monopoly ownership of all industries, including media. While the claim that most media are produced by only a handful of companies is a wildly overstated claim, when it comes to Internet service provision, there are many communities with quasi-monopolies. Five percent of Americans live in areas with no Internet providers, 13% have only one Internet provider, and 78% have only two choices. Since consumers have few choices, companies have no real incentive to compete on either speed or pricing.[12]

This problem may change over time as consumers shift more of their usage to mobile Internet providers like AT&T, Verizon, and Sprint—a market with significantly more competition. If broadband providers come to see mobile companies as a real threat to the residential broadband market, they may begin to invest in infrastructure upgrades to compete on speed. However, in 2017, with only half of Americans using 4G service, mobile web is not yet a viable competitor for home Internet in many places.

In addition to regulating ownership in Internet, the FCC also issues rules about market shares of broadcast media like TV and radio within communities (as discussed in Chapter 4). Those rules are then enforced by the DOJ and FTC.

## Content

Last but not least, states also regulate content. Comedian George Carlin famously claimed there are seven words you can never say on television. In fact, there was not then nor is there now a list of words you cannot say on television or radio. But federal law prohibits the broadcast of "obscene, indecent and profane" content and, since the FCC issues broadcast licenses, they are able to maintain "obscenity guidelines" and fine broadcasters that violate them. Though people disagree about what constitutes "obscene," legislators and courts have decided that it is in the public interest to prohibit the broadcast of material that is offensive or could be harmful to children.

American visitors to Europe are often surprised by the amount of casual nudity on, say, orange juice commercials, while visitors from many European countries are surprised that U.S. television allows advertising to children under 12. In authoritarian regimes, such as China, broad categories of content—including Google, Facebook, and all books with the word "capitalism" in the title—are blocked or banned. All societies put some limits on what can be said or shown in media in the name of whatever they define as the public interest.

In the U.S., we have a fairly expansive definition of free speech protected by the Constitution. However, Congress can act to ban certain types of content. For example, in 1971, Congress passed the Public Health Cigarette Smoking Act, which banned tobacco advertisements from broadcast TV and radio. Contrary to popular belief, the FCC and the DOJ do not regulate content on non-broadcast media, like cable television. Basic cable channels, like Comedy Central, are self-regulating, censoring their own content not because of the FCC, but out of fear of advertiser and viewer complaints.

Still, there are forms of content that the FCC does censor. The Supreme Court has ruled that the First Amendment does not protect obscene speech. In Miller vs. California (1973), the Supreme Court created a three-pronged test for obscenity: "It must appeal to an average person's prurient interest; depict or describe sexual conduct in a "patently offensive" way; and, taken as a whole, lack serious literary, artistic, political or scientific value." While "obscene" content is always prohibited from broadcast media, the FCC prohibits two other categories of content between 6AM and 10PM when children might be watching. The first is "indecent" content, which "portrays sexual or excretory organs or activities in a way that does not meet the three-prong test for obscenity," and the second is "profane" content, which "includes 'grossly offensive' language that is considered a public nuisance."[13]

The FCC also has the power to mandate that broadcast media present certain types of content. Between 1949 and 1987, the FCC required broadcasters to adhere to the Fairness Doctrine, which held that TV and radio stations must provide a) adequate coverage of important public issues, and b) equitable time for a range of contrasting views on the subject.[14] In 1987, during the Reagan administration, the FCC repealed the policy as an "intrusion by government [restricting] the journalistic freedom of broadcasters."[15] Supporters of the repeal also argued that in such a large and diverse media landscape as had developed by the late-1980s, citizens are exposed to a wide range of views anyway.

The repeal of the Fairness Doctrine allowed for the rise of openly partisan broadcast media, especially conservative talk radio (e.g., Rush Limbaugh). For this reason, a number of Democratic politicians, including Former President Bill Clinton, House Minority Leader Nancy Pelosi, and former Secretary of State John Kerry have argued for the reinstatement of the Fairness Doctrine. Republicans, on the other hand, have described the Fairness Doctrine as an affront to the free speech of broadcasters. Even if the Fairness Doctrine were reinstated, because the FCC only regulates broadcasters, it would have no power over newspapers, web sites, or cable networks like Fox News and MSNBC, let alone social media.

On the whole, in the U.S., regulating content in the public interest tends to mean censoring content that is viewed as "obscene" and
requiring little else. By contrast, the Ministry of the Interior in Saudi
Arabia has vast control over all publications, web sites, television, and
radio to ban anything that is seen as either immoral, against Islam, or
critical of the Saudi government. Their definition of the public interest seems to be maintaining the current religious and political order.

Most European countries have more lax, self-regulating standards
around naughty words and nudity than either Saudi Arabia or the
U.S., but have much more stringent rules about the amount and type
of advertising that is allowed. In 2012, the European Commission
updated the European Data Protection Directive to include a provision
creating "the right to be forgotten."[16] This provision allows EU citizens to request that Google, YouTube, and other web sites remove
damaging, private information about them.[17] Aimed at protecting citizens' right to privacy, the law also poses a substantial regulatory burden
to companies like Google, which have to process the requests for
removal. Combined with the substantial funding for public media
throughout Europe, these policy decisions reflect a European definition
of public interest that emphasizes an informed public, protected from
corporate excesses.

How countries choose to regulate media for access, ownership, and
content are indicative of their prevailing ideologies and their understanding of what is in the "public interest." In the U.S., we see a regulatory
approach that usually favors free markets and free speech. The European
paradigm, by comparison, tends to limit corporations in the name of
expanding information and protection for the individual.

## Cat and Mouse

If deciding on a regulatory approach to TV and radio broadcasters involved
difficult trade-offs, the Internet brings with it new complexities in the relationship between the state and media. Like other authoritarian countries,
Iran has always been able to monitor and revoke the licenses of newspapers
that published stories that were seen as being critical of the ruling regime
and, in 1994, they even banned the use of satellite television.

However, it has proven more difficult to ban sites on the Internet. In
2009, as members of the Iranian public began to protest fraudulent vote
counts in their presidential election, the Iranian government blocked
Twitter. Both activists in Iran and around the world had been tweeting
in Farsi and English, organizing the protests via Twitter.[18] Though the
government's efforts to block Twitter may have impeded some users,
many were able to use Twitter anyway by using tools that shield their IP
addresses. Even in countries like China where they maintain "The Great

Firewall," blocking many web sites, citizens regularly get around these barriers using digital tools of their own.

Over the past decade, this cat-and-mouse pattern has played out again and again. The Internet and social media have created new platforms for people to communicate. Every time a state attempts to suppress media content, activists, citizens, and consumers find new tools to uncover the blocked material. Media scholar Eric Jardine found that the use of the anonymity-granting browser, Tor, is highest in countries with very low and very high political repression. In countries with low political repression, including most developed, western nations, users adopt anonymity-granting technology, well, because they can. There are no penalties for doing so. By contrast, even though there are penalties for using Tor in high repression countries (like Iran or China), users adopt technologies like Tor because they have to in order to access information. In moderate political repression countries, like Burkina Faso, there are penalties for using Tor, but not enough political repression to make its use necessary.[19]

Even as information and communication technologies have made it harder for states to regulate media, the digital footprints we leave behind combined with their immense computing power have made it easier for governments to conduct surveillance on the public. After the events of September 11, 2001, the USA Patriot Act granted the U.S. government far more powers to conduct electronic surveillance over the Internet and cellular phone networks.[20] These forms of surveillance were often carried out without warrants (which require evidence of criminal activity) or with secret warrants issued by a secret Foreign Intelligence Surveillance Act (FISA) court.[21] In 2013, former National Security Agency (NSA) contractor Edward Snowden revealed to journalists for *The Guardian* newspaper that the NSA had been collecting data on millions of Americans by demanding metadata on phone calls from Verizon and through direct access to email, photos, videos, and the search histories from Google, Facebook, and Apple. Snowden (and at least one federal court) saw the NSA's surveillance practices as in direct violation of the Fourth Amendment right to privacy and protection from unlawful search. However, sociologist Zygmunt Bauman and co-authors have argued that, in western nations today, we have a growing expectation of being surveilled by the state and that we view it as "domesticated, normal, [and] unremarkable."[22]

State surveillance is not without consequences. In 2017, researchers Alex Marthews and Catherine Tucker found a "chilling effect" on the public's web search habits in the wake of the Snowden revelations in 2013. Tracking Google searches over time, they document a decline in searches for potentially personally-sensitive words (e.g., atheism, abortion, body odor, gay rights) and government-sensitive words (e.g., anthrax, border patrol, epidemic, dirty bomb) after Snowden revealed the extent of government surveillance.[23] To the extent that the public is less willing to use communication technologies out of fear of state surveillance, it hurts both democracy and the bottom line of tech giants.

All of which brings us back to Apple's legal battle with the U.S. government. Apple, like all businesses, cooperates with search warrants that require them to turn over specific evidence. However, as a technology company, they also try to make products with highest encryption and security standard to protect their customers' privacy. In the case of the San Bernadino shooter, the FBI argued in court that Apple should be forced to write code to break their own lock-screen security, creating "a back door" that would allow Apple to aide police in future investigations. From the perspective of executives at Apple, the FBI was asking them to make their product weaker by creating a "back door" that could be exploited by hackers and foreign governments. As Apple executives indicated to *The New York Times*, "[Apple's] defiance was not a business choice … cooperating with the government now could quickly lead to murkier situations internationally, especially in China."[24] But there are also business implications for Apple. They found themselves trapped in the middle of a battle between the state's interest in surveillance and customers' desire for products that protect their privacy.

## Media Management

Beyond states' formal approach to supporting and regulating media, the state and powerful political actors aim to manage media, shaping public opinion in the process. The White House press briefing room offers an instructive look into these media management tactics by political actors. When President Woodrow Wilson held the first presidential news conference in 1913, both journalism and public relations were emerging as new professions.[25] All presidents following Wilson have used press conferences as a way of getting their narrative on current events into mainstream news coverage. The press, who often fancy themselves a "watchdog" of the powerful, are drawn to presidential news conferences because of the unusual access to the leader of the free world. Of course, a common critique of such conferences is that they turn these watchdogs into lapdogs by having reporters simply print whatever the President says.[26]

Whatever critiques of this arrangement existed, as television emerged as the dominant medium, in 1969, President Richard Nixon ordered a permanent press briefing room built in the White House. Since that time, press briefings have grown into a ritual practice with a dedicated set of White House correspondents from all the major media outlets, a formal seat chart, multiple briefings each day, and a topical theme of the week. Given this structure and journalistic labor that news outlets grant to it, it is unsurprising that presidents can count on the White House being quoted on a daily basis in nearly every news source. It is a supremely powerful tool of agenda-setting for the president. While editors and reporters recognize this fact and attempt to counteract it by asking challenging questions at the time, it is simply difficult for them to give up such good access to important actors.

Likewise, in wartime, the U.S. military has traded access to journalists for news coverage that emphasize their preferred narratives. During the war in Iraq, the Pentagon introduced an embedding program that allowed journalists to join military units during the major combat period of the war. While journalists made no pledge to produce any particular type of coverage, as embedded reporters, they depended on the military units for their safety and were able to report in unprecedented depth on the soldiers' experience of the war. The coverage that was beamed back home to the U.S. public was astonishing. Never before had the U.S. public been given such a powerful first-hand glimpse of a military action in real time.

However, as a 2009 study by one of this book's authors, Andrew Lindner, found, embedded reporters cover all dimensions of the soldiers' experience of the war, but largely failed to capture Iraqi civilians' perspectives. By contrast, independent reporters—a more expensive, dangerous, and far more rare type of journalism—were able to provide more balanced coverage, capturing both U.S. soldier and civilian experiences of the war. While focusing on the soldier's perspective does not guarantee favorable coverage, it does tend to depict the war from the U.S. government's preferred vantage point.[27] Whether in the White House press room or sitting in a tank across the world, these media management strategies are effective ways for the state to use the press to communicate their preferred messaging to the public.

Increasingly, in the age of social media, political actors bypass the press and communicate directly with the public. No politician is more infamous for his use of social media than President Donald Trump. In conflict with the press for what he claims is unfair coverage, the Trump administration has threatened to kick the press out of the White House to a government building across the street.[28] Instead, Trump's preferred method of communication is Twitter, tweeting 356 times in his first hundred days as president (http://trumptwitterarchive.com). Using Twitter, Trump is able to communicate directly with his followers, avoiding the watchdog functions typically performed by the press. Naturally, journalists view the tweets of a president as important news and, so, Trump's 280-character narratives get reported in mainstream news outlets as well. As a media management strategy, it offers Trump the best of both worlds. He is able to issue unfiltered communications, but all his opinions reported by the mainstream press. For the public, this is, perhaps, the most dangerous media management strategy of all. The president's power to disseminate his message is greater than ever, but the public does not benefit from the fact-checking and critical follow-up questions of experienced reporters.

In ways both formal and informal, states and political actors exert great influence over mass media. The nature of that influence differs dramatically between democracies and authoritarian states, but also differs between states with competing visions of what's in the public interest. The Internet has also complicated the picture by creating more spaces outside the state's control, while also producing all new ways for governments to spy on their people and for politicians to get their messages directly to the public.

## Notes

1  Elliott, Stuart. 1995. "The Media Business: Advertising; A New Ranking of the '50 Best' Television Commercials Ever Made." *New York Times Business.*; Goldberg, Fred S. 2013. *The Insanity of Advertising: Memoirs of a Mad Man.* Council Oak Books.
2  FCC Strategic Plan 2015–2018. https://apps.fcc.gov/edocs_public/attach match/DOC-331866A1.pdf.
3  Klinenberg, Eric. 2007. *Fighting for Air.* Metropolitan Books; Dunbar-Hester, Christina. 2014. *Low Power to the People: Pirates, Protest, and Politics in FM Radio Activism.* MIT Press.
4  The Code of Federal Regulations Title 47 Section 73.3542 www.gpo.gov/fdsys/granule/CFR-2012-title47-vol4/CFR-2012-title47-vol4-sec73-3542.
5  Hargittai, Eszter, and Yuli Patrick Hsieh. 2013. "Digital Inequality." In William H.(ed.), *The Oxford Handbook of Internet Studies*, Dutton: Oxford University Press, pp. 129–150.
6  Robinson, Laura, and Jeremy Schulz. 2013. "Net Time Negotiations Within the Family." *Information, Communication, and Society* 16(4): 542–560.; Robinson, Laura. 2014. "Freeways, Detours and Dead Ends: Search Journeys Among Disadvantaged Youth." *New Media & Society* 16(2): 234–251.
7  Goldman, David. 2014. "Slow Comcast Speeds Were Costing Netflix Customers." *CNNMoney.*
8  FCC. "National Broadband Plan—Chapter 4: Broadband Competition and Innovation Policy." *Broadband.gov.*
9  Fiegerman, Seth. 2017. "FCC Unveils Plan to Roll Back Net Neutrality." *CNNMoney.*
    Kang, Cecilia. 2018. "F.C.C. Repeals Net Neutrality Rules." *The New York Times*, January 20.
10  Hafer, T. J. 2019. "What You Need to Know about Net Neutrality in 2019." *PC Gamer.* Retrieved January 9, 2019. Available at: https://www.pcgamer.com/the-net-neutrality-fight-isnt-over-even-after-the-repeal/.
11  Wyatt, Edward. 2013. "U.S. Struggles to Keep Pace in Delivering Broadband Service." *New York Times Technology.*
12  FCC. "National Broadband Plan." https://www.fcc.gov/general/national-broadband-plan
13  FCC. 2017. "Obscene, Incident and Profane Broadcasts." *FCC.*
14  Jung, D.L. 1996. *The Federal Communications Commission, the Broadcast Industry, and the Fairness Doctrine 1981–1987.* New York: University Press of America, Inc.
15  Hershey Jr., Robert D. 1987. "F.C.C. Votes down Fairness Doctrine a 4–0 Decision." *New York Times.*
16  European Commission. 2012. "Regulation of the European Parliament and of the Council." *European Commission.*

17  Mantalero, Alessandro. 2013. "The EU Proposal for a General Data Protection Regulation and the Roots of the Right 'To be Forgotten'." *Computer Law & Security Review* 29(3), 229–235.

18  While subsequent analyses have cast doubt on how many of the tweets originated in Iran, it is clear that at least some influential organizers were based in Tehran; Murthy, Dhiraj. 2013. *Twitter: Social communication in the Twitter age*. John Wiley & Sons.

19  Jardine, Eric. 2016. "Tor, what is it good for? Political Repression and the use of Online Anonymity-Granting Technologies." *New Media & Society* 1–18.

20  Kerr, Orrin S. 2002. "Internet Surveillance Law After the USA Patriot Act: The Big Brother that isn't." *Nw. UL Rev.* 97, 607.

21  Risen, James, and Eric Lichtblaue. 2005. "Bush Lets U.S. Spy on Callers Without Courts." *NY Times.*; NPR. 2013. "FISA Court Has Approved Majority of Surveillance Warrants." *NPR.*

22  Bauman, Zygmunt, Didier Bigo, Paulo Esteves, Elspeth Guild, Vivienne Jabri, David Lyon, and Rob BJ Walker. 2014. "After Snowden: Rethinking the Impact of Surveillance." *International Political Sociology* 8(2), 121–144.

23  Marthews, Alex, and Catherine E. Tucker. "Government Surveillance and Internet Search Behavior." (2015). Working Paper.

24  Khamooshi, Arash. 2016. "Breaking Down Apple's iPhone Fight with the U.S. Government." *NY Times.*

25  Kumar, Marth Joynt. "Presidential Press Conferences: Windows on the Presidency and Its Occupants." *The White House Historical Association.*

26  Clayman, Steven E., John Heritage, Marc N. Elliott, and Laurie L. McDonald. 2007. "When Does the Watchdog Bark? Conditions of Aggressive Questioning in Presidential News Conferences." *American Sociological Review* 72(1), 23–41.

27  Lindner, Andrew M. 2009. "Among The Troops: Seeing the Iraq War Through Three Journalistic Vantage Points." *Social Problems* 56(1):21–48.

28  Grynbaum, Michael M. 2017. "Trump Team Considers Moving Press Corps, Alarming Reporters." *New York Times.*

# Chapter 6

# The Makers and the Breakers

Since the time journalism emerged as an American profession in the early 1900s, its practitioners have worked within a field that is constantly in the making. Through technological innovation, the boom and bust of business models, political debate and constraint, and the churn of high-profile news stories that shape public discourse, the culture of journalism has generally remained consistent in its mission and method.

Over time, so-called "crises" in journalism have helped distinguish it from other media professions. Around the time of the First World War, the success of government propaganda and corporate advertising, in addition to some high-profile failures of sensational and intentionally misleading "yellow" journalism, drove those committed to the craft to better define journalism as a field unto itself. One of the first steps was to begin training reporters formally, rather than expecting they learn the tricks of the trade while on the job. By 1920, nearly a dozen American public universities were offering degrees in journalism.[1] The growth of such programs not only improved the quality of reporting, but also helped establish journalism as a professional field with a distinct identity.

What marked the boundaries of journalism from other media industries was, among other things, an emphasis on public service. This meant that journalists should prioritize stories that would affect people most, such as healthcare, housing crises, inequality, tax legislation, war, etc., over more trivial topics like celebrity gossip. Along with an obligation to the public good came a set of professional norms, such as independence, objectivity, and the method of verification that were ultimately oriented toward providing a broad and diverse public with the information they needed to do the work of democracy.[2] To accomplish this, journalists worked hard to maintain a distance from those they reported on, to keep fact separate from opinion, and to confirm accounts through multiple independent sources. Yet, journalism also shared many parallels with its cousins elsewhere in the media industry, including common communication platforms, professional style, and profit-orientation, among others. These similarities and differences are all consequential in delineating journalism's boundaries and professional identity. Indeed, the practice and profession of journalism can no more be defined by what it aims to do than what it does, or how it does it.

Whereas other sectors of the media industry have fully embraced the priorities of maximizing profits and persuading audiences, as evidenced by the political and advertising-driven nature of their content, those working under the label "journalism" have done so with mixed enthusiasm. In other words, for much of the past century journalism has strived for economic independence by constructing a "wall" between the news and business desks that, like the separation of church and state, seeks to create an environment where the work of the institution can proceed autonomously, unhindered by competing interests or outside influences. This meant creating organizational structures and workflows that ensured editorial decisions about news stories were not affected by the desires of advertisers. Nevertheless, so-called "native advertising"—a euphemism for paid content made to look like independent journalism—has found its way onto the pages of some of the nation's most prominent newspapers, including *The New York Times*.[3]

For these reasons and more, journalism scholar Jay Rosen was driven to ask in his book by the same name, *What Are Journalists For?* The question is both a search for the values driving journalism as well as an inquiry into its social functions. Like many scholars of journalism that came before him, and we suspect, many who will come after, Rosen found little in the way of definitive answers. However, in seeking to explain the popularity of "public journalism," a popular buzzword at the time of its writing in 1999, the book concluded that while the media industry as a whole was in the business of creating audiences and gaining their attention, no matter the content, journalism "is where the media gets democratic in principle—that's why it's important."[4] This is the impression one gets from the bulk of scholarship on journalism.

But in order to know what journalism is *for*, we must first understand what journalism *is*. According to the prominent media sociologist Michael Schudson,

> journalism is the business or practice of producing and disseminating information about contemporary affairs of general public interest and importance. It is the business of a set of institutions that publicizes periodically (usually daily) information and commentary on contemporary affairs...to a dispersed and anonymous audience so as to publicly include the audience in a discourse taken to be publicly important.[5]

Of course, such a definition is steeped in the profession's own ideology (notice how Schudson's conception relies on its democratic function) and is biased toward a particular kind of supposedly homogenous organization (as if journalism can only be produced by profit-oriented institutions). While there is good reason for Schudson to emphasize these aspects of journalism, there is more to the story.

But to see the larger picture for what it is, we must first come to understand in greater detail how the various media "fields" relate to one another, and how they govern the actions of those who occupy them. Accordingly, this chapter will expand on the theory of the journalistic field, first introduced in Chapter 2, before discussing what researchers have come to know about the reality of modern media work. We end by examining how various aspects of the media fields shape action within it.

## The "Field" of Journalism

French sociologist Pierre Bourdieu, famous for his work on the study of culture and power within numerous social institutions, was among the first to conceptualize journalism as a "field" and to develop a theoretical toolkit to better understand its workings. While his own work on the subject of journalism was sparse and more oriented toward public than scholarly dialogue, Bourdieu provided a glimpse into how his version of "field theory" might apply to the study of media. Indeed, his book, *On Television*, a transcript from a series of televised lectures he gave on the topic, was a brief but critical assessment of the limitations of French journalism in the age of television.

Despite its limitations, Bourdieu's theorizing inspired many—most notably sociologist Rodney Benson, who is widely credited with popularizing field theory in media and journalism studies—to seek answers to various questions about the "journalistic field." Rather than approaching the study of news as resulting from the biases of individual journalists or overbearing owners, research on the journalistic field emphasizes the complex interplay of these and other factors. As Benson and Neveu write in the introduction to their edited volume applying field theory to the study of journalism, "fields are arenas of struggle in which individuals and organizations compete, unconsciously and consciously, to valorize those forms of capital which they possess."[6] Accordingly, Bourdieu conceived of a variety of separate but interrelated fields, including the political, economic, educational, intellectual, as well as various cultural fields like the artistic, literary, scientific, religious, and journalistic, among others.

Each field operates within a broader field of power, defined by the economic and political context of the nation-state, which helps shape what information is reported, and by whom. As an expression of this power, the World Press Freedom Index, compiled each year by the organization Reporters Without Borders, publishes information about how political and monetary interests in each country hinder the flow of information (or not). While journalism is often found to be relatively free from constraint in liberal Western democracies, due in part to First Amendment-like protections, the U.S. ranked 45th out of 180 countries in 2018.[7] Although American journalists are sometimes arrested, attacked, or otherwise hindered from doing their jobs, their work can also be hindered by the political and economic cultures of the organizations for which they work. Nevertheless, the field's own values also play a powerful role in guiding the actions of those who work within it. This is precisely why Jay Rosen's question "what are journalists for?" is more difficult to answer than it may seem at first glance: not only are journalists far from a homogenous group, but their actions are shaped by both the values of their profession as well as those of the political and economic context they exist within. Indeed, as Bourdieu put it, "to understand what happens in journalism, it is not sufficient to know who finances the publications, who the advertisers are, who pays for the advertising, where the subsidy comes from, and so on." Rather, we must conceptualize the world of journalism as a "microcosm" with its own rules and to consider how those rules bear upon the actors and actions that exist within it.[8]

With his theory of fields, Bourdieu offered a sophisticated way of accounting for the dynamics of structure and agency that have long guided sociological analysis. While the concept of *structure* has come to signify the large-scale social forces that shape (if not determine) the action of individuals, yet exists outside of them, *agency* denotes the ability of individuals to determine their own actions, even though they always exist within and in relation to various social structures. Thus, individual journalists may have enough agency to decide who they interview and what quotes to include, but rank-and-file newsworkers rarely have the power to determine what stories are newsworthy in the first place. Furthermore, the norms of independence and objectivity, as normative structures of the journalistic field, all but require reporters to keep their own opinion out of the story. In short, as Benson has put it, "strategy follows structure."[9]

While Bourdieu's concept of a field offered a view of structure that was bounded by specific constraints while remaining open to change, his concepts of capital, habitus, and doxa provided a practical understanding of the ways those structures guide human behavior. For Bourdieu, there are four primary types of *capital*—economic (money), cultural (education and other class-related resources), social (human connections), and symbolic (reputation and status)—that operate as a form of power by "govern[ing] success in the field."[10] With their accumulation of capital, individuals are said to possess a *habitus*—a "system of embodied dispositions" that structure how they perceive and act in the world—based on their experiences and social location.[11] For example, as the son of a postal worker who attended some of the most elite academies in France, Bourdieu's own capital and habitus were formed based on his own unique mix of working-class and upper-class experiences. To the extent that dispositions are normalized, and therefore taken-for-granted within a particular field, they are said to be part of the field's *doxa*.

Whether or not studies draw directly on Bourdieu's field theory, a large portion of the works in media sociology take into consideration many of the factors described above. Like Bourdieu's own analyses of various cultural fields, including art, literature, and education, field theory can explain all kinds of social relations. For example, scholars have examined how the institutions of journalism,[12] music,[13] reality television,[14] and even higher education[15] are shaped by a combination of other institutional factors. Yet today, when various industries exist together in a converged landscape of media platforms, "one thing all these fields have in common is the fact that journalism, advertising, broadcasting, film, and game development are all examples of the production of culture."[16]

## The Reality of Media Work

The tradition of media sociology, first popularized in the 1960s and 1970s, has from the very beginning had a deep devotion to the critical examination of media work. While studies of media content have long been of interest to scholars in the field, it is an interest in the media workers themselves—where they work, what they do, why, and to what effects—that animated the bulk of media sociology, especially during this early, formative period. Though studies of individual journalists have often painted the profession as inherently activist[17] and investigative, functioning as civil society's "custodians of conscience,"[18] those that take the newsroom as the primary object of study are less likely to find uniformity in journalistic style than they are to find larger patterns in the structures and practices that govern work in the media industries.

Among the early slate of research into the realities of media work were numerous newsroom studies—some anonymized, others not—of the nation's most prominent news organizations, including popular newspapers such as *The New York Times*, television stations like CBS and NBC, and news magazines such as *Newsweek* and *Time*, among countless others. Because those studies relied heavily on qualitative observations and interviews with news workers, and sometimes complemented by analyses of media content, the knowledge produced was richly descriptive and full of practical as well as theoretical insights. This combination is perhaps one of the greatest strengths of media sociology: it offers the critical perspective of an outsider, while being informed primarily by the views and experiences of insiders. In addition to painting a vivid picture of news work, this allowed early media sociologists to study how the social structures particular to the field shape the actions of journalists working in it. For example, after studying interactions in numerous newsrooms in the Northeastern U.S., sociologist Gaye Tuchman concluded that news workers do not intend to frame the news so as to support either private economic or state interests, but, because of their institutional position and organizational practices, they are likely to serve those interests, and to reproduce their structural and power bases.[19]

A lesson learned from the bulk of this scholarship is that journalistic values, however (un)conscious, play a notable role in shaping the actions of newsworkers.

Though early newsroom studies have been criticized for focusing on the most influential news outlets and for exaggerating organizational constraints, they provide an important window into the "'black box' of news production."[20] As media sociology has experienced a resurgence in the last few decades, more recent studies have yielded a host of interesting findings, much of which relate to the fact that news is now produced in what reporter and blogger Doc Searls first called the age of "post-industrial journalism," where reporting is "no longer organized around the norms of proximity to the machinery of production."[21] If taken literally, this point is highly debatable, since the work of reporting still relies greatly on the tools journalists use to produce and disseminate their work. Nevertheless, the broader point inferred by Searls and others is that the field is undergoing significant change due to shifts in economic and technological factors. Thus, news organizations are beginning to work more creatively and collaboratively with the hope of remaining relevant and profitable in a changing, post-industrial context.[22]

From these newsroom studies, we have learned a great deal about the structure of media institutions as well as the practices of media workers. Structurally, we have come to understand how labor is divided within organizations, including the gatekeeping role played by writers and editors in determining what content gets published, and how. On a practical level, we have learned about the norms, conventions, and routines that govern the actions of media workers. Let's examine each of these factors in greater detail.

## Norms that Make the News: Conventions, Routines, and Editorial Gatekeeping

There are many factors that structure work within the journalistic field, from the external rhythms of current events to the profession's own norms and routines. Just as the news cycle is relatively predictable, covering pre-planned events, breaking news, and public interest stories by the day, hour, or minute, so too are the responses of newsworkers when news breaks. Rather than having to reinvent the wheel for each new story, experienced reporters follow a set of journalistic conventions and routines that invariably guide and simplify their work.

To say that something is *conventional* is to suggest that it is normalized, or as Bourdieu might say, part of the doxa and habitus particular to the field. Accordingly, the *conventions* of professional journalism are those practices, stated or implied, that are used widely by newsworkers from a variety of media organizations. For example, journalists practice a method of *verification*, where each stated fact is confirmed independently by multiple sources, in order to ensure their reporting is accurate and truthful.[23] In addition to tapping into their network of contacts to obtain information, reporters patrol their *beat*. Like police officers assigned to a particular neighborhood, journalists are often assigned a beat—it could be a location, such as the local government offices, or a topic, such as sports or education—that they are expected to follow closely and report on. To do this, beat reporters often make *rounds*, visiting the people and places that are likely to produce news. Together, these conventions make up a reporter's *routine*, which structures their work and how they approach it.

While each of these conventions serves a function, they also have unintended consequences that invariably shape the content produced. And while *objectivity*—the norm that deters reporters from injecting their opinion into news stories—is also a core convention of American journalism, bias in the framing and selection of news is unavoidable.[24] Indeed, from the selection of story ideas and the contacting of sources to the decisions regarding the framing of a story and its placement in the broadcast, the gatekeeping process plays a central role in shaping the news.

The concept of *gatekeeping*—central to the production of news since at least 1950—refers to the process whereby content is selected, shaped, accompanied with imagery, and positioned in the news by a number of newsworkers who are assigned various roles in the process.[25] Gatekeepers rarely have to be told when a story is newsworthy—they just know, because they have developed what media sociologist Ida Willig described as a "journalistic gut feeling" through their location and experience in the field.[26] Because professional reporters generally work within a well-defined organizational structure, the work is often distributed in a manner that delegates responsibility for certain tasks—writing, photography, copyediting, page layout, promotion and distribution, etc.—to others in the newsroom who each have their own, albeit similar, gut feelings. Thus, the process of gatekeeping may be as much about the diffusion of responsibility as it is about establishing a hierarchy to maintain order and ensure a quality product. And perhaps surprisingly, given the rise in amateur media production following the mainstreaming of blogs and social media, citizen journalism sites have also been shown to follow gatekeeping norms in a manner similar to those upheld by professional organizations.[27]

Today's media workers exist in a drastically different world (and professional field) than the one their 20th century counterparts knew. Whereas the routine of a journalist in the early 1940s may have entailed phoning potential sources, typing up stories on a typewriter, and submitting them to publishers via telegraph or telephone (see Figure 6.1), 75 years later, much has changed. While journalists still maintain telephone contact with many sources, today their work (much like their personal life) is primarily mediated through digital screens (see Figure 6.2).

*Figure 6.1* The New York Times Newsroom in September 1942

[Photo by Marjory Collins. Source: https://loc.gov/pictures/resource/cph.3c12969/]

*Figure 6.2* CNN Newsroom in November 2011

[Photo by Conxa Rodà. Source: www.flickr.com/photos/25730976@N06/6356811909 Licensed under Creative Commons (CC BY-SA)]

In short, media work has adapted to the information age, but the newsroom is not all that has changed. As the next section will show, along with the profound technological transformations, the media fields have seen significant shifts in the structures and practices that guide their work.

## The Modern Newsroom (and Beyond): Risk Minimization, Profit Maximization, and McDonaldization

Today's newsrooms are a far cry from the imagery of the past. While the pulse of the newsroom was once driven in large part by journalism's deep-seated belief in democracy, today's newsrooms also run on the culture of convergence and the click-based logics of profit-seeking companies trying to survive in a rapidly changing post-industrial economy. Indeed, the proliferation of new media and communication technologies has given rise to what media scholar Henry Jenkins has termed a "convergence culture."

The concept of *convergence*, an early 21st century buzzword in the media industries, refers to "the flow of content across multiple media platforms, the cooperation between multiple media industries, and the migratory behavior of media audiences."[28] As embraced by the bulk of media institutions, this convergence culture means that media companies do not necessarily control the channels used to disseminate their content, and instead work with a variety of publishers and platforms, including many social media sites and the amateur media makers who inhabit them.[29] This is as much an effort to adapt to the enduring shifts in technological and market dynamics as it is an attempt to stay in tune with what Jay Rosen calls "the people formerly known as the audience," who are increasingly likely to participate in the media production and distribution processes.[30]

Audience *engagement*, another popular buzzword in the media industries, has become a central focus in recent years. But the desire to engage is hardly selfless—the more an audience member connects with the brand, the more visible it is in the network (i.e. free advertising) and the more likely they will be return customers. Thus, while the work of media gatekeepers has not been radically transformed, they are by many accounts more attuned to the thoughts and actions of outsiders than ever before, even going as far as to track the sentiment of comments made about their brand and content.

As cultural sociologist David Grazian argues, "decision making in the media industries is primarily driven by the minimization of risk."[31] In their classic study of pilot episodes created for prime-time television, sociologists William and Denise Bielby found that the process for determining which shows get produced is far from scientific. Even though gatekeepers can easily determine which scripts are most innovative, or which producers have earned high ratings in the past, programmers have "no reliable basis for predicting whether audiences, advertisers, and critics will accept the series."[32] As a former president of CBS Entertainment put it, "all hits are flukes."

Nevertheless, media companies do what they can to ensure they are producing the most viable products, and thus maximizing revenues. For blockbuster films, music, and TV shows, this often entails enlisting stars because their notoriety will increase the likelihood of audience interest, and emulating the trends set by previously successful releases. Hollywood movies and popular music are obvious examples, with their affinity for sequels and common melodies,[33] although a similar logic is also applied by many popular news organizations.

While the growth of digital technologies has increasingly allowed content producers to reach audiences directly through podcasts, streaming platforms (Netflix, Hulu, Amazon Prime, Spotify, BandCamp, etc.) and social media (Facebook, Twitter, YouTube, Instagram, Snapchat, etc.) they must also go through the gatekeepers of traditional media channels to reach mass audiences. And at every step in the process, from writing the script to recording, producing, and publishing, and everything in between, the content is subject to strict editorial standards. To be sure, for every piece of content published, there's another—perhaps a dozen more—that will never see the light of day. Instead, this content will likely end up "on the cutting room floor," if it is even produced at all. This is the process of gatekeeping in practice, and in short, the now-familiar economic logic that underlies it works like this: by minimizing risk, producers maximize the likelihood that their content will produce profits.

The news business is hardly any different. Innovations in the dissemination and tracking of web traffic has given rise to click-based logics that, as discussed in Chapter 3, foreground the need to drive traffic to stories or sites in order to generate advertising revenue. Much of the workings of the digital media industry, whether focused on producing news or entertainment, can be explained by Hirsch's "culture industry system," introduced in Chapter 2. As you may recall, Hirsch explains how managerial gatekeepers like programmers and casting directors, institutional gatekeepers like DJs and talk show hosts, and members of the audience each act as "filters" that direct the flow of consumer attention to media products. For the market-driven (heteronomic) portion of the journalistic field, gatekeepers decide what becomes news, industry elites/influencers drive traffic, and consumers click, read, comment, and share (or not). Using online platforms to track web analytics, producers monitor what content is successful, and use this knowledge to inform future decisions.

Just as the commitment to traditional journalistic values has shaped the practices of those working in various media fields, the introduction of new metrics has quickly entered the journalistic consciousness. Through qualitative observations and interviews at three prominent media institutions—the leading metrics company Chartbeat, the now-defunct online publisher Gawker Media, and *The New York Times*—sociologist Caitlin Petre finds that analytics now play a key role in the decision-making of online news outlets.[34]

Although journalists generally maintain their traditional focus on truth and verification, decisions about which stories get told, how, when, and by whom, are increasingly shaped by the lessons learned from running detailed analytics on each piece of content published. While this can have transformative and profitable effects, the role that audience metrics can play in the newsroom is complicated at best. It is easy for newsworkers to place excessive emphasis on web analytics, and this tendency, when combined with a profit-oriented metrics platform designed to play to the mindsets of journalists and editors (as Chartbeat's analytics platform "Publisher" is), may lead to distractions from an organization's mission. And while decision-making based on digital data, which is often automated through the use of algorithms, offers a tempting opportunity to maximize efficiency and minimize individuals' subjectivity, the trend poses significant risk to the culture and practice of journalism.[35] Perhaps this is one reason why, as sociologist Angèle Christin found, many reporters do not go out of their way to view the analytics on their stories.[36] But this has not stopped media industry insiders from raising concerns about the potential consequences of technological innovations like web analytics and automated content production.

These concerns may be symptomatic of what sociologist George Ritzer has termed McDonaldization. Building off of Max Weber's classical sociological contention that modern institutions are bound by the logics of rationalization and bureaucratization—to such an extent that they can become an irrational "iron cage"[37]—Ritzer argues that the work of modern institutions is guided by the principles of efficiency, calculability, predictability, and control.[38] The hyper-rational fast food industry serves as a clear example, since robots can now cook hamburgers and fries with greater efficiency than humans, and customers can place their own orders using in-store consoles or mobile apps—both trends which may render many fast food workers' jobs obsolete.

Just as the growth of artificial intelligence is enabling further automation in the fast food industry, jobs in the news industry may soon be replaced by robots. In considering the role McDonaldization is playing in the media industries, Bob Franklin coined the term "McJournalism" to describe the routinization of newswork.[39] Since Franklin's writing in 2005, changes in the media industries appear to have accelerated the McDonaldization he described. For example, in addition to the traditional reporting tasks, media managers in the Netherlands expect their journalists to create infographics and animations, curate and share news content from other sources, maintain social media profiles, use "search engine optimization" to maximize the visibility of online content, and even to make sure advertisers and investors are happy.[40] Journalists in Austria, Germany, Spain, like those in many other countries, are expected to engage in similar efficiency-increasing measures as their newsrooms adapt to the era of convergence.[41]

Far beyond the consolidation of many journalists into one, as symbolized by the "backpack" or "iPhone" journalists who play the role of multiple media workers at once, one increasingly common solution to media institutions' lack of human capital is to use computer algorithms to create and disseminate content. Believe it or not, news organizations are now building automated "bots" designed to collect information, create short videos, write and post their own news stories, and even engage and respond to audiences.[42] While many of these automated applications may save media companies time and money by reducing the human role in content creation, they are also bound to have unintended consequences.

If Franklin was concerned with the rise of "junk journalism" in 2005, then we wonder what he might say about the recent growth of so-called "fake news," which uses false or potentially misleading information to simultaneously generate revenue and manipulate public opinion. Consider the example of American News, a small Miami-based company operating several liberal and conservative websites, which all publish nearly identical, fake news stories that capitalize on social media users' political preferences.[43] Like other media companies that use fictitious authors to give their computer-generated stories added legitimacy, the main goal of American News and other purveyors of fake news appears to be to generate advertising revenue by driving traffic to their websites.[44]

Although fake news may not sit well with media professionals, the strategy —producing low-cost content that is likely to generate a high volume of clicks by gaming the filters of the 21st century culture industry system—is all too familiar. Furthermore, like the early forms of propaganda, which played a central role in journalism's formative crisis nearly a century ago, today's more sophisticated counterparts may well have a similar effect. Perhaps, as the popular aphorism goes, only time will tell.

## Notes

1  Winfield, Betty Houchin, ed. 2008. *Journalism 1908: Birth of a Profession*. Columbia: University of Missouri Press.
2  Kovach, Bill and Tom Rosenstiel. 2014. *The Elements of Journalism, Revised and Updated 3rd Edition: What Newspeople Should Know and the Public Should Expect. 3 Rev Upd edition*. New York: Three Rivers Press.
3  Sebastian, Michael. 2014. "Five Things to Know About The New York Times' New Native Ads." *Ad Age*, January 8. Retrieved June 14, 2017. Available at: http://adage.com/article/media/york-times-debuts-native-ad-units-dell/290973/.
4  Rosen, Jay. 1999. *What Are Journalists For?* New Haven: Yale University Press, p. 295.
5  Schudson, Michael. 2003. *The Sociology of News*. Norton, p. 11.
6  Benson, Rodney and Erik Neveu. 2005. *Bourdieu and the Journalistic Field*. Cambridge; Malden, MA: Polity, p. 4.
7  Anon. n.d. "2018 World Press Freedom Index | Reporters Without Borders." *RSF*. Retrieved February 8, 2019. Available at: https://rsf.org/en/ranking.

8 Bourdieu, Pierre. 2005. "The Political Field, the Social Science Field, and the Journalistic Field" pp. 29–47 In Rodney Benson and Erik Neveu (eds.), *Bourdieu and the Journalistic Field*. Polity Press: Cambridge, UK. p. 33.

9 Benson, Rodney. 2014. "Strategy Follows Structure: A Media Sociology Manifesto." In Silvio Waisbord (ed.), *Media Sociology: A Reappraisal*. Polity Press, pp. 26–44.

10 Bourdieu, Pierre. 1993. *The Field of Cultural Production: Essays on Art and Literature*. Columbia University Press. p. 30.

11 Nash, Roy. 1990. "Bourdieu on Education and Social and Cultural Reproduction." *British Journal of Sociology of Education* 11(4):431–47. Page 432.

12 Benson, Rodney. 2006. "News Media as a 'Journalistic Field': What Bourdieu Adds to New Institutionalism, and Vice Versa." *Political Communication* 23(2):187–202.

13 Prior, Nick. 2008. "Putting a Glitch in the Field: Bourdieu, Actor Network Theory and Contemporary Music." *Cultural Sociology* 2(3):301–19.

14 Skeggs, Beverley. 2009. "The Moral Economy of Person Production: The Class Relations of Self-Performance on 'Reality' Television." *The Sociological Review* 57(4):626–44.

15 Sterne, Jonathan. 2005. "Digital Media and Disciplinarity." *The Information Society* 21(4):249–56.

16 Deuze, Mark. 2007. *Media Work*. Malden, MA: Polity. p. 11.

17 Russell, Adrienne. 2016. *Journalism as Activism: Recoding Media Power*. Cambridge, UK; Malden, MA: Polity.

18 Ettema, James S. and Theodore Lewis Glasser. 1998. *Custodians of Conscience: Investigative Journalism and Public Virtue*. Columbia University Press.

19 Tuchman, Gaye. 2002. "The Production of News." In Klaus Bruhn Jensen (ed.), *A Handbook of Media and Communication Research: Qualitative and Quantitative Methodologies*, London: Routledge, pp. 78–90 quoted in Stonbely, Sarah. 2015. "The Social and Intellectual Contexts of the U.S. 'Newsroom Studies,' and the Media Sociology of Today." *Journalism Studies* 16(2):259–74.

20 Stonbely, Sarah. 2015. "The Social and Intellectual Contexts of the U.S. 'Newsroom Studies,' and the Media Sociology of Today." *Journalism Studies* 16(2):259–74.

21 Bell, Emily and Nausicaa Renner. 2014. "Post Industrial Journalism: Adapting to the Present." *Tow Center for Digital Journalism*. December 3. Retrieved June 20, 2017. Available at: http://towcenter.org/research/post-industrial-journalism-adapting-to-the-present-2/.

22 Anderson, C. W. 2013. *Rebuilding the News: Metropolitan Journalism in the Digital Age*. Philadelphia: Temple University Press.
Usher, Nikki. 2014. *Making News at The New York Times*. Ann Arbor:- University of Michigan Press.

23 Kovach and Rosenstiel. 2014.

24 We will discuss this topic in greater depth in Chapter 7.

25 Vos, Tim P. 2015. "Revisiting Gatekeeping Theory during a Time of Transition." Pp. 3–24 In Tim P. Vos and Francois Heinderyckx (eds.), *Gatekeeping in Transition*. New York, NY: Routledge, p. 4.

26 Schultz, Ida. 2007. "The Journalistic Gut Feeling: Journalistic doxa, news habitus and orthodox news values." *Journalism Practice* 1(2): 190–207.

27 Lindner, Andrew M. 2016. "Editorial Gatekeeping in Citizen Journalism." *New Media & Society* 1,461,444,816,631,506.

28 Jenkins, Henry. 2008. *Convergence Culture: Where Old and New Media Collide*. Revised edition. New York, NY: NYU Press, p. 2.

29 Kleis Nielsen, Rasmus and Sarah Anne Ganter. 2017. "Dealing with Digital Intermediaries: A Case Study of the Relations between Publishers and Platforms." *New Media & Society* 1,461,444,817,701,318.
30 Rosen, Jay. 2006. "PressThink: The People Formerly Known as the Audience." Retrieved January 26, 2011. Available at: http://archive.pressthink.org/2006/06/27/ppl_frmr.html.
31 Grazian, David. 2010. *Mix It Up: Popular Culture, Mass Media, and Society.* New York: W. W. Norton & Company, p. 113.
32 Bielby, William T. and Denise D. Bielby. 1994. "'All Hits Are Flukes': Institutionalized Decision Making and the Rhetoric of Network Prime-Time Program Development." *American Journal of Sociology* 99(5):1287–1313. Page. 1290.
33 Michaels, Sean. 2012. "Pop Music These Days: It All Sounds the Same, Survey Reveals." *The Guardian*, July 27. Retrieved November 17, 2017. Available at: http:www.theguardian.com/music/2012/jul/27/pop-music-sounds-same-survey-reveals.
34 Petre, Caitlin. 2015. "The Traffic Factories: Metrics at Chartbeat, Gawker Media, and The New York Times." *Columbia Journalism Review.* Retrieved June 14, 2017. Available at: http://www.cjr.org/tow_center_reports/the_traffic_factories_metrics_at_chartbeat_gawker_media_and_the_new_york_times.php.
35 Carlson, Matt. 2017. "Automating Judgment? Algorithmic Judgment, News Knowledge, and Journalistic Professionalism." *New Media & Society.* Retrieved June 15, 2017. Available at: http://journals.sagepub.com/doi/10.1177/1461444817706684.
36 Christin, Angèle. 2017. "Algorithms in Practice: Comparing Web Journalism and Criminal Justice." *Big Data & Society* 4(2):2,053,951,717,718,855.
37 Weber, Max. 2003. *The Protestant Ethic and the Spirit of Capitalism.* Mineola, N.Y: Dover Publications.
38 Ritzer, George. 2013. *The Mcdonaldization Of Society: 20th Anniversary Edition.* SAGE.
39 Franklin, Bob. 2005. "McJournalism: The Local Press and the McDonaldization Thesis." In Stuart Allen (ed.), *Journalism: critical issues.* Maidenhead, UK: Open University Press, pp. 132–150.
40 Bakker, Piet. 2014. "Mr. Gates Returns." *Journalism Studies* 15(5):596–606.
41 García-Avilés, José A., Andy Kaltenbrunner, and Klaus Meier. 2014. "Media Convergence Revisited." *Journalism Practice* 8(5):573–84.
42 Keohane, Joe. 2017. "A Robot May Have Written This Story." *WIRED.* Retrieved June 15, 2017. Available at: http://www.wired.com/2017/02/robots-wrote-this-story/.
43 Silverman, Craig. 2017. "This Is How Your Hyperpartisan Political News Gets Made." *BuzzFeed.* Retrieved December 12, 2017. Available at: http://www.buzzfeed.com/craigsilverman/how-the-hyperpartisan-sausage-is-made.
44 Cohen, Nicole S. 2015. "From Pink Slips to Pink Slime: Transforming Media Labor in a Digital Age." *The Communication Review* 18(2):98–122.

# Section 3

# Content

## Chapter 7

# Fear and Loathing on Cable News

In October 3, 2017, a group of 12 U.S. Special Forces soldiers left their base in the Nigerien capital and joined approximately 50 Nigerien troops on a routine patrol to a village in the remote area of Tongo Tongo. A desert climate, Niger is dry and hot, reaching 100° F most days in October. The area they were visiting is a rural one with most people living in huts without running water. The joint U.S.-Nigerien group stayed overnight in the village, eager to speak with a village elder about the whereabouts of known terrorist leader Adnan Abu Walid al-Sahrawi. Without electrical lighting, it must have been very dark at night, but U.S. soldiers had patrolled this territory 29 times before without incident.

The next morning on October 4, after speaking with the local leader, they began to return to their base in Niamey. Shortly after leaving the town, 50 combatants, armed with light machine guns and rocket-propelled grenades, ambushed the patrol and the U.S.-Nigerien coalition engaged them in open combat. At this point, the details of the incident in Niger become hazy. But it took an hour to call for help and another hour for back-up to arrive. When the skirmish ended, five Nigeriens and four American servicemen were dead. Sergeant La David Johnson had become separated from the group and it took 48 hours to recover his body.[1]

This tragic story raises important questions for the American public to grapple with. At the time of writing, we still lack details on precisely what happened in Niger. Many Americans had no idea that the U.S. military even maintains a base with 800 soldiers in Niger. What were the objectives of this mission? What went wrong operationally and/or strategically on October 4? Are we willing to accept the human costs of a geographically-widening War on Terror?

These are the questions the American public ought to discuss in an inclusive, civil, and reasoned debate. But, of course, that's not what happened in the immediate aftermath of the incident in Niger. President Trump, responding to a journalist's question pressing for details on the fatalities in Niger, instead falsely accused previous presidents of not making condolence calls to the families of the fallen service members. Subsequently, Trump's own condolence call to the widow of Sgt. Johnson then became the subject of controversy when Democratic Congresswoman Frederica S. Wilson (Florida) criticized him for being insensitive when he said, "[Sgt. Johnson] knew what he signed up for" on the call with Ms. Johnson.[2]

The rest of the story is terribly predictable. Trump denied he ever made the comment (though his chief of staff later acknowledged that it was said). Fox News and other conservative media claimed that the news media has a "liberal bias" for reporting Wilson's critique.[3] The White House chief of staff, John Kelly, called Wilson an "empty barrel"—whatever that means. Wilson demanded an apology. The scandal took a turn toward the absurd when cowboy hat-wearing Trump-supporter Sheriff David Clarke criticized Congresswoman Wilson for looking "whacky" because she wears a cowboy hat.[4]

The political culture in the U.S. is deeply broken. In Chapter 2, we described social theorist Jurgen Habermas' ideal "public sphere" as one that is inclusive, disregards statuses in evaluating arguments, is rational-critical, and takes up issues of common concern. Political discourse in the U.S. today is so far from a functional public sphere that Habermas' vision seems like a pipe dream.

Up to this point in this book, we have been examining production of media, the macro and micro forces that contribute to making media content the way it is. In the next few chapters, we now turn to exploring the content itself. In this chapter, we consider the current state of the U.S. political environment, the role of media in shaping our political debates, and how we got to such a bad place where sensationalism, hyper-partisanship, and conflict reign.

## State of the Public Sphere

To understand the state of our public sphere, we need look no further than popular television shows about politics. As recently as the early 2000s, there was still a substantial audience for depictions of Washington, D.C. politics like *The West Wing*, the naively optimistic NBC show that ran from 1999–2006. Focused on a centrist Democratic president, the show told the story of earnest, intelligent, hard-working White House staffers achieving reasonable compromises to help all Americans amidst a tide of rising polarization on the left and right. On the one hand, the show was a sort of gratifying fantasy for liberals during the Bush administration (former *The Daily Show* host Jon Stewart once referred to it as "John Kerry fanfiction"). On the other hand, the show depicted political actors in D.C. as honorable people, acting in the public interest, with Republicans winning some battles and Democrats winning others.

Ten years later, the most popular political shows are like a dark inversion of *The West Wing*. *Scandal* (2012) is a romantic melodrama focused on a political fixer for hire, Olivia Pope, who is having an affair with the married president, while also concealing the election fraud that brought him to power. *House of Cards* (2013) features a ruthless president who will stop at nothing (even personally committing murder!) to seize more power. And HBO's comedy *Veep* (2012) envisions D.C. as a place where petty, cynical, incompetent people make decisions purely to better their political standing. The view from the couch makes politics today seem pretty terrible.

While this new wave of TV shows caricature politics to a degree that is hyperbolic, reality ain't so great either. In particular, three important changes have taken place in recent decades that have profoundly undermined the public sphere. The most central change, well-documented in social scientific research, is growing political polarization in the U.S.. Beginning in the late-1970s, elected officials in the two parties, the Republicans and the Democrats, began to adopt more consistently conservative and consistently liberal views respectively. With the growth of a strong grassroots conservative movement, this pattern was especially true for Republicans in the House of Representatives, with the average Republican congressperson in 2015 being roughly twice as conservative as the average Republican in 1980.[5] As late as the mid-2000s, it was still possible to say that the American people were largely politically moderate—that it was just our elected officials who were so polarized.

But even that's not true anymore. In 1994, there was substantial overlap in the policy views of Democrats and Republicans in the wider public. Approximately 36% of Republicans were more liberal than the median Democrat, while 30% of Democrats were more conservative than the median Republican. By 2017, the equivalent numbers were only 1% and 3% (see Figure 7.1). As Americans have grown more divided on the issues, we have also seen growing political animosity. According to Pew Research, 36% of Republicans and 27% of Democrats see the other party as a threat to the nation's well-being![6] An era with such hyper-partisanship and social distrust makes it very difficult to have discussions that bridge differences and find mutual solutions.

In such a conflictual political atmosphere, it is no surprise that many people want no part of it. A second important change has been a retreat from the public sphere. In 2000, political scientist Robert Putnam published a landmark book titled *Bowling Alone*. The title, drawn from the decline of bowling leagues, spoke to the wider decrease in many forms of civic engagement from voting to attending Parent-Teacher Association (PTA) meetings to spending time with friends. After a brief post-9/11 boost to civic engagement, the patterns Putnam documented have largely continued. Many Americans are not only disengaged from politics, but from the life of their

Ideological Consistency by Party

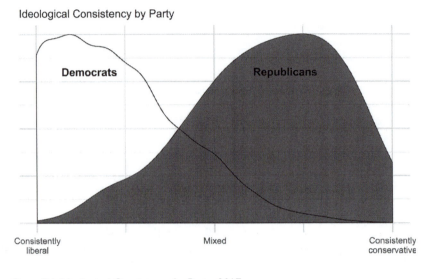

Consistently                      Mixed                     Consistently
liberal                                                     conservative

*Figure 7.1* Ideological Consistency by Party, 2017
[Source: Pew Research Center]

communities. For Putnam, the primary culprit for the decline of civic engagement is television. And, indeed, social scientists who study time usage have found that the average American watches about 2.7 hours of television per day, or about 50% of their free time.[7]

Even those interested in issues sometimes feel reluctant to participate in our toxic political climate. Sociologist Nina Eliasoph, in a qualitative study of political participation in one community, found that people were only willing to speak to issues that were "close to home," avoiding issues that were seen as political. Many of her interview subjects reported that politics felt too big and distant to reasonably do anything about. Moreover, they often felt they lacked the technical expertise to enter into wonky and antagonistic political debates. As Eliasoph writes, "nearly all of the people I met…wanted to care about *people*, but did not want to care about *politics*."[8]

As partisans have become more extreme and many Americans have dropped out from engaging with politics, we have also seen a third important change: a decline in trust of *transpartisan institutions*, particularly the mass media. Transpartisan institutions are "mainstream institutions devoted to gathering and disseminating knowledge … [and are] appointed [by society] as referees in matters of factual dispute."[9] These institutions include the news media and journalism, scientific institutions (e.g., NASA and the National Weather Service), and the academy (e.g., researchers at colleges and universities). Perfect objectivity may not exist, but each of these institutions attempts to serve as a "neutral arbiter," helping society determine what's true and what's fake. We simply cannot have a reasoned public sphere without natural and social scientists who help us understand what's going on in the world, and journalists who investigate and fact-check our politicians. Increasingly, however, Americans have doubts about the referees. In 2000, over half of Americans reported that they have a "fair amount" or "great deal" of trust in the mass media (including TV, newspapers, and radio). By 2016, according to Gallup, that proportion had dropped to 32%.[10] Partially, that decrease is reflective of wider declining trust across all institutions, including organized religion, Congress, labor, corporations, the military, the police, banks, etc. Still, the decline in trust in mass media has been unusually steep. As we shall see, the political right sees the mainstream news media and universities as hotbeds of liberal bias. To a lesser extent, the political left believes the news media advances the interests of corporations and other elites.

With polarization, a retreat from the public sphere, and declining trust in transpartisan institutions, the U.S. has largely lost its capacity to have effective, democratic debates. That is not to say that we once had an ideal public sphere in the past that merely needs to be revived. In the mid-20th century, a period of less partisan polarization, more civic engagement, and greater faith in institutions, the U.S. was a society with

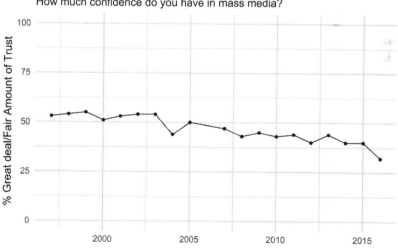

*Figure 7.2* Americans' Confidence in Mass Media
[Source: Gallup]

extreme exclusion of women and racial minorities and a troubling culture of conformity. A return to the 1950s is not and should not be on the table. Still, there are ways in which the U.S. public sphere has become less functional and effective. Unsurprisingly, how we got here and what to do about it are deeply contested.

## How Did We Get Here?

*It's a fact that our mainstream-media newsrooms, our nation's faculties, and even the elite college student bodies that disproportionately produce the newsrooms and faculties are overwhelmingly left-wing. The result is an ideological monoculture so narrow and so uniform that its members often view much of the rest of the country like an anthropologist visiting an obscure tribe in the Amazon rain forest.*[11]

David French, *National Review*, 2017

Beginning in the late 1970s, a revitalized conservative movement began to mobilize, transforming the Republican Party from a center-right party to the far more conservative party it is today. The new movement emphasized an unregulated free market, extreme reductions in welfare state spending, a politics of racial and ethnic resentment, and outreach to a growing evangelical Christian base with "culture war" issues (e.g., same-sex marriage, abortion, the "war on Christmas," etc.). Leaders of the new conservative movement also took umbrage with the very concept of "transpartisan institutions." To them, the academy and the media were fundamentally left-wing institutions, stacked against conservative causes.

This argument was not new. Whether in the form of William F. Buckley's famous 1951 book, *God and Man at Yale*, which critiques the dominance of left-wing, secular thought in the Ivy Leagues or the Nixon administration's grumblings about the "closed fraternity of privileged men" who run the news, Republicans have long bemoaned the "liberal bias" of the news media and the academy.[12] However, the newly emergent conservative movement of the late 1970s decided to make "media bias" a permanent campaign issue supplied with constant ammunition by a set of conservative organizations, like the Media Research Council and Newsbusters. Meanwhile, it began the process of constructing a parallel media system with Fox News as its crown jewel.

The primary argument of those claiming that the media are liberally biased is that most journalists are affluent liberal elites, largely based in large cities in the Northeast. This "progressive monoculture" leads to biased coverage of conservative policies and conservative politicians. It is true that journalists in general lean Democratic. According to a 2014 study, 28.1% of journalists were Democrats, 50.2% were independents, 14.6% defined themselves as "other," and only 7.1% were Republicans.[13]

Some, like Tim Graham, the executive editor of Newsbusters, believe these numbers underestimate the liberal skew of newsrooms. As he told the *Washington Post*, "Journalists have gotten incredibly reluctant to identify with a party. I suspect liberals check the 'independent' box to avoid being properly identified."[14] Surveys of journalists are rare, but one 2004 Pew study of national reporters found that 34% identified as liberals, 54% as moderates, and only 7% as conservatives.[15] As the *New York Times* public editor Daniel Okrent once wrote, "[On] social issues [like] gay rights, gun control, abortion and environmental regulation ... if you think The Times plays it down the middle on any of them, you've been reading the paper with your eyes closed."[16]

To many on the right, these surveys seem like slam-dunk evidence of liberal bias. Those who accept the media bias argument see this dynamic play out in nearly every news cycle. Considering the political fall-out over President Trump's condolence call to Sgt. Johnson's widow, some conservatives saw the news coverage as a wild overreaction by a mainstream media with a liberal bias. Trump himself reacted to the coverage by saying, "The Fake News is going crazy." White House Chief of Staff John Kelly, for example, told the press corps that he was "stunned" by the criticism of the phone call, saying that President Trump had attempted to express his condolences "in the best way that he could" and the press simply does not give him the benefit of the doubt with an unartful turn-of-phrase.[17]

Even if we acknowledge that members of the press lean Democratic in their personal views, there are several reasons to be skeptical of claims of media bias. First, that 2004 Pew study found that the journalists were only substantially more liberal than the country as a whole on a few issues. Whereas only 51% of Americans at the time believed that "homosexuality should be accepted by society," 88% of national reporters and 74% of local reporters believed that. By contrast, on a survey question that pits personal freedom vs. a social safety net, 34% of the general public favored a social safety net compared with 42% of national reporters and 35% of local reporters. These findings tend to suggest a bigger gap between journalists and the general public on social issues than on economic policy. As Okrent himself argued, the *New York Times* doesn't have a liberal bias, but it does have a cosmopolitan and "'urban' viewpoint." That may help explain why pro-corporate, but also pro-diversity and pro-globalization conservatives like Marco Rubio and Mitt Romney receive somewhat more friendly treatment than nationalist and anti-immigration politicians like Donald Trump.

However, all of this relies on the assumption that the personal partisan leanings of journalists directly translate into biased coverage. The trouble with that assumption is that the work of investigating and reporting stories occurs in structured context that makes it difficult to interject strong partisan views. For starters, most journalists are employed by publishers and corporate owners that lean Republican (recall the discussion of media owners in Chapter 4). More importantly, as we have seen in Chapter 6, one of the most strongly held codes in the field of journalism is the "objectivity norm," which requires reporters to be dispassionate observers, treating "both sides" equally. This norm is not only performed by the journalists whose names appear on an article's byline, but is enforced by the multiple layers of editors who vet journalistic work before it reaches the public. Moreover, most journalists are not political reporters. Does it matter who the Knicks beat reporter or the food critic voted for in the last election?

Conservative media criticism organizations will counter these arguments by showing the results of content analyses, indicating liberal bias in coverage. The Media Research Center, for example, in a study of 588 evening television news stories from the 2016 election found that network news devoted more airtime to Trump than Clinton (440 minutes vs. 185 minutes) and had more opinionated statements about Trump (686 statements, 91% negative) than Clinton (184 statements, 79% negative).[18] Of course, it is difficult to separate out any bias in coverage from the effects of Trump being a more controversial candidate. In the 2012 presidential election, one analysis found that there were 17% more negative statements about Obama than Romney, and Republicans were quoted 44% more than Democrats.[19] The relative partisan balance of coverage seems to be affected more by dominant narratives in the specific campaign and personalities of the candidates than by a consistent partisan lean of the press.

None of this is to say that the prevailing shared social, political, and moral values of the mass media has no effect on their coverage. Rather, we are often led astray by looking for partisan bias in coverage. Instead, journalism scholar Robert Jensen argues that American journalism is shaped by three dominant ideological commitments, which he describes as *fundamentalisms*, or "any intellectual, political, or moral position that asserts a certainty in the truth and/or righteousness of a belief system."[20] The first is national fundamentalism, the belief that the United States' use of power around the world is legitimate, morally justified, and for the betterment of humankind. The second, economic fundamentalism, is the view that capitalism and the power American capitalism grants to corporations is the only viable, efficient, and rational system possible. Finally, technological fundamentalism is the belief that an increasingly technological society is beneficial and that most problems can be solved by further technology. While you may agree or disagree with these assumptions, they are truly deeply held by the news media and, unlike either Republican or Democratic politicians, are rarely questioned. Even in cases of corporate malfeasance or a military quagmire, the U.S. press is more likely to chalk it up to a few bad apples rather than any faults in the underlying systems.

In the case of the incident in Niger, using Jensen's argument, we should take note that the political controversy focused on Trump's performance of the ritual of the condolence call and, in more sophisticated news outlets, why there was an operational or intelligence failure. What we did not see was any deeper questioning of the extension of U.S. military power throughout the world, its consequences for people in countries like Niger, or whether the goals achieved are worth the sacrifice made by service men and women like Sgt. Johnson. Through this lens, in covering the controversy over Trump's condolence call, the press was not engaged in a petty partisan attempt to embarrass a Republican president. Instead, media outlets have a bias toward conflict and, given that the conflict involved the president, a prominent Congresswoman, and a Gold Star widow, they viewed it as highly newsworthy.

It is not that there is no bias in journalism. But the biases that really matter for affecting news coverage have more to do with a deep belief in the economic and political systems that undergird U.S. power as well as the urbanity, cosmopolitanism, and professional norms of many journalists. While there are, of course, occasional examples of left-leaning bias by individual journalists that motivated critics can cherry-pick to make their case, there simply is inadequate evidence for the claim that there is a liberal bias in media that systematically disadvantages conservatives and their policies. That has not stopped conservatives from using the claim of "media bias" to their benefit.

## Reacting to the Charge of Liberal Bias

Regardless of the evidence concerning the existence of liberal bias in the press, the conservative movement's plan to make media bias a permanent issue has worked. It has worked by weakening public trust in the press. And it has worked by changing journalists' behavior. Just as NBA referees sometimes give "make-up calls" after star players vocally complain about an allegedly bad foul call, so too has the press reacted to years of being accused of liberal bias in ways that undermine good reporting.

Though few serious reporters see themselves as perfectly objective, as discussed in Chapter 6, the "objectivity norm" in American journalism has the noble goal of encouraging journalists to transcend their personal viewpoint and report verifiable facts that support an understanding of some objective truths. Unfortunately, after decades of being accused of bias, journalists are in a defensive crouch and will go to any length to be seen as "objective" and, therefore, trustworthy. But, according to media scholar Jay Rosen, this defensiveness has mutated the objectivity norm into a type of false objectivity he calls "the View From Nowhere." As Rosen writes, "the View From Nowhere is a bid for trust that advertises the viewlessness of the news producer. Frequently it places the journalist between polarized extremes, and calls that neither-nor position 'impartial.'"

This stance is not merely a silly affectation. It leads to bad journalistic practices. When reporters have spent days, weeks, or months investigating a story, following leads, cultivating sources, and verifying facts, it would not be surprising if they developed a point of view about it. That informed point of view doesn't damage the story, Rosen argues, it strengthens it. For example, if after deeply studying a proposed healthcare bill, a reporter comes to the conclusion that it would be harmful to many people's health, it would be helpful to the reader for the reporter to come out and say it.

> When NPR forbids its 'news analysts' from expressing a view on matters they are empowered to analyze—that's dumb. When reporters have to 'launder' their views by putting them in the mouths of think tank experts: dumb ... American journalism is dumber than most journalists.[21]

Perhaps most troublingly, "the View From Nowhere" leads to a great deal of "both sides" reporting in which either side of an argument is represented equally regardless of the amount of evidence on each side. In cases where the evidence is not equal, this style of reporting produces a *false equivalency*. For example, there is a tremendous amount of evidence that the global climate is warming due to human activity and peer-review studies show that 97% of actively publishing climate scientists agree with that claim.[22] But because climate change is a debated political issue, for years, many news outlets adopted the practices of offering a quote from one climate scientist and one climate change denier. The upshot was that, to a reader unfamiliar with the subject, opinion seemed to be divided 50/50, while, in fact, there is an overwhelming scientific consensus.

"Both sides" reporting is also misleading in an era when the two parties are not equal. The typical journalistic frame for reporting on D.C. politics is to depict both Democrats and Republicans as equally to blame for Congressional gridlock, as equally polarized and extreme, and as equally untrustworthy about science, facts, and evidence.[23] But—and, unfortunately, it may make one sound (yikes!) biased to even say it—there is substantial political science evidence to show that on every one of those counts, the Republican Party is worse. While both parties have polarized in recent decades, the Republican Party is far more polarized and has widely adopted far more ideologically extreme views.[24] The Republican Congress during the Obama administration used the filibuster to block widely-supported bills and judicial nominees in a simply unprecedented way.[25] Republicans increasingly doubt reporting from transpartisan institutions like mainstream newspapers and scientific research. Journalist David Roberts explains, "The US is experiencing a deep epistemic breach, a split not just in what we value or want, but in who we trust, how we come to know things, and what we believe we know." According to Roberts, the primary cause of this breach is that the right no longer believes in transpartisan institutions and "has created its own parallel set of institutions, most notably its own media ecosystem."[26]

As accusations of "media bias" have weakened trust in media, the press has tried to win it back by studiously offering up "the View From Nowhere," which goes to great pains to report on "both sides" and avoid analysis at all costs. In a society where both sides were actually equal, that wouldn't be so bad. But that is simply not the case today. Even as the journalists have doubled down on objectivity to avoid accusations of bias, the mainstream press has already lost much of their audience to a rival: Fox News.

## Fox News and the Growth of Partisan Media

While the conservative movement has tried to delegitimize the mainstream press through claims of media bias, they also took another strategy: building a separate, parallel, conservative media ecosystem. There had always been publications with a conservative bent, like the *National Review*, just as there are periodicals with a liberal bent, like *The Nation*. Such publications, though they have an ideological perspective, tend to be serious and intellectual, but, most importantly, use evidence and are grounded in reality. The new partisan media that emerged beginning in the late-1980s were, and still are, something different. They were propagandistic, inspired fear and outrage in their audiences, and had a wanton disregard for fact.

As discussed in Chapter 5, in 1987, the FCC repealed the Fairness Doctrine, which required broadcasters to offer equitable time for contrasting views of public issues. This change allowed radio stations around the country to begin broadcasting openly right-wing hosts, like Rush Limbaugh, without views from the other side. Over the years, right-wing radio has produced a steady stream of stars of conservative media including Sean Hannity, Glenn Beck, and Mark Levin. Though conservative radio listenership peaked in 2012, Rush Limbaugh had approximately 13.25 million listeners per week and Sean Hannity had 12.5 million listeners in 2016.[27]

Unlike traditional news programs aimed at informing the public, the right-wing radio hosts offer up a daily rundown of stories that outrage their mostly older, mostly white, mostly Christian audience. With stories about immigrants pouring across the border, horrific reports of violent crime, and people saying, "Happy Holidays" instead of "Merry

Christmas," the fundamental narrative on right-wing radio is that the
U.S. is changing rapidly and for the worse. And—crucially—these
changes are caused by out-of-touch, secular, left-wing elites and racial
minorities. Sociologist Sarah Sobieraj and political scientist
Jeffrey M. Berry describe this kind of programming as outrage rhetoric,
"a particular form of political discourse involving efforts to provoke vis-
ceral responses (e.g., anger, righteousness, fear, moral indignation) from
the audience through the use of overgeneralizations, sensationalism, misleading or patently inaccurate information, ad hominem attacks, and
partial truths about opponents."[28]

The formula created on radio was carried over to television in 1996
when conservative media mogul Rupert Murdoch hired longtime
Republican media consultant Roger Ailes to create a partisan cable news
channel. With the slogan "Fair and Balanced," the Fox News Channel
asserted that it was the only unbiased news source. In fact, Fox News was
quite apparently a partisan media outlet, airing almost exclusively Republican talking points, often misrepresenting facts, and offering a steady
stream of outrage rhetoric. Not surprisingly, a number of studies have
shown that exposure to Fox News has made people more likely to vote
Republican and to favor more far-right Republicans.[29] But Fox News
viewers are also more misinformed about facts regarding the news. Over
half of Fox News viewers believe that American forces found weapons of
mass destruction in Iraq (they did not). As late as 2015, four years after
President Obama released his birth certificate, 30% of Fox News viewers
did not believe Obama was born in the U.S..[30] This kind of misinformation is particularly troubling given that since 2002, Fox News has been
the annually most-watched news channel with an average of 2.8 million
viewers in 2017.[31]

Many argue that liberals have their own partisan news channel in
MSNBC. Originally a partnership between Microsoft and NBC News,
the channel searched for identity in its early years, settling into its incar-
nation as a progressive news channel in the mid-2000s as opinionated liberal anchor Keith Olbermann grew in popularity. In some ways,
MSNBC does seem like a mirror image to Fox News. Its primetime line-
up of Chris Matthews, Chris Hayes, Rachel Maddow, and Lawrence
O'Donnell are all avowed liberals who have past experience in the
Democratic Party or progressive politics. A Pew study of 2012 election
coverage found that Fox and MSNBC were far more extreme than other
media outlets in covering one party positively and the other negatively.[32]
However, MSNBC's parent company, NBC News, is a transpartisan
news division and has always been uneasy about allowing MSNBC to
become a partisan station. Unlike Fox, MSNBC's CEO Phil Griffin is
a career television executive, not a former political operative. Moreover,

their morning news program is hosted by a former Republican congress-man, Joe Scarborough, and their entire daytime line-up is unopinionated reporting presented by the NBC News division.[33]

Aside from staffing, there are other important differences between left and right partisan media. In a content analysis of partisan news across several media (TV, radio, blogs, and op-ed columns), Sobieraj and Berry found that both left and right partisans engage in outrage rhetoric, but that the right does it significantly more. Left media engaged in an average of 10.32 outrage incidents per segment/article/post and right media had an average of 15.47 outrage incidents per segment/article/post. While the left did more verbal fighting/sparring, more belittling, and more slippery slope argumentation, the right had significantly higher levels of insulting language, name calling, emotional display, emotional language, character assassination, misrepresentative exaggeration, open conflict, and ideologically extremizing language.[34] Such outrage rhetoric does not help to inform citizens in a democracy. It only serves to inspire anger and fear and to vilify others.

The final difference between left and right partisan media involves the audience. For most on the left, MSNBC is one source in a relatively diversified media diet. Liberals and moderates alike get their news from a range of sources probably including mainstream TV news (e.g., ABC, NBC, CBS), national newspapers (e.g., *New York Times, WSJ, USA Today*), as well as blogs, digital news sites, and cable news. For Republicans, increasingly, their only source is Fox News and other highly partisan conservative media. A 2017 study conducted by a team of researchers at Harvard's Berkman Klein Center for Internet & Society examined patterns of linking and social media sharing on the web during the 2016 election. They found that even the most left-wing media sources linked to a diversified set of sources, spanning from left to the center. Right-wing media sources linked almost exclusively to other highly partisan right-wing sources. This pattern was even more extreme on Facebook. Conservative Facebook users shared links exclusively to right-wing media, while liberal Facebook users had much more exposure to the center.[35] The real concern, then, with the growth of partisan news on the right is not merely that it is misleading, emotional, and tribal, but that its viewers consume it exclusively, shutting down information from other sources.

In coverage of the Niger incident, liberals who turned on MSNBC during primetime did encounter a hyperbolic, outraged treatment of Trump's insensitive treatment of a Gold Star widow, but they probably also read a newspaper article describing the strategic failure in more detail and, perhaps, saw some "both sides" reporting on ABC Nightly News about the back and forth between Congresswoman Wilson and President Trump. Fox News viewers saw a version of the story that focused on the "whacky" congresswoman and the biased media unfairly picking on the president again. Unfortunately, for many of those viewers, that partisan take was the only one they got.

## New Agents Enter the Field

Thus far, we have discussed important changes in systems—newspapers, television, radio—that have existed for some time. Equally important are media systems that have emerged more recently. Part of the great promise of the Internet is the sweeping democratization it offers. One did not have to own a TV station to create a video series nor own a printing press to distribute commentary on political events. In the early days of the Internet, some media theorists imagined that such openness would help usher in precisely the type of digital public sphere that Habermas envisioned. Though there are many examples of citizens and journalists throughout the world using the Internet to expand reasoned democratic discourse, the open architecture of the web allows malicious actors to commit acts of vandalism, disinformation, and abuse.

Among the more positive developments of the Internet age have been the emergence of citizen journalists, members of the public who contribute to the gathering, reporting, and analysis of news. Some citizen journalists, those media scholar Melissa Wall calls "The Resistance," create news that directly challenges professional media's "fundamentalisms" and routine practices like the "objectivity norm."[36] In places like Tahrir Square in 2012 in the midst of mass protests of the Egyptian government, or Ferguson, Missouri, protesting police violence against African Americans, activist citizen journalists have reported events critically. This type of "advocacy in violation of objectivity" allows people whose voices usually are underrepresented in the press to be heard.[37]

Other citizen journalists act as "hyperlocal deputy journalists" who "do not reject journalism but instead want more of it." Whether in big cities where the professional news outlets don't have the capacity to cover every neighborhood or, in rural areas, where there may not be a daily newspaper, citizen journalists have stepped in to cover local events, act as a watchdog for local governments, and provide important civic information. Multiple content analyses have shown that citizen journalist sites are not adequate "newspaper substitutes" since they lack the access to government officials and investigative resources that professional media outlets have.[38] Nonetheless, citizen journalism has served to augment and sometimes challenge existing media organizations in many communities in the U.S. and throughout the world.

The Internet has also enabled the growth of a new breed of digital native news sites, including *Buzzfeed*, *Vox*, *Vice*, *FiveThirtyEight*, *The Intercept*, *ProPublica*, and *The Marshall Project*. These news sites, web-based since their founding, diverge in many ways from the norms of journalism as practiced by legacy media outlets. *FiveThirtyEight*, for example, is the most prominent practitioner of "data journalism," using statistical analysis rather than traditional punditry to analyze politics, sports, and society. *Vox* specializes in "explanatory journalism," focusing on explaining the bigger picture, not just the most recent events. *The Intercept*, which claims to practice "fearless, adversarial journalism," challenges the objectivity norm. So do *Buzzfeed* and *Vice*, which blend analysis and reporting as well as first-person stories in a way that is uncommon in mainstream news. However, unlike citizen journalism, these digital news sites are all staffed by professional reporters and editors.

Digital native news sites have added to the diversity of the journalistic field. Following the Niger incident, *Vox* ran a story titled, "Why were US soldiers even in Niger? America's shadow wars in Africa, explained." *The Intercept* became the first outlet to break the news that Sgt. Johnson had survived the initial ambush and ran with the provocative lead, "WHAT DID OFFICIALS at U.S. Africa Command know about the fate of Sgt. La David Johnson, and when did they know it?" *FiveThirtyEight* and *ProPublica*, a public interest investigative journalism site, simply did not cover the story as it was not part of their beat.

These news sites of the Internet era have been a net positive for democratic discourse, bringing different methods, voices, and styles into journalism. But not all of the digital native news sites have been a force for good. In particular, the Breitbart News Network, a right-wing site founded by Andrew Breitbart, has become the nation's most prominent advocate for white supremacist views and a propaganda site for the Trump administration. Though it is ostensibly a "news" site, since Steve Bannon took over leadership in 2012, it has become the primary mouthpiece of the alt-right political movement, according to the Southern Poverty Law Center.[39] Breitbart's modus operandi is clear from their response in the wake of the military fatalities in Niger. They ran stories distancing the operation from the Trump administration ("Donald Trump Says He Did Not 'Specifically' Authorize Niger Mission"), blaming it on the Obama administration ("Green Berets in Niger Were Part of Mission Obama Authorized"), and criticizing "Leftists" for "Politicizing Niger."[40]

What distinguishes Breitbart from other opinionated news sites are the extremist white ethno-nationalist views frequently posted on the site and how closely Breitbart echoes Trump administration talking points. A site like *Vox*, by contrast, while clearly left-leaning, is well within the political mainstream and was often critical of the Obama administration. There are plenty of fringe web sites on the Internet, espousing extremist views from the right or the left. Breitbart is unusually concerning because it presents itself as a news site and is the 56th most popular web site in the U.S., only slightly less popular than the *Washington Post* (48th).[41]

If Breitbart is extreme and propagandistic, some news is outright fake. Though President Trump has often used "Fake News" to describe mainstream media reports he merely dislikes or that were unintentionally erroneous, the origin of the term comes from a rash of malicious, verifiably untrue news reports created with the intent of deceiving readers. Though fake news stories have long been circulated, the 2016 presidential election revealed just how widespread fake news could be in the Internet era. Among the most frequently shared fake stories were "Pope Francis shocks world, endorses Donald Trump for president," "Donald Trump sent his own plane to transport 200 stranded marines," and "WikiLeaks confirms Hillary sold weapons to ISIS." Like the vast majority of the fake news items, these stories favored Donald Trump over Hillary Clinton and were posted on web sites designed to look like mainstream news web sites. One attempt to study fake news stories during the election found that 115 pro-Trump fake stories were shared 30 million times on Facebook, while 41 pro-Clinton fake stories were shared 7.6 million times. These sites registered 0.64 visits per American adult.[42] Another analysis finds that about one in four American adults visited a fake news site during the final month of the campaign. However, these visits were highly concentrated in a small subset of very conservative people. According to political scientist Andrew Guess and his co-authors, "six in ten visits to fake news websites came from the 10% of Americans with the most conservative information diets."[43]

While researchers have shown that fake news stories are unlikely to have changed the result of the presidential election, these stories increase distrust, hostility, and polarization across groups. Unfortunately, fake news didn't end with the 2016 campaign. As news broke about the incident in Niger, a fake and racially incendiary story, widely circulated among conservatives on social media, claimed, "BREAKING: Black Soldier Killed In Niger Was A Deserter." Later, the author argued it was merely "satire."[44] Nonetheless, it was shared on Facebook as fact, contributing to misinformation and stoking racial antagonism.

Why would anybody want to spread such fake stories? For a group of teenagers in a small town in Macedonia who ran over a hundred fake news sites, the answer was money. Fake news stories that appealed to political partisans were more likely to go viral, allowing them to earn more than $30,000 from advertisements.[45] For others, including Russian political operatives who ran a troll farm actively pushing fake and politicized stories, the goal was to help Donald Trump win.[46]

The scourge of fake news is not a uniquely American problem. In the Philippines, authoritarian leader Rodrigo Duterte has paid $200,000 to employ 500 online trolls to spread false stories and attack political activists critical of his regime.[47] An Oxford University study of 28 countries found disinformation campaigns to be widespread in both authoritarian societies and democracies alike, carried out by a mixture of "cyber troops" (real people) and "bots" (fake accounts with content produced by robots who pretend to be human users).[48]

There are many proposed solutions to the United States' broken political culture. Some argue that social media giants ought to do a better job of policing their sites for false and extremist content better. Others believe we need media literacy courses in schools. Conservatives claim that there ought to be more political diversity in newsrooms, while some liberals would like to bring back the Fairness Doctrine. None of these solutions is likely to be a cure-all, but most of them point in the direction of an important first step: restoring trust in transpartisan institutions like the news media.

## Notes

1  Account of Nigerien ambush based on: Schmitt, Eric and Thomas Gibbons-Neff. 2017. "Deadly Ambush of Green Berets in Niger Belies a 'Low-Risk' Mission." *New York Times*. Oct. 5. (www.nytimes.com/2017/10/05/world/africa/green-berets-killed-niger.html); Schmitt, Eric and Thomas Gibbons-Neff. 2017. "Fourth U.S. Soldier Is Found Dead After Ambush in Niger." *New York Times*. Oct. 6. (www.nytimes.com/2017/10/06/world/africa/green-berets-niger-soldiers-killed.html); Gibbons-Neff, Thomas and Helene Cooper. 2017. "U.S. Troops Ambushed in Niger Waited an Hour to Call for Help." *New York Times*. Oct. 23. (www.nytimes.com/2017/10/23/world/africa/niger-attack-dunford.html); Stoller, Paul. 2017. "Niger Nightmare: The Cost of Cultural Ignorance." *Huffington Post*. Oct. 23. (www.huffingtonpost.com/entry/niger-nightmare-the-cost-of-cultural-ignorance_us_59ed3ad3e4b034105edd4fef).

2  Landler, Mark and Yamiche Alcindor. 2017. "Trump's Condolence Call to Soldier's Widow Ignites an Imbroglio." *New York Times*. Oct. 18. Available at: http://www.nytimes.com/2017/10/18/us/politics/trump-widow-johnson-call.html.

3  Fetzer, Barry. 2017. "Opinion: Media got it wrong on Trump phone call." *Havelock News*. Oct. 25.Available at: http://www.havenews.com/opinion/20171025/opinion-media-got-it-wrong-on-trump-phone-call.

4  Holmes, Jack. 2017. "Big Hat Enthusiast Attacks Political Opponent for Her Big Hat." *Esquire*. Oct. 20. Available at: http://www.esquire.com/news-politics/a13057198/sheriff-clarke-attacks-frederica-wilson/.

5  Poole, Keith. 2018. *Voteview.org*. Available at: http://www.voteview.org/political_polarization _2015.htm.

6  Pew Research Center. 2014. "Political Polarization in the American Public." Available at: http://www.people-press.org/2014/06/12/political-polarization-in-the-american-public/.

7  Bureau of Labor Statistics. 2017. "American Time Use Survey." Available at: http://www.bls.gov/news.release/atus.nr0.htm.

8  Eliasoph, Nina. 1998. *Avoiding Politics: How Americans Produce Apathy in Everyday Life*. Cambridge University Press, pp. 12–13.

9  Roberts, David. 2017. "America is Facing an Epistemic Crisis." *Vox*. Nov. 2. Available at: http://www.vox.com/policy-and-politics/2017/11/2/16588964/america-epistemic-crisis.

10  Swift, Art. 2016. "Americans' Trust in Mass Media Sinks to New Low." *Gallup News*. Sept. 14. Available at: http://news.gallup.com/poll/195542/americans-trust-mass-media-sinks-new-low.aspx.

11  Times editors. 2017. "Selected Readings from the Left and from the Right." *Tampa Bay Times.* Retrieved January 15, 2020. Available at: https://tampabay. com/opinion/columns/Selected-readings-from-the-left-and-from-the-right_163500014/.

12  Hemmer, Nicole. 2014. "The Conservative War on Liberal Media Has a Long History." *The Atlantic Monthly.* Jan. 17. Available at: www.theatlantic.com/polit ics/archive/2014/01/the-conservative-war-on-liberal-media-has-a-long-history/ 283149/.

13  Willnat, Lars and David H. Weaver. 2013. "The American Journalist in the Digital Age.". Available at: http://archive.news.indiana.edu/releases/iu/2014/ 05/2013-american-journalist-key-findings.pdf.

14  Wemple, Eric. "Dear Mainstream Media: Why so liberal?" *Washington Post.* Jan. 27. Available at: www.washingtonpost.com/blogs/erik-wemple/wp/ 2017/01/27/dear-mainstream-media-why-so-liberal/.

15  Pew Research Center. 2004. "Values and the Press." *Bottom-Line Pressures Now Hurting Coverage, Say Journalists.* Available at: www.people-press.org/ 2004/05/23/iv-values-and-the-press/.

16  Okrent, Daniel. 2004. "Is the New York Times a Liberal Newspaper?" *New York Times.* July 25. Available at: www.nytimes.com/2004/07/25/opin ion/the-public-editor-is-the-new-york-times-a-liberal-newspaper.html.

17  Fox News. 2017. "Trump: Media 'going crazy' with Wilson's 'total lie' about call to widow." Available at: www.foxnews.com/politics/2017/10/20/ trump-media-going-crazy-with-wilsons-total-lie-about-call-to-widow.html.

18  Noyes, Rich. 2016. "MRC Study: Documenting TV's Twelve Weeks of Trump Bashing." *Newsbusters.* Oct. 25. Available at: www.newsbusters.org/blogs/nb/rich-noyes/2016/10/25/mrc-study-documenting-tvs-twelve-weeks-trump-bashing.

19  Romensko, Jim. 2012. "Claim: Campaign Coverage is Biased Toward Republicans." *JimRomensko.com.* Aug. 6. Available at: http://jimromenesko. com/2012/08/06/campaign-coverage-and-liberal-media-bias.

20  Jensen, Robert. 2015. "American journalism's ideology: Why the 'liberal' media is fundamentalist." *ZNET.* June 10. Available at: https://zcomm.org/znetarticle/ american-journalisms-ideology-why-the-liberal-media-is-fundamentalist/.

21  Rosen, Jay. 2010. "The View from Nowhere: Questions and Answer." *Press-Think.* Nov. 10. Available at: http://pressthink.org/2010/11/the-view-from-nowhere-questions-and-answers/.

22  NASA. 2018. "Scientific consensus: Earth's climate is warming." *Global Climate Change: Vital Signs of the Planet.* Available at: https://climate.nasa.gov/scientific-con sensus/.

23  Gans, Herbert J. 2014. "The American news media in an increasingly unequal society." *International Journal of Communication* 8:12.

24  Barber, Michael, and Nolan McCarty. 2015. "Causes and consequences of polarization." *Political Negotiation: A Handbook*, p. 37.

25  Mann, Thomas E., and Norman J. Ornstein. 2016. *It's even worse than it looks: How the American constitutional system collided with the new politics of extremism.* New York: Basic Books.

26  Roberts 2017.

27  Ho, Rodney. 2016. "Rush Limbaugh still on top of Talkers talk Show Rankings for 10th year." *Atlanta Journal-Constitution.* May 4. Available at: http://radiotvtalk.blog.ajc.com/2016/05/04/rush-limbaugh-still-on-top-of-talkers-talk-show-rankings-for-10th-year/.

28  Sobieraj, Sarah and Jeffrey M. Berry. 2011. "From Incivility to Outrage: Political Discourse in Blogs, Talk Radio, and Cable News." *Political Communication* 28(1):19–41. Pg. 19.
29  Schroeder, Elizabeth and Daniel F. Stone. 2015. "Fox News and political knowledge." *Journal of Public Economics* 126:52–63.; Hopkins, Daniel J. and Jonathan M. Ladd. 2012. "The Consequences of Broader Media Choice: Evidence from the Expansion of Fox News." *Working Paper*. (www.jonathanm ladd.com/uploads/5/3/6/6/5366295/foxpersuasion102612.pdf).
30  Breitman, Kendall. 2015. "Poll: Half of Republicans Still Believe WMDs found in Iraq." *Politico*. Jan. 7. (www.politico.com/story/2015/01/poll-repub licans-wmds-iraq-114016).
31  Fox News. 2017. "FOX News Channel Marks Ratings Milestone." *Fox News*. Jan. 31. Available at: www.foxnews.com/entertainment/2017/01/31/ fox-news-channel-marks-ratings-milestone.html.
32  Pew Research Center. 2012. "The Final Days of the Media Campaign 2012." Available at: www.journalism.org/2012/11/19/final-days-media-campaign-2012/.
33  Wemple, Eric. 2012. "MSNBC Chief: Fox Cheerled; we didn't." *Washington Post*. Nov. 21. (www.washingtonpost.com/blogs/erik-wemple/post/msnbc-chief-fox-cheerled-we-didnt/2012/11/21/fe2bf52a-3358-11e2-9cfa-e41bac906cc9_blog. html).; Ariens, Chris. 2015. "MSNBC Begins 'Pivot Towards Live, Breaking News Coverage.'" *Adweek*. Aug. 3. Available at: www.adweek.com/tvnewser/ msnbc-begins-pivot-towards-live-breaking-news-coverage/268736.
34  Sobieraj, Sarah, and Jeffrey M. Berry. 2011. "From Incivility to Outrage: Political Discourse in Blogs, Talk Radio, and Cable News." *Political Communication* 28(1):19–41.
35  Faris, Rob, Hal Roberts, Bruce Etling, Nikki Bourassa, Ethan Zuckerman, Yochai Benkler. 2017. "Partisanship, Propaganda, and Disinformation: Online Media and the 2016 U.S. Presidential Election." *Berkman Klein Center for Internet & Society at Harvard University*. Available at: https://cyber.harvard.edu/publica tions/2017/08/mediacloud.
36  Wall, Melissa. 2015. "Citizen journalism." *Digital Journalism* 3:797–813.
37  St. John, Burton. 2007. "Newspapers' struggles with civic engagement: the U.S. press and the rejection of public journalism as propagandistic." *The Communication Review* 10(3):249–270.
38  Fico, Frederick, Stephen Lacy, Steven S. Wildman, et al. 2013. "Citizen journalism sites as information substitutes and complements for United States newspaper coverage of local governments." *Digital Journalism* 1(1): 152–168.
39  Piggott, Stephen. 2016. "Is Breitbart.com Becoming the Media Arm of the 'Alt-Right'?" *Hatewatch*. April 28. Available at: www.splcenter.org/hate watch/2016/04/28/breitbartcom-becoming-media-arm-alt-right.
40  Spiering, Charlie. 2017. "Donald Trump Says He Did Not 'Specifically' Authorize Niger Mission." *Breitbart*. Oct. 25. Available at: www.breitbart.com/big-gov ernment/2017/10/25/donald-trump-says-he-did-not-specifically-authorize-niger-mission/; Wong, Kristina. 2017. "Green Berets in Niger Were Part of Mission Obama Authorized." *Breitbart* Nov. 3. Available at: www.breitbart. com/big-government/2017/11/03/green-berets-niger-part-mission-obama-authorized/.; Delingpole, James. 2017. "Former Green Beret's Post Blasting Leftists for Politicizing Niger Goes Viral." *Breitbart*. Oct. 24. Available at: www. breitbart.com/tech/2017/10/24/ex-green-beret-says-what-special-forces-really-think-about-niger-goes-viral-on-twitter/.
41  All web traffic information from Alexa Available at: www.alexa.com/.

42  Allcott, Hunt and Matthew Gentzkow. 2017. "Social Media and Fake News in the 2016 Election." *Journal of Economic Perspectives* 31(2):211–236.
43  Guess, Andrew, Brenden Nyhan, and Jason Reifler. 2018. "Selective Exposure to Misinformation: Evidence from the consumption of fake news during the 2016 U.S. presidential campaign." *Working Paper* Available at: www.dartmouth.edu/~nyhan/fake-news-2016.pdf.
44  Palma, Bethania. 2017. "Was the 'Black Soldier' Killed in Niger a Deserter?" *Snopes*. Oct. 27. Available at: www.snopes.com/was-soldier-killed-deserter-satire/.
45  Subramanian, Samanth. 2017. "Inside the Macedonian Fake-News Complex." *Wired*. Feb. 15. Available at: www.wired.com/2017/02/veles-macedonia-fake-news/.
46  Karpf, David. 2017. "People are hyperventilating over a study of Russian propaganda on Facebook. Just breathe deeply." *Washington Post*. Oct. 12. Available at: www.washingtonpost.com/news/monkey-cage/wp/2017/10/12/people-are-hyperventilating-over-a-new-study-of-russian-propaganda-on-facebook-just-breathe-deeply/.
47  Syjuco, Miguel. 2017. "Fake News Floods the Philippines." *New York Times*. Oct. 24. Available at: www.nytimes.com/2017/10/24/opinion/fake-news-philippines.html.
48  Bradshaw, Samantha and Philip N. Howard. 2017. "Troops, Trolls and Troublemakers: A Global Inventory of Organized Social Media Manipulation." *Computational Propaganda Research Project, University of Oxford*. Available at: http://comprop.oii.ox.ac.uk/wp-content/uploads/sites/89/2017/07/Troops-Trolls-and-Troublemakers.pdf.

## Chapter 8

# Doing Gender and Sexuality in Media

For any given movie, ask yourself this question: are there two or more female characters with names who ever speak to each other about something other than a man? This question is known as the "Bechdel Test," named after graphic artist, Alison Bechdel, and it originated from her 1985 comic strip, *Dykes to Watch Out For*. The answer to this question for most popular Hollywood movies is "no." While 13% of the most widely distributed movies of the 2000s failed to have two women, 28% of the movies never showed these women talking to each other, and, in another 15%, they only talked about men. The view from Hollywood is a world based around men.

The underrepresentation of women in media is only half of the story. A movie like *Twilight* (2008), an adaptation of a book series about a damsel-in-distress who needs to be rescued by her vampire boyfriend, actually *passes* the Bechdel Test. Mere representation is far from a guarantee that women will be presented in an equitable or positive light. Likewise, even as representations of members of the LGBTQ community in movies and television have increased in recent years, many still remain mired in stereotype.

Unlike the top-down media of TV and movies, the bottom-up nature of the web has created new opportunities for alternative representations of women and men as well as members of the LGBTQ community. At the same time, a torrent of sexist, often threatening trolling deluges comment sections and Twitter feeds of prominent women online every day. With a $10 billion domestic pornography industry, which produces material watched by two-thirds of American men on at least a monthly basis, the web is also a place where gender stereotypes and simulated violence against women are reproduced.

In this chapter, we examine gender and sexual identity inequalities in media representations and consider the various mechanisms that produce such representations. We also explore some of the possibilities and problems of gender and sexual identity representations in the digital world.

## Representing Women

How often are women represented? How well are women represented? And how visible are those representations? Sociologist Maryann Erigha argues that in order to make sense of how women are represented in media we must consider three types of representation. First, *numerical representation* is the extent to which a social group is included or excluded both as part of media content and as media creators. We could ask what proportion of Hollywood movies have female leads? (About 25% in 2013).[1] Or what percentage of *New York Times* articles had women as first authors? (About 34% in 2013–2014).[2] But mere numerical representation doesn't tell us anything about the *quality of representation* or the types of roles that social groups have both in media content and as media workers. Do women get to play complex characters in movies or are they relegated to being sex objects for men? Do female reporters get to do serious investigative journalism or are they stuck covering families, fashion, and food?

Finally, women may be represented well, but it doesn't make much of a difference if nobody sees it. Erigha says we also need to pay attention to *centrality of representation*. Do women get to direct big franchise movies like *Star Wars* or do they tend to direct documentaries that get shown in 25 movie theaters? Do female politicians get invited to appear on a national show like *Meet the Press* or are they lucky if they get a write-up in their local newspaper? Each of these forms of representation matters and we will take on each one in turn.

### Numerical Representation

The short answer here is that, across a range of media, both in content and as creators, women are deeply underrepresented. As Figure 8.1 reveals, whether in news or entertainment, on the big screen, the small screen, or in print, women rarely constitute more than 30% of the talent or sources in media content. In primetime medical dramas like *Grey's Anatomy*, men dominate every role: 57% of the patients, 62% of the bystanders, and 60% of the caregivers.[3] In news, one study by Eran Shor and his colleagues tracked the number of mentions of male and female names in 13 top U.S. newspapers from 1983 to 2009. They found that female names increased from 19% in 1983 to 27% in 2009. However, even in the news sections where female names were most frequently mentioned, they only constituted 37% in 2008. In the sports section, females were less than 10% of all names![4]

At least part of the reason for the underrepresentation of female talent on-screen may be because of the lack of female media workers behind the scenes. While women now represent about 40% of TV news employees and newspaper reporters, less than a third of the leadership positions in both TV and print news are held by women. In fact, in an extensive study of newspaper,

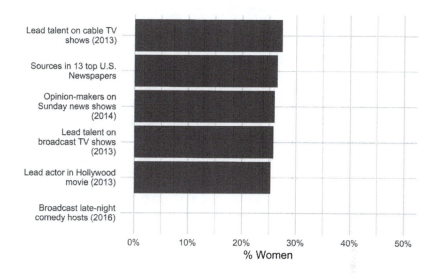

Figure 8.1 Numerical Representations of Women in Media Content
[Source: State of Women, 2015; Shor et al., 2015; Hunt et al., 2014]

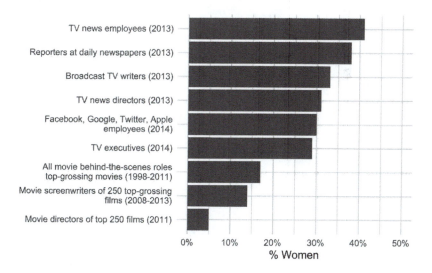

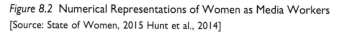

Figure 8.2 Numerical Representations of Women as Media Workers
[Source: State of Women, 2015 Hunt et al., 2014]

wire service, and online news sources, there was only one media outlet with greater than 50% female writers (the Huffington Post, which had 53%). Women are severely underrepresented as writers and directors in the film industry and represent less than a third of the creators of entertainment TV.

Women are 51% of the population, but by most metrics represent only about a quarter to a third of the people represented in media and those creating it. One could argue that the underrepresentation of women might be due to females being less interested in media careers. However, women represent two-thirds of the journalism school graduates. Based on Internal Revenue Service data, there are roughly equivalent numbers of men and women pursuing media occupations. The lack of representation is not a lack of aspiration, but a dearth of opportunities.

TV and movie studio executives presented with the underrepresentation of women in media often point to market demand for male-centric entertainment. To take the example of movies, anecdotal evidence suggests that media executives believe that female-driven films don't earn as much profit. In 2007, industry blog *Deadline Hollywood* reported that Warner Brothers' president of production Jeff Robinov had bluntly informed his staff, "We are no longer doing movies with women in the lead." While Warner Brothers issued a denial of the statement, several columnists noted that the comment reflected a common sentiment among studio executives.

Is it true? Do movies featuring women earn less? Based on a study of a thousand movies released from 2000–2009, the answer is yes. Movies that pass the Bechdel Test earn $11 million less at the box office on average than those that don't pass. However, contrary to the studio executives' beliefs, it's not because audiences are disinterested. Rather, one of the best predictors of box office performance is the size of the production budget. Bechdel movies tend to have much smaller production budgets. But comparing movies with similar production budgets, movies featuring women do not do any worse at the box office than other films. In other words, we can't blame the underrepresentation of women in films on market demand. The inequalities that produce the underrepresentation of women seem to exist in the creation process.[5]

### Quality of Representation

Even when women are represented, the depictions are often stereotypical. In 1992, offering a review of research to date, critical media scholar Fred Fejes found that men were more likely to be portrayed as dominant over women and to "occupy high-status positions, initiate action and act from the basis of rational mind as opposed to emotions, are found more in the world of things as opposed to family and relationships, and organize their lives around problem solving."[6] Since that time, a few studies have noted tepid progress with the introduction of more feminist characters and themes in television beginning in the 1980s and the creation of more "tough girl roles."[7] *New Yorker* TV critic Emily Nussbaum argues that some ambiguous depictions may be a form of progress. "[T]he vast majority of iconic 'single girl' characters on television, from *That Girl* to Mary Tyler Moore and Molly Dodd, had been you-go-girl types—which is to say, actual role models," she writes. By contrast, more recent women on TV—Carrie Bradshaw on *Sex and the City*, Nancy Botwin on *Weeds*, Carrie Mathison on *Homeland*, Olivia Pope on *Scandal*—represent complicated, at times morally dubious, female anti-heroes. Far from offering a simple social mobility story like in *The Mary Tyler Moore Show*, these female characters offer nuanced representations of women and show that being a woman can involve contradictions. Despite some more complex portrayals, much of current television programming traffics in antiquated gender stereotypes.[8] Popular reality television shows of the past decade like *Wife Swap*, *Trading Spouses*, and *Supernanny* depict women in domestic roles, doing the cooking, cleaning, and caregiving.[9]

Beyond television, researchers have documented the sexualization and subordination of women across a variety of media. In the realm of video games, communications researchers Edward Downs and Stacy Smith found in 2010 that 98% of the 489 female gaming characters they studied engaged in either sexual talk or behavior. Unsurprisingly, many of these characters had bodies with unrealistic proportions.[10] Women also play subordinate roles in the storylines of video games. A prominent YouTube video series by cultural critic Anita Sarkeesian titled *Tropes vs. Women in Video Games*[11] has noted the trope common in video games of the "damsel-in-distress" or a helpless woman saved by a male hero. A variant on this trope features women abused, sexually assaulted, or killed within the game's storyline in order to motivate a male hero into action.

In part because of such critiques, things have been changing within video game culture, though not without controversy and some disturbing hostility. The most prominent example of this is the set of events that have come to be known as Gamergate. The ostensible beginning of Gamergate came in 2013 when game developer Zoë Quinn released *Depression Quest*, an interactive browser game that centered on the experience of a person dealing with depression. The game received mostly positive reviews. However, some in the online gaming community saw the positive reviews as reflecting an unwanted imposition of feminist values and unmerited praise for female developers. While some made these arguments in relatively civil (if misguided) essays, there was also a violent backlash that targeted Quinn, Sarkeesian, and other women with ties to the gaming community. This took the form of threatening phone calls, rape threats on Twitter, and what one report called "an ambient hum of menace." The *New Yorker* reported one threat directed at Quinn as saying, "Next time she shows up at a conference we … give her a crippling injury that's never going to fully heal."[12] And for what? Making a good game that raises awareness about depression while being a woman.

Low quality representations of women extend into news coverage as well, whether in politics or something as mundane as sports. Apart from media, both politics and sports are male-dominated fields. But news coverage of them doubles down on gender inequality. Empirical studies have shown that both cable news pundits and even reputable newspapers are far more likely to mention women politicians' appearance, age, and children as compared to men. Former Secretary of State Hillary Clinton, for example, was subjected to scrutiny of her hairstyles and clothing that neither her 2008 or 2016 primary challengers experienced (President Obama and Senator Bernie Sanders respectively). Clinton had to walk a careful line, emphasizing that she is a caring friend and mother to seem likable, without letting these domestic roles undermine her seriousness as a politician.[13]

In sports coverage, basketball commentators are more likely to praise female athletes for their good teamplay and "heart," while emphasizing men's "pure athleticism."[14] In the Olympics, female athletes are often compared to male athletes, while the reverse almost never happens.[15] In other words, sports announcers will say "she's the female Lebron James," but not the "he's the male Serena Williams." Even more notable is the sheer difference in numerical representation. In 2014, only 2% of ESPN coverage was devoted to women's sports, down from 1999 levels.[16]

It would be a mistake to regard all women as receiving equally low quality of representation. Upper-middle class, heterosexual, white women can find a number of complex, counter-stereotypic representations of women like them across the media landscape. But we must be alert to *intersectionality* or the way that statuses like gender, race, social class, sexual orientation, etc. are interconnected in media representations. For working class women, women of color, and LBTQ women, there are numerically fewer representations and those that exist are often token or highly stereotypical.

### Centrality of Representation

There are so many media platforms today that surely there must be some high quality representation of most types of women somewhere. It matters though whether that representation is a YouTube video or on prime-time broadcast TV. Erigha's *centrality of representation* directs our attention to whether representations of women—and various kinds of women—are at the center or the margins of the various media sectors.

In Hollywood, the most renowned actors and directors tend to make big budget blockbusters that earn substantial box office revenue and make big budget dramas to win Oscars. J.J. Abrams' *Star Trek* and *Star Wars* movies were large investment, large return projects at the very heart of the industry. Alejandro González Iñárritu, director of

*Birdman* and *The Revenant*, is widely respected for his auteur filmmaking. He is able to work with the most in-demand actors and garner sizable production budgets for his projects. To see men in these central positions is not strange. Meanwhile, Kathryn Bigelow, director of *The Hurt Locker* and *Zero Dark Thirty*, is the rare female director to work in gritty genres and earn industry recognition. Female directors are underrepresented in box office busting genres like action, sci-fi, and animation and are far more likely to direct in less central genres like romance and documentaries.[17]

In the music industry, we can easily think of women in very central positions. Taylor Swift, Beyoncé, Lady Gaga, among others. But behind the scenes, women represent only 30% of leadership roles in the music industry.[18] Take Beyoncé, for example, a self-described feminist and a symbol of powerful womanhood. While she is an executive producer on her solo albums, her co-executive producers have also been men and more than three-quarters of her other producers are men. Nearly all of her songs are co-written by professional songwriters who are also mostly men. Of the 22 songwriters who have contributed to Beyoncé's seven biggest hit songs, 20 of them are male.[19] While Beyoncé is an accomplished performer, creative artist, and among the most central figures in music today, we would be wrong not to observe the influence that men wield even when working with the most powerful female performers.

In news, the story is somewhat better. The news anchor, the most central position on TV news, was traditionally a male-dominated role. However, in 2014, with a female co-anchor team on PBS *NewsHour*, Diane Sawyer on ABC *World News*, women anchored 40% of news broadcasts, a new high. Women are also better represented in central roles at top national newspapers than at newspapers in general. For the past decade, at least half of the news masthead at the *New York Times* are women.[20] Still, even at top newspapers, where women are almost equally numerically represented, they are more likely to write in less central sections like lifestyles, fashion, or arts rather than news.

To summarize, compared to men, women are represented less, represented less well, and represented less centrally, though the degree of gender inequality differs by representation type, by medium, and by industry. The three types of representation are linked. It is unlikely that we would see a huge increase in numerical representation of women without some corresponding improvement in quality and centrality. But we must be attentive to all three in order to understand more fully gender inequality in media.

## The Good, the Bad, and the Ugly of Digital Cultures

For media researchers, the emergence of digital cultures have made it far more difficult to answer the question, "how are women represented in media?" When there were three broadcast TV channels and relatively widespread newspaper readership, it was fairly easy to conduct a content analysis that reported on representation in primetime TV or the front page of the country's top newspapers.

New media, with its sprawling diversity and multimedia formats, is a much greater challenge to document. New media includes digital news sites, social media, videos, a wide range of apps, as well as software. There's simply no way to arrive at any sort of universal measure of representation for new media or even, more narrowly, the web.

On top of that, "representation" sometimes feels like the wrong word. Many of the activities we do online blur the distinction between personal communications (like a phone call or a letter) and mass media (like TV and radio) as well as the line between creators and receivers. Homer Simpson is quite clearly a representation of men. But are we representing men every time we tweet? The answer is yes. Our tweets ensure that men are numerically well represented; in a teeny-tiny way the content of our tweets contribute to the overall quality of representation of men, and how often they are retweeted speaks to the centrality of representation.

Even with some of the difficulties of examining gender representations online, we do know that the web has created new possibilities for more representations of women and of a higher quality, while also producing some patterns of gender representation far worse than what was possible with earlier media.

What's the good news? There is no question that the medium of the web has helped feminist communities flourish, created opportunities for female writers and filmmakers, and supported activism around issues of gender inequality. Web sites like Feministing (feministing.org), Feministe (feminist.us), and Our Bodies Our Blog (ourbodiesourblog.org) represent different brands of feminism and serve different groups of women and male allies, but all of them are explicitly oriented toward covering women and issues of gender inequality in ways that traditional media outlets do not. Such web sites offer not only news, but also discussion boards and comment sections where real communities of support and activism can form. More recently, people have left "old-fashioned" discussion boards for Twitter, Facebook, Tumblr, and the rest.

The promise of web for women extends beyond the U.S. In traditional Muslim cultures, women and men are separated in most social settings, making cross-gender discussion of politics very limited. However, in Tunisia and Egypt during the 2011 Arab Spring uprisings, Arab feminist activists played an important role on social media, mobilizing people to attend demonstrations and offering citizen reporting on ongoing events. Without the hierarchies and social divisions that exist offline, social media empowered women to enter "men's spheres of influence."[21]

Despite these promising developments, the web also has a dark side. Like the women at the center of Gamergate, many women online are victims of what feminist media scholar Karla Mantilla calls *gendertrolling*, a particular type of the aggressive online behavior known as "trolling." Conventional trolling is provocative, inflammatory, or otherwise disruptive and carried out for one's own amusement. Mantilla argues that gendertrolling is different because it does have a purpose. Gendertrolls are usually privileged individuals (i.e., men) who deliberately aim to silence women's voices and discussion of issues of gender inequality with demeaning comments and/or implicit or explicit threats of violence.[22]

The web is not an inherently civil space. Almost any semi-public figure, including writers, is going to experience some degree of trolling. But women receive more negative comments and of a violent nature. In 2016, the British newspaper *The Guardian* conducted an analysis of the 70 million comments that readers had posted to articles on their site to date. *The Guardian* has a policy to block comments that engage in "author abuse," which they define as "demeaning and insulting speech targeted at the writer of the article or another comment." At the time of writing, the site had blocked 1.2 million (2%) of comments due to writer abuse. Articles by female writers receive approximately 33% more comments that moderators ban than articles by male writers. Some of the comments are playground insults like "you suck" or "you're stupid." More extreme comments include threats of murder and rape. For women who write professionally, each abusive comment is what Zoë Quinn described as "a snowflake in an avalanche."[23]

It's not just celebrities and writers who are the victims of gendertrolling. Among young women (18–24), 70% had been victims of at least one of six forms of online harassment tracked by Pew Research Center. While experiencing some of these forms of harassment, like being called an offensive name, were as common among men, young women were particularly likely to be victimized by the more serious forms of harassment. The study showed 26% have been stalked online and 25% experienced sexual harassment. Whether in online gaming, dating apps, social media, or comments sections of web sites, becoming the victim of gendertrolling is a common part of the experience of being a woman online.[24]

At times, the brutal treatment of women on the web makes the stereotypical representations of moms on TV sitcoms look quaint. But the web is bigger, more diverse, and less regulated than TV. These qualities have contributed to the creation of feminist communities online with the power to challenge ideas in the political area, but also a dominant online culture where women can be demeaned and threatened with little consequence.

## LGBTQ Identities in Media

On the whole, representations of women have made slow, uneven progress over time in terms of quality, centrality, and by sheer numbers. By contrast, while there is still much room for growth, there is no question that LGBTQ representations have improved dramatically since the 1990s both numerically and qualitatively. In one sense, changing representations of LGBTQ people are a natural outgrowth of rapid transformation in the public's attitudes about sexual orientation. At the same time, advocates and opponents alike believe that mass media played a key role in changing popular views about gays and lesbians and, more recently, transgender people.

Analyzing representations of sexual identity can be a bit more complicated than gender for a few reasons. First, while women represent 51% of the population, estimates of the number of LGBTQ people in the U.S. vary. The best estimates put the population of Americans who self-identify as lesbian, gay, bisexual, or transgender at 3–4% of the public.[25] Given these very small numbers, shows like *Modern Family*, *Scandal*, and *Glee* end up numerically *over*-representing gays and lesbians despite having only one or two LGBTQ characters. It is, perhaps, for this reason that Americans on average estimate that gays and lesbians make up 23% of the population![26]

Another reason representations of sexual identity are difficult to track is that those identities are not always visible. When you turn on the TV news, it's usually possible to tell the news anchor's gender and race, but unless the anchor explicitly mentions it, her or his sexual orientation isn't clear. Moreover, because of continuing homophobia and discrimination, many LGBTQ media workers stay in the closet in professional contexts, complicating efforts to collect data on representations.

What we do know is that for much of the history of popular radio, TV, and film, the only gay characters were effeminate, incompetent men used as a punchline. Many media scholars point to Ellen DeGeneres coming out on *Ellen* in 1997 and *Will & Grace* in 1998 as watershed moments in LGBTQ representation. However, the first progressive representations of gays and lesbians began in the early 1970s when shows like *All in the Family* and *M\*A\*S\*H* devoted episodes to discrimination against gays. But just as often from the 1970s through the 1990s, gay characters were portrayed as child molesters and psychopathic killers.[27]

What marked *Ellen* and *Will & Grace* as different is rather than having gay guest characters for a "very special episode" on homophobia, these were the first two primetime broadcast shows with LGBTQ lead characters at a time when 27% of the public favored same-sex marriage. The popularity of *Will & Grace* in particular paved the way for more LGBTQ characters in the next decade, including groundbreaking shows like *Queer as Folk* and *The L Word*.

Religious leaders who opposed acceptance of same-sex marriage often decried Hollywood and the "liberal media" for what they saw as promoting "the gay lifestyle." And, to the extent that the TV and film industries as well as the elite news media offered normalizing, sympathetic representations of LGBTQ people before a majority of Americans supported same-sex marriage, they were right. As former *New York Times* Public Editor Daniel

Okrent wrote in 2004, "*The [New York] Times* present the social and cultural aspects of same-sex marriage in a tone that approaches cheerleading."[28]

In these ways, LGBTQ representations are unquestionably better than a mere two decades ago. However, LGBTQ characters are still numerically underrepresented in media as a whole and these portrayals are often of a lower quality and centrality. According to a study by GLAAD, only 17.5% of major studio release films in 2014 had at least one character who identified as LGBT. Moreover, most of those characters were minor ones like "the gay best friend," with 73% of portrayals having less than 10 minutes of screen time.[29] Considering intersectionalities, it's also important to note that, according to GLAAD, across both TV and film more than three-quarters of all LGBTQ representations are white males. As Fred Fejes wrote, entertainment media's vision of homosexuality is a "young, white ... preferably with a well-muscled, smooth body, handsome face, good education, professional job, and a high income."[30] While white, affluent, male gay identities are now regularly represented in mass media, there are too few black, low income, and female LGBTQ experiences represented numerically for us to even consider their quality or centrality.

In conclusion, it's probably not surprising that those who are more privileged in society are also privileged in media representations. What should be troubling is the magnitude. Forty years after women entered the work force in mass numbers, women are still underrepresented numerically and in the most central positions as media creators, and the world represented on screens big and small is still one that revolves around men. Meanwhile, the great promise of the Internet to promote equality and inclusivity has yielded mixed results for women. Prominent examples of LGBTQ representations may have advanced the cause of gay rights, but those examples remain exceptional and, to a large extent, represent only affluent white male experiences. As we will see in the next chapter, the privileging of whites and the affluent is true not only in LGBTQ representations, but is a current that runs throughout mass media.

## Notes

1  Women's Media Center. 2015. "The State of Women in the U.S." *Media*. Available at: https://www.womensmediacenter.com/reports/2015-statistics.
2  Cohen, Philip. 2014. "Gender at the NY Times: The Most Comprehensive Analysis Ever." *The Society Pages*. Available at: https://thesociety pages.org/socimages/2014/05/27/gender-at-the-new-york-times-the-most-comprehensive-analysis-ever/.
3  Hether, Heather and Sheila Murphy. 2010. "Sex Roles in Health Storylines on Prime Time Television: A Content Analysis." *Sex Roles*. 62:810–821.
4  Shor, Eran, Arnout van de Rijt, Alex Miltsov, Vivek Kulkarni, and Steven Skiena. 2015. "A Paper Ceiling Explaining the Persistent Underrepresentation of Women in Printed News." *American Sociological Review* 80(5):960–984.

5  Lindner, Andrew M., Melissa Lindquist, and Julie Arnold. "Million Dollar Maybe? The Effect of Female Presence in Movies on Box Office Returns." *Sociological Inquiry* 85(3): 407–428; Lauzen, Martha M. 2008. *Women @ the Box Office: A Study of the Top 100 Worldwide Grossing Films*. San Diego, CA: Center for the Study of Women in Television and Film.

6  Fejes, Fred. 1992. "Masculinity as Fact: A Review of Empirical Mass Communication Research on Masculinity." In Steve Craig, ed., *Men, Masculinity, and the Media*, pp. 9–22. Newbury Park, CA: Sage.

7  Mendes, Kaitlynn and Cynthia Carter. 2008. "Feminist and Gender Media Studies: A Critical Overview." *Sociology Compass* 6:1701–1718; Osgerby, Bill and Anna Gough-Yates. 2001. *Action TV: Tough Guys, Smooth Operator and Foxy Chicks*. New York: Routledge.

8  Nussbaum, Emily. 2013. "Difficult Women." *The New Yorker*. July 29. Available at: http://www.newyorker.com/magazine/2013/07/29/difficult-women.

9  Brancato, Jim. 2007. "Domesticating Politics: The Representation of Wives and Mothers in American Reality Television." *Film & History: An Interdisciplinary Journal of Film and Television Studies* 37:49–56.

10  Downs, Edward and Stacy Smith. 2010. "Keeping Abreast of Hypersexuality: A video game character content analysis." *Sex Roles* 62:721–733.

11  Sarkeesian, Anita. 2015. *Tropes vs. Women in Video Games*. Available at: https://feministfrequency.com/tag/tropes-vs-women-in-video-games/.

12  Parkin, Simon. "Zoe Quinn's Depression Quest." *The New Yorker*. September 9. Available at: www.newyorker.com/tech/elements/zoe-quinns-depression-quest.

13  Lawrence, Regina G. and Melody Rose. 2010. *Hillary Clinton's Race for the White House: Gender Politics and the Media on the Campaign Trail*. Boulder, CO: Lynne Rienner Publishers.

14  Denham, Bryan E., Andrew C. Billings, and Kelby K. Halone. 2002. "Differential accounts of race in broadcast commentary of the 2000 NCAA men's and women's final four basketball tournaments." *Sociology of Sport Journal* 19(3):315–332.

15  Jones, Ray, Audrey J. Murrell, and Jennifer Jackson. 1999. "Pretty versus powerful in the sports pages print media coverage of US women's Olympic gold medal winning teams." *Journal of Sport & Social Issues* 23(2):183–192.

16  Cooky, Cheryl, Michael A. Messner, and Michela Musto. 2015. "'It's Dude Time!' A Quarter Century of Excluding Women's Sports in Televised News and Highlight Shows." *Communication & Sport* 2,167,479,515,588,761.

17  Erigha, Maryann. 2014. Unequal Hollywood: African Americans, Women, and Representation in a Media Industry. PhD dissertation, University of Pennsylvania.

18  Lindvall, Helienne. 2010. "Behind the music: the gender gap shows no sign of closing." *The Guardian Online*. May 7. Available at: http://www.theguardian.com/music/musicblog/2010/may/07/behind-the-music-gender-gap.

19  Eggert, Jessica. 2016. "Here Are the Writers Who Helped Make Beyoncé the Ultimate Fame Queen." *Music.Mic*. February 15. Available at: http://mic.com/articles/135091/here-are-the-writers-who-helped-make-beyonc-the-ultimate-fame-queen.

20  Women's Media Center, 2015.

21  Newsom, Victoria A. and Lara Lengel. 2012. "Arab Women, Social Media, and the Arab Spring: Applying the framework of digital reflexivity to analyze gender and online activism." *Journal of International Women's Studies*, 13(5):31.

22  Mantilla, Karla. 2013. "Gendertrolling: Misogyny adapts to new media." *Feminist Studies* 39(2):563–570.

23 Gardiner, Becky, Mahana Mansfield, Ian Anderson, Josh Holder, Daan Louter and Monica Ulmanu. 2016. "The dark side of Guardian comments." *The Guardian.* April 12. Available at: http://www.theguardian.com/technol ogy/2016/apr/12/the-dark-side-of-guardian-comments.
24 Duggan, Megan. 2014. "Online Harassment." *Pew Research Center.* October 22. Available at: www.pewinternet.org/2014/10/22/online-harassment/.
25 Brody, Ben. 2015. "Americans Vastly Overestimate Size of Gay and Lesbian Population." *Bloomberg Politics.* May 22. Available at: http://www.bloomberg. com/politics/articles/2015-05-22/americans-vastly-overestimate-size-of-lgbt-population; Volokh, Eugene. 2014. "What percentage of the U.S. population is gay, lesbian or bisexual?" *The Washington Post: The Volokh Conspiracy.* July 15. Available at: www.washingtonpost.com/news/volokh-conspiracy/wp/2014/07/ 15/what-percentage-of-the-u-s-population-is-gay-lesbian-or-bisexual/.
26 Newport, Frank. 2015. "Americans Greatly Overestimate Percent Gay, Lesbian in U.S." *Gallup Social Issues.* May 21. Available at: http://www.gallup. com/poll/183383/americans-greatly-overestimate-percent-gay-lesbian.aspx.
27 Hart, Kylo-Patrick R. 2000. "Representing gay men on American television." *The Journal of Men's Studies* 9(1):59–79.
28 Okrent, Daniel. 2004. "Is The New York Times a Liberal Newspaper?" *The New York Times.* July 25. Available at: http://www.nytimes.com/2004/07/25/ opinion/the-public-editor-is-the-new-york-times-a-liberal-newspaper.html.
29 GLAAD. 2016. *The Studio Responsibility Index 2016.* Available at: http:// www.glaad.org/files/2016_SRI.pdf.
30 Fejes, Fred. 2000. "Making a Gay Masculinity." *Critical Studies in Mass Communication* 17(1):113–17.

# Chapter 9

# Unequal Images in an Unequal Age

In a so-called "post-racial" era, race sure does matter an awful lot. We live in a time defined by what sociologist Eduardo Bonilla-Silva described as "color-blind racism." In his influential book *Racism Without Racists*, Bonilla-Silva describes a world—indeed, our world—where statements like "I don't see color" and "I'm not racist, but ..." are too often followed by discriminatory remarks. Couched in an ideology of color-blindness, Bonilla-Silva argues, these statements are able to denigrate entire racial groups without ever mentioning race.[1] They do this through racial codes that "prime racial stereotypes, fears, and resentments while appearing not to do so."[2] The fuzziness of racial codes allow them to invoke racialized sentiments while appearing to be non-racial.

Perhaps the most famous racially-coded image in American media is the mug shot of convicted criminal Willie Horton. During the 1988 presidential campaign, a conservative political action committee opted to use Horton's mug shot to stoke fear amongst the public and tip the scales of the election. They succeeded. Since then, racialized imagery has become a common strategy that is used, however intentional, to stoke fear and galvanize public opinion, whether on social media or the nightly newscast.

But imagery is only a piece of the puzzle. Whether or not a picture is actually "worth a thousand words," it is true that for every racially-charged picture, there are many more racially-coded words printed in newspapers, and even more published on the web. Today, the word "thug" is commonly used to demean people of color without actually making an explicitly racial reference.[3] Similar rhetorical strategies were used by those insisting President Barack Obama was "un-American."[4]

Where do these codes come from? Given the constant interplay between media, culture, and society, it is difficult to decipher where the problem originates. But, to what extent are media complicit in creating these unequal images? And to what extent are they simply reflecting back to society the images they see in the world? The answer, according to most media scholars, is that news and entertainment media are only partially responsible for the perpetuation of inequality.

This chapter digs into the ways media (mis)represent issues of race, ethnicity, and class, and the role such representations play in the perpetuation of inequality. In addition to considering recent and classic examples from American popular culture, the chapter draws on a wide body of scholarship from both entertainment and news media.

## Not All Images Are Created Equal

Whether we're talking about news or entertainment media, there is plenty of evidence to conclude that representations are far from equal. In addition to the unequal representations of gender and sexuality discussed in the previous chapter, race and class are two other clear sites of inequality created and perpetuated in media messages. Studies of popular media have shown that stereotypes work in both directions, although not equally, as White and upper class characters are portrayed in mostly flattering or normalizing ways while non-White and working class or working poor characters are typically depicted in a less flattering manner.

Like the previous chapter's discussion of numerical representation and quality representation, we use the concept of *representation* in this chapter to describe two key aspects of inequality in the media. First, it pertains to the issue of inclusion itself, and asks to what extent actors from particular backgrounds are cast in a production, and to what degree they advance to positions of power where casting decisions are made (i.e., directors and producers). It may come as no surprise that American media, like other sectors of American society, still struggles with inclusion. As sociologist Maryann Erigha found through an analysis of over 1,600 American films released between 2000 and 2011, "Black directors comprised of 7% of directors compared with 88% White directors"—a disproportionate representation given that African Americans make up 12.6% of the non-Hispanic U.S. population while White Americans make up 63.7%.[5] This disparity grows even greater when considering the most popular and profitable films and film genres, such as science fiction and action adventure. As Erigha and other scholars argue, disparities in inclusion contributes to a racial hierarchy, whereby non-White directors are less likely to have access to opportunities with the greatest cultural and economic influence.

Second, while the matter of inclusion may be an indicator of diversity in and of itself, it is perhaps best seen as a means to a larger end. That is, inclusion in the production of media content allows people of color and from working class backgrounds greater opportunities in the media industry. In the UK, research has shown that the acting profession is increasingly dominated by people from privileged classes. For example, 88% of the British actors included in the Great British Class Survey were White

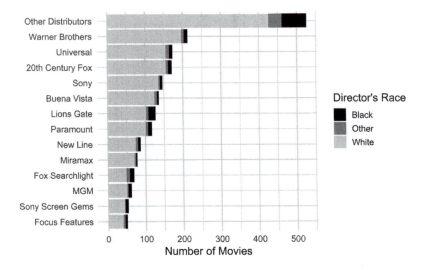

*Figure 9.1* Director's Race for Films by Top Hollywood Film Distributors
[Source: Erigha, 2017]

and 73% had parents with professional or managerial occupations. Not only are actors from working class backgrounds less likely to "make it" in the profession, but their relative lack of resources, both economic and cultural capital, puts them at a disadvantage during casting.[6]

Having in-group representation in media management positions increases the chances that minorities and people of color will be represented more equally on screen. For example, one study of the 100 top-grossing films of 2013 found that films with Black directors were 35% more likely to cast Black actors in speaking roles than those with directors of other races.[7] Thus, being represented in the process of media production is perhaps a necessary but insufficient condition for equal representation in media products. In the world of news, this concern is particularly consequential, as there is a growing body of evidence demonstrating that the lack of diversity among media makers results in a lack of equity in media stories and frames.[8]

On the other hand, when the conversation turns to inequality in entertainment media, many people may be inclined to respond with a sense of shock or disinterest. I mean, what's the big deal? It's just a TV show, right? Despite the temptations to excuse creators for their artistic choices, there is reason to believe that fictional representations can indeed have a significant (and perhaps amplified) impact on people's perception of real social issues.[9] As sociologist Diana Kendall explains, "we use information we gain from the media to construct a picture of class and inequality that we come to accept as reality."[10] The process works much the same for race, ethnicity, and other markers of difference.

## (South) Asian Invasion?

In Aziz Ansari and Alan Yang's Emmy Award winning comedy series *Master of None*, there is an episode dedicated to the topic of "Indians on TV." In the episode, Ansari's character, Dev, is perpetually frustrated by the limitations he faces as an up-and-coming Indian-American actor. After bombing a casting for refusing to do an Indian accent, Dev meets up with his friend and fellow Indian-American actor, Ravi (played by Ravi Patel), to vent about the experience. Not only are they generally limited to the few stereotypical roles cast for South Asian men, but they are often forced to compete with White actors wearing "brown-face makeup." Later in the episode Dev and Ravi both audition for a new sitcom, *Three Buddies*, but the plot thickens when they learn that one producer's rationale also limits the number of roles allowed for Indians and other minorities in any one production.

As Ravi described the decision, "There can't be two Indians on TV."

This strategy is commonly referred to as *typecasting*, where "studios stereotype creative talent in a few narrow roles, limiting them to small segments of work," often based on obvious identity characteristics such as race, ethnicity, and class.[11] Typecasting works hand in hand with the media strategy of narrowcasting. Whereas the age of broadcasting was defined by the creation of content designed to reach a diverse "mass"

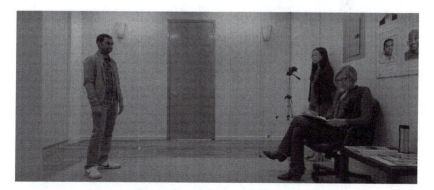

*Figure 9.2* Dev (Aziz Ansari) Auditioning for the Role of a Cab Driver in *Master of None*

[Source: Ansari, Aziz and Alan Yang. 2015. Master of None, 1(4). Netflix]

audience, *narrowcasting* includes targeting a niche audience with tailor-made content. According to the logic of narrowcasting, these niche audiences are attracted to programming that features people who look, act, and talk like them. However, this strategy is not applied equally to all target markets, since the bulk of Americans, and certainly the bulk of American culture, is defined by hegemonic Whiteness. This means that, unless otherwise specified, Whiteness is assumed to be the norm and thus taken for granted.

Sociologist Boomi Thakore argues that it is not necessarily explicit racism that explains the patterns of typecasting. Rather, she argues that they likely come from media producers' unconscious biases, shaped by their personal experiences:

> While [media producers] may have been less likely to run into South Asians who were scientists, professors, or even doctors, they were more likely to run into South Asians who were behind the counter of a local convenience store or driving their cab in an urban city.[12]

Given how little diversity there is in media production, it becomes clear why we see such unequal representations in media content, even as the American population grows more diverse.

### Marking and Stigmatizing Difference (from the White Upper-Middle Class)

In his path-breaking book, *Stigma*, sociologist Erving Goffman distinguished between personal identities that are discredited (marked with obvious, often physical, deformities) and those that are discreditable when socially undesirable character traits are made public.[13] Through a qualitative examination of case studies and autobiographies, Goffman uncovered how stigmatized people experience and manage a life lived outside perceived social norms. Of course, stigma is first and foremost a *social* phenomenon—the meanings attached to these traits are not inherent, but a product of unequal status systems created (and constantly recreated) through social interaction. Whether based on race, class, or other signifiers of difference, stigmas effectively place an undue burden on the "other"—a trend that applies as much to news and entertainment media as it does to "real life."

Goffman was also one of the first scholars, and indeed the first sociologist, to develop the concept of "frames."[14] To Goffman and others, frames are significant because of the work they do in coloring and contextualizing society's view of a person, event, or issue. While the topic of framing will be taken up in greater detail in Chapter 10, it is mentioned here because of the role frames play in representing and highlighting markers of difference.

This kind of treatment, where certain identity traits are emphasized in minorities and downplayed in others, is a perfect illustration of social marking and mental coloring. According to sociologist Wayne Brekhus, *marking* is a social process that calls attention to difference from a perceived norm (i.e. skin color), perceived as an embodied or symbolic "mark." By contrast, the "unmarked" lack such identifiers of difference, and are therefore (falsely) perceived as generic.[15] The process of social marking may help explain why certain identity characteristics are paid disproportionate attention in media representations. This includes the writing and casting of a disproportionately low number of so-called "ethnic" characters, thus leaving the bulk of roles to be played by (and for) a White majority.

But the process of social marking cannot account for the full story of unequal media representations. As Brekhus found through qualitative observation and interviews regarding the management of gay identity in suburbia, the process of stereotyping individuals based on one identity trait is best understood as *mental coloring*. According to Brekhus, "mental coloring involves figuratively painting an entire marked category so that it is represented only by the most colorful stereotypical images of the category."[16] For example, South Asian actors being repeatedly cast as immigrant cab drivers or convenience store clerks. As Ansari put it, "If you're a minority actor, your casting is oftentimes based on what you're [sic] ethnicity is perceived to do in a mostly-white world."[17]

### We're (Still) Not Post-Racial

Just as social marking is prominent in films and in everyday life, it is also prominent in the world of politics. For example, the 2008 presidential primaries were populated by a diverse array of candidates. In the running for the Democratic Party nomination were Hillary Clinton (a woman) and Barack Obama (a biracial man). The top candidates for the Republican Party were Mitt Romney (a Mormon), and John McCain (an elderly man). While each candidate's platform had many similarities and differences, it was their identities—indeed, their marked identity traits, often tied to physical (i.e. racial) or religious characteristics—which received significant attention in the spectacle of media coverage.[18]

Cable TV news stories asked whether Obama is "black enough" and wondered "is America ready for a black president?" Stories about Clinton were framed around questions like: "Is America ready for a female president?" "Is she qualified to be president?" "Will she represent the country adequately?" Pundits asked if McCain was "too old for office?" And so on. Thus, Obama was widely known as the Black candidate; Clinton, the female candidate; Romney, the Mormon candidate; and McCain, the old candidate.

Following the 2008 election, much of the American news media engaged in what sociologist Enid Logan calls "post-racial triumphalism." As she describes, "pundits hailed the age of Obama as the dawn of a new era in racial politics, and as evidence of the nation's definitive triumph over the problem of race."[19] Believe it or not, the question, "Are we post-racial?" was debated in media outlets across the country. The day after the election, CNN ran a segment about how Obama broke the mold of previous Black politicians by running a campaign that was not defined by race. After examining how poll numbers varied by race, one pundit exclaimed that although "race is important; it's not a barrier."[20] If the illusion of a post-racial America lasted through Obama's presidency, it was shattered following the election of Donald Trump, whom *The Atlantic* has called "the first White president" because he flagrantly embraces his (privileged) White identity through openly racialized language, which he uses to appeal to White voters.[21] Nevertheless, the veil of post-racialism was already thin to begin with, as evidenced by the resurgence of racial tensions following a number of high-profile police shootings in the final years of Obama's presidency.

Recent studies have shown that unarmed Black men are between 2.5 and 3.5 times more likely to be shot by police than unarmed White men.[22] According to the UK newspaper *The Guardian*, American police killed 1,146 people in 2015, making the U.S. number one in the world by a wide margin. By comparison, just 42 police were killed by gunfire in 2015, a decrease of 14% from the previous year and a near-record low.[23] Although the majority of those killed by police in 2015 were White (584 or 50.9%), a closer look at the *rates* of police shootings by race reveals a significant disparity. Indeed, while just 26.7% of those killed by police in 2015 were Black they only made up 12.6% of the U.S. population, whereas Whites made up 73.6%.[24] This means that in 2015, Blacks were just over three times more likely than Whites to die as a result of police actions.

News media began devoting more coverage to police shootings and their related protests following the death of Michael Brown in August 2014.[25] Nevertheless, coverage of police shootings was far from equal. In one study of the nation's top ten newspapers, researchers found that while Native Americans and indigenous people were killed at a similar rate as Blacks, newspapers published less than one article per fatality, while Blacks received an average of eight times more coverage.[26] This is not to downplay the unequal treatment of any group, nor to suggest that one group has it worse than another. It is not the "oppression Olympics," after all. Rather, such findings shed light on the way most news and entertainment media have come to treat indigenous people in recent years: with nearly complete erasure.

The disparity minorities face persists when *circumstances* are factored in: Black Americans killed by police are twice as likely to be unarmed compared to Whites.[27] But rather than assuming each incident can be explained by overtly racist officers, scholars have attributed much of this disparity to implicit or unconscious biases, derived from a lifetime of experiences in a highly racialized (media) society. This same implicit bias is also what is said to shape media makers' depiction of various races and racial issues.

Although scientific evidence of this disparity is growing, media coverage is quite mixed. In fact, studies of newspaper reporting yield mixed results. On the one hand, Tracy Everbach, Meredith Clark, and Gwendelyn Nisbett found that *The New York Times* (the newspaper with the second largest circulation in the U.S.) and the *St. Louis Post-Dispatch* (the most proximate major newspaper to the protests in Ferguson, Missouri) relied primarily on elite sources such as police and government officials.[28] While information from official sources is often newsworthy, relying solely or primarily on them means that other important perspectives, such as those from activists, researchers, and witnesses, will be largely ignored. By contrast, Mohamad Elmasry and Mohammed El-Nawawy found that coverage in the same publications was mostly sympathetic to protesters, in large part because they were quoted as sources more frequently than officials.[29] While this disparity may be explained in part by different sampling techniques, including relying on sources from social media compared to traditional interviews, the stark contrast is an indication of just how consequential methodological choices can be.

Despite the debate over newspaper coverage of the protests in Ferguson, Missouri, there is a much longer and well-documented history of racialized representations in the news media. It should come as no surprise, then, that members of the African American community in Ferguson are aware of (and troubled by) the trend. Indeed, the prominence of media portrayals that perpetuate the "thug" stereotype and disproportionately associate it with Black men, especially during the height of the #BlackLivesMatter movement, is what has contributed to the rise of the viral hashtag #IfTheyGunnedMeDown.[30]

*Figure 9.3*  #IfTheyGunnedMeDown Image by @CapriSun_Rell
[Source: https://twitter.com/CapriSun_Rell/status/498584169065091072]

As the tagline suggests, social media users on Twitter, Facebook, and Tumblr posted two contrasting photos—one, a supposedly realistic depiction of themselves, and another a thug-like representation, alongside the hashtag #IfTheyGunnedMeDown. The rhetorical question asked, unsurprisingly often by men of color, was which picture news media would use to commemorate them if they were "gunned down" by police. The message was clear, even if the answers were not: people of color had reason to be concerned about their treatment, not just by police, but also by media institutions.

## Poverty in the News: It's (Almost) Always Intersectional

As Max Rose and Frank Baumgartner found through their close reading and computer-assisted analysis of 560 poverty-related stories published in *The New York Times* between 1960 and 2008, there has been a steady shift toward more negative framing of poverty issues over time.[31] While the *Times'* framing was overwhelmingly generous towards those in poverty in the early 1960s, frames depicting welfare recipients as lazy or as cheating the system grew significantly thereafter. Given that four other major U.S. papers paid comparable attention to poverty over the same time period, Rose and Baumgartner maintain that these findings hold relevance beyond any one publication.

Of course, media coverage of poverty-related issues does not occur in isolation. Rather, as discussed in Chapter 8, media representations must be seen as more or less intersectional. For example, in *Why Americans Hate Welfare*, political scientist Martin Gilens demonstrates the pervasiveness of unequal media representations of the poor and poverty-related social programs broadly characterized as "welfare." At just the same time as Rose and Baumgartner identified an increase in negative representations of poverty in the mid-1960s, Gilens observed a "racialization of poverty" and welfare, where newsmagazine pictures of the poor quickly became overwhelmingly Black. In this instance, the media were not simply mirroring realities in society. In fact, this imagery far outpaces African Americans' representation amongst the poor in the U.S.: while African Americans made up roughly 30% of impoverished Americans, they made up over 70% of newsmagazine pictures in 1967. Furthermore, this imagery was most likely to be used alongside negative stories about "waste, inefficiency, or abuse of welfare," whereas depictions of Whites were more likely to be included in more neutral stories about poverty and social programs.[32] It is unequal representations like this that contributed to the racialization of welfare, and as a consequence, the growth of narratives about the "undeserving poor."

Nevertheless, it is important to remember that the concept of race is not only applicable to those seen as "other." Indeed, as discussed above, while the process of social marking goes a long way to obscure the significance of race for the so-called majority, it does not actually succeed in erasing their race. White/Caucasian is just as significant a racial category as Black/African American. And while largely unmarked, representations of Whiteness are also apparent in popular media. Seeing them, however, may require many to adopt a more critical, less hegemonic lens.

The example of the racialization of poverty provides a clear illustration of the intersectionality of identity, and by consequence, inequalities in media representation. Another example that demonstrates this is the way race and ethnicity combine with class to shape representations of crime in the U.S. Within the social sciences and humanities, there has long been a rich tradition of documenting and critiquing the role of media in distorting the public's view of crime as a social problem, and by consequence, those who are likely to commit such crimes. According to criminologists Jeffrey Reiman and Paul Leighton, the media function as part of a "carnival mirror" that misrepresents the reality of crime by systematically presenting the most egregious crimes as those committed by the poor.[33] Relatedly, sociologist Barry Glassner contends that such media frames, and the disproportionate attention media programs pay to them, distort the image of the typical crime and criminal in the eyes of the public.[34]

Exposure to these kinds of representations are bound to have some influence on people's perception of reality. In fact, researchers have found that the more television someone watches, the more likely they are to fear crime and perceive it as a greater risk in their neighborhood.[35] This should come as no surprise, given how much television Americans watch, and how loose and fast media producers play with facts. In fact, according to a 2016 report from the Bureau of Labor Statistics, Americans spend an average of 2.8 hours per day watching television, the most of any leisure activity.[36]

### Outclassed: On Television and Off

Like race in contemporary America, class often operates under the guise of hidden codes. Even when unspoken, the techniques used to invoke class-based tropes are easily discernable for many viewers. But again, the process of social marking plays a significant role, as representations of class are easier to identify when they differ significantly from the viewer's social location. By this logic, working class viewers are likely to pick up on the salience of class in a show like *Modern Family*, whereas a viewer from an upper-middle class background may not.

Although ABC's *Modern Family* has been praised for its supposed diversity (the sitcom focuses on three related families: one nuclear, one biracial, and one same-sex), its depiction of class is hardly representative of modern

America. While one parent from each family stays at home, their partners' professions—construction company owner, real estate agent, and lawyer—allow them to live comfortably upper-middle class lifestyles. For example, the families are often seen going on expensive vacations, staying in hotels near their homes just for fun, obsessing over the latest Apple devices, and getting into frequent car accidents—all with few financial woes.[37]

*Modern Family* is just one example of the way that many popular television situation comedies (sitcoms) depict issues of class. By and large, popular sitcoms begin with an assumption of (upper-) middle class status—the contemporary American version of unmarked class status according to most media—while creating an apparently classless context around which the plot can unfold. In this way, the bulk of fictional programming normalizes, even romanticizes, the American Dream, as characterized by hard work, economic opportunity, upward social mobility, and the ideology of individualism.

In her book *Framing Class*, Diana Kendall analyzed how newspapers and entertainment television shows framed issues of class and inequality by doing an extensive analysis of content dating as far back as the 1850s and up to the early 2000s. Perhaps predictably, Kendall concludes that media coverage of six distinct class categories—upper class, upper-middle class, middle class, working class, working poor, and poor and homeless—tend to be framed in ways that invoke and perpetuate common stereotypes.

> Rather than providing a meaningful analysis of inequality and showing realistic portrayals of life in various social classes, the media either play class differences for laughs or sweep the issue of class under the rug so that important distinctions are rendered invisible. By ignoring class or trivializing it, the media involve themselves in a social construction of reality that rewards the affluent and penalizes the working class and the poor.[38]

In other words, like the vast majority of marked characteristics, the burden of class is placed disproportionately upon those individuals at the bottom of the class hierarchy, whereas those at the top are celebrated for success and their tendency to live a life of excess. A decade after the Great Recession, realistic representations of the middle class are fewer and far between. Those programs that do depict the middle class—a class that has been steadily shrinking over the past two decades—tend to address the issue of class subtly, if at all.[39]

On the other hand, the issue of class is seated at the forefront of many shows featuring working class characters, despite the characters rarely discussing economic issues explicitly. Beyond the occasional reflections on the characters' cultural tastes and humble economic means, their social class is made visible through clothing and home décor, which proves quite a contrast to the average (upper-middle class) fictional family shown in American media. Kendall discovers five frames that are commonly used to characterize those in the lower and working classes as: 1) *shady*, 2) *heroes and victims*, 3) *white trash*, 4) *buffoons, bigots and slobs*, and 5) *dissatisfied or downwardly mobile.*[40]

Whether we're talking about popular sitcoms like *Shameless* or *Raising Hope*, or common depictions on "reality" television shows, there are plenty of examples showing poor and working class families living a life of crime, cheating, and general chaos. Unsurprisingly, the shady frame often corresponds strongly with the white trash frame, which is a common but politically incorrect reference "to low-income individuals who [tend to be] judged by the more privileged members of society to be tasteless, uneducated, lazy, and otherwise inferior."[41] Those depicted in the media as relatively low status are said to function as a comparison group against which typical viewers can relate, and most likely, feel better about their own situation. This strategy raises the classic sociological issue of manifest and latent functions. According to sociologist Robert Merton, while manifest functions are those that are generally apparent and often intentional, latent functions are more hidden/implicit, and are thus commonly unintentional or ignored. A latent function of media representations of the lower classes, whether through reality television programs like *Here Comes Honey Boo Boo* or sitcoms like *2 Broke Girls*, is the repetition and further perpetuation of the "white trash" frame.

Kendall describes how some working class sitcoms like the cult-classic *Roseanne* and *The King of Queens* extend beyond the white trash frame, instead characterizing many as buffoons and slobs, if not bigots. While the buffoon is a classic caricature dating back many centuries, it remains a common frame most often used to depict working class men.[42] From the 1970s classic *All in the Family*'s bigoted Archie Bunker to *The Simpsons*' Homer, a literal caricature of slobbish buffoonery, it is easy to see how media portray members of the working class in extreme and undesirable ways.

There are certainly bigots on American news and political television as well as talk radio, but in an age of color-blindness, there appear to be fewer outright bigots in American popular culture and entertainment. Yet, there are always exceptions. For example, in a 2017 episode of NBC's *The Carmichael Show*, a Black father makes light of slavery by suggesting that his ancestors' forced migration to America now provides his family with considerable economic opportunity. While neither the scene nor the show portray the father's character as obviously bigoted, his apparent comfort with post-racial rhetoric, especially coming from a Black man, is the color-blind equivalent of racial ignorance.

One common theme that frequently cuts across each of these frames is the constant pursuit of upward mobility. But, as with the majority of

Americans, television's fictional characters are not very likely to achieve this goal. This theme, in which people are expected to "pull themselves up by their bootstraps," despite whatever challenges they face, symbolizes a core element of the American Dream. The common portrayal of working class people as buffoons leads viewers to believe they are responsible for their own fate. And because these characters are also relatable, the implicit message is that you, the viewer, are likewise responsible for your own fate. Thus, working class characters are commonly depicted as struggling for the ever-elusive step up the class ladder. There may be no better example of this than the popular sitcom *2 Broke Girls*, which features two best friends living a life on the hustle, sharing a one-bedroom apartment and working long hours as waitresses while constantly searching for ways to earn extra money to start their own business together. In each episode, it is clear that the characters are dissatisfied with their class status, and their constant struggle to climb the economic ladder raises the ever-present threat of downward mobility.

Contrastingly, programs that frame the working class as heroes and victims predictably paint such characters in a more positive light. This is possible in large part because depictions of the heroes, if not the victims, typically occur in relatively class-less—that is, implicitly (upper-) middle class—contexts. While the majority of crime dramas fit this mold, NBC's popular slate of Chicago-themed series (including *Chicago PD*, *Chicago Fire*, *Chicago Med*, and *Chicago Justice*) provide a clear example. Despite the professions of police officer and firefighter being befitting of working or middle class status, the programs inconsistently depict the characters' lifestyles as such. For example, while characters in *Chicago Fire* are frequently shown on the hustle (writing books, running a bar, etc.), the firefighters, along with their blue collar colleagues from *Chicago PD*, are also shown attending fancy events and rubbing elbows with elite professionals.

Overall, while popular television's working class characters have unquestionably endearing qualities—they all have to be likeable in some way—the fact is that their programming mirrors these frames all too often. And while these characters are almost always complicated and often morally ambiguous, rarely do audiences see programs that mix or break the mold of common working class frames. This kind of nuance, while undoubtedly part of everyday American life, appears to be less appealing to television audiences—or rather, television writers and producers.

Such patterns in media representation are bound to have some effect on American audiences, no matter their ethnicity, race, or class. As sociologists W.I. Thomas and Dorothy Swaine Thomas famously explained nearly a century ago, "if [people] define situations as real, then they are real in their consequences."[43] In today's increasingly mediated society, there is notable reason to believe that what happens on the page (or screen) has the potential to help shape real-world realities in some way. But, to what extent can we say that media have deterministic effects on us when we have an undeniable sense of agency over our lives? This is precisely the question that drives our next chapter.

## Notes

1  Bonilla-Silva, Eduardo. 2013. *Racism without Racists: Color-Blind Racism and the Persistence of Racial Inequality in America.* 4 edition. Lanham: Rowman & Littlefield Publishers.

2  Mendelberg, Tali. 2001. *The Race Card: Campaign Strategy, Implicit Messages, and the Norm of Equality.* Princeton University Press, p. 4.

3  Smiley, Calvin John and David Fakunle. 2016. "From 'Brute' to 'Thug:' The Demonization and Criminalization of Unarmed Black Male Victims in America." *Journal of Human Behavior in the Social Environment* 26(3–4):350–66.

4  Hughey, Matthew W. 2012. "Show Me Your Papers! Obama's Birth and the Whiteness of Belonging." *Qualitative Sociology* 35(2):163–81.

5  Erigha, Maryann. 2016. "Do African Americans Direct Science Fiction or Blockbuster Franchise Movies? Race, Genre, and Contemporary Hollywood." *Journal of Black Studies* 47(6):550–69.

6  Friedman, Sam, Dave O'Brien, and Daniel Laurison. 2016. "'Like Skydiving without a Parachute': How Class Origin Shapes Occupational Trajectories in British Acting." *Sociology* 0038038516629917.

7  Smith, Stacy, Marc Choueiti, and Katherine Pieper. 2015. "Race/Ethnicity in 600 Popular Films: Examining On Screen Portrayals and Behind the Camera Diversity." *Media, Diversity & Social Change Initiative, USC Annenberg.* Retrieved November 29, 2017. Available at: http://latinodonorcollaborative. org/usc-annenberg-raceethnicity-in-600-popular-films-examining-on-screen-portrayals-and-behind-the-camera-diversity/.

8  Smiley and Fakunle, 2016.

9  Moyer-Gusé, Emily. 2008. "Toward a Theory of Entertainment Persuasion: Explaining the Persuasive Effects of Entertainment-Education Messages." *Communication Theory* 18(3):407–25.

10  Kendall, Diana Elizabeth. 2005. Framing Class: Media Representations of Wealth and Poverty in America. Rowman & Littlefield. Page 6.

11  Erigha, Maryann. 2016.

12  Thakore, Bhoomi K. 2014. "Must-See TV: South Asian Characterizations in American Popular Media." *Sociology Compass* 8(2):149–56. Page 152.

13  Goffman, Erving. 1986. *Stigma: Notes on the Management of Spoiled Identity.* Reissue edition. New York: Touchstone.

14  Goffman, Erving. 1974. *Frame Analysis: An Essay on the Organization of Experience.* Harvard University Press.

15  In American popular culture, unmarked and so-called generic traits are typically white, male, heterosexual, cisgender, middle class, Christian, and able-bodied.

16  Brekhus, Wayne H. 1996. "Social Marking and the Mental Coloring of Identity: Sexual Identity Construction and Maintenance in the United States." *Sociological Forum* 11:497–522. Page 512.

17  Stern, Marlow. 2017. "Aziz Ansari on His Excellent New Series 'Master of None,' Sexism, and Race in America." *The Daily Beast.* Retrieved May 3, 2017. Available at: www.thedailybeast.com/aziz-ansari-on-his-excellent-new-series-master-of-none-sexism-and-race-in-america.

18 Kellner, Douglas. 2009. "Media Spectacle and the 2008 Presidential Election." *Cultural Studies* ↔ *Critical Methodologies* 9(6):707–16.
19 Logan, Enid Lynette. 2011. *"At This Defining Moment": Barack Obama's Presidential Candidacy and the New Politics of Race.* NYU Press. Page 29.
20 CNN.com. November 5, 2008. "Transcripts." Retrieved November 29, 2017. Available at: www.cnn.com/TRANSCRIPTS/0811/05/ec.05.html.
21 Coates, Ta-Nehisi. 2017. "The First White President." The Atlantic, October. Retrieved January 11, 2019. Available at: www.theatlantic.com/maga zine/archive/2017/10/the-first-white-president-ta-nehisi-coates/537909/.
22 Ross, Cody T. 2015. "A Multi-Level Bayesian Analysis of Racial Bias in Police Shootings at the County-Level in the United States, 2011–2014." *PLOS ONE* 10(11):e0141854.
   Lowery, Wesley. 2016. "Analysis | Aren't More White People than Black People Killed by Police? Yes, but No," *Washington Post,* July 11. Retrieved May 11, 2017. Available at: www.washingtonpost.com/news/post-nation/wp/2016/07/11/arent-more-white-people-than-black-people-killed-by-police-yes-but-no/.
23 Chappell, Bill. December 29, 2015. "Number Of Police Officers Killed By Gunfire Fell 14 Percent In 2015, Study Says." *NPR.Org.* Retrieved November 29, 2017. Available at: www.npr.org/sections/thetwo-way/2015/12/29/461402091/number-of-police-officers-killed-by-gunfire-fell-14-percent-in-2015-study-says.
24 U.S. Census Bureau. 2015. "American FactFinder—Results." Retrieved November 29, 2017. Available at: https://factfinder.census.gov/faces/tableser vices/jsf/pages/productview.xhtml?src=bkmk.
25 Schroedel, Jean Reith and Roger J. Chin. 2017. "Whose Lives Matter: The Media's Failure to Cover Police Use of Lethal Force Against Native Americans." *Race and Justice.* Advanced online publication. https://doi.org/10.1177/2153368717734614.
26 Schroedel and Chin. 2017.
27 Swaine, Jon, Oliver Laughland, and Jamiles Lartey. 2015. "Black Americans Killed by Police Twice as Likely to Be Unarmed as White People." *The Guardian,* June 1. Retrieved November 29, 2017. Available at: www.theguar dian.com/us-news/2015/jun/01/black-americans-killed-by-police-analysis.
28 Everbach, Tracy, Meredith Clark, and Gwendelyn S. Nisbett. 2017. "#IfTheyGunnedMeDown: An Analysis of Mainstream and Social Media in the Ferguson, Missouri, Shooting of Michael Brown." *Electronic News* 1,931,243,117,697,767.
29 Elmasry, Mohamad Hamas and Mohammed el-Nawawy. 2017. "Do Black Lives Matter?" *Journalism Practice* 11(7):857–75.
30 Everbach, et al. 2017.
31 Rose, Max and Frank R. Baumgartner. 2013. "Framing the Poor: Media Coverage and U.S. Poverty Policy, 1960–2008." *Policy Studies Journal* 41(1):22–53.
32 Gilens, Martin. 2009. *Why Americans Hate Welfare: Race, Media, and the Politics of Antipoverty Policy.* University of Chicago Press. p. 116–117.
33 Reiman, Jeffrey and Paul Leighton. 2012. *The Rich Get Richer and the Poor Get Prison: Ideology, Class, and Criminal Justice.* 10 edition. Boston: Routledge.
34 Glassner, Barry. 2010. *The Culture of Fear: Why Americans Are Afraid of the Wrong Things: Crime, Drugs, Minorities, Teen Moms, Killer Kids, Mutant Microbes, Plane Crashes, Road Rage, & So Much More.* 10 Anv edition. New York: Basic Books.

35  Callanan, Valerie J. 2012. "Media Consumption, Perceptions of Crime Risk and Fear of Crime: Examining Race/Ethnic Differences." *Sociological Perspectives* 55(1):93–115.

36  Bureau of Labor Statistics. 2018. American Time Use Survey Summary, 2017. Washington, D.C.: U.S. Department of Labor. Retrieved May 17, 2017. Available at: www.bls.gov/news.release/atus.nr0.htm.

37  D'Addario, Daniel. September 24, 2013. "'Modern Family' Is a Class-Blind Fantasy World." *Salon.* Retrieved November 30, 2017. Available at: www. salon.com/2013/09/24/modern_family_is_a_class_blind_fantasy_world/.

38  Kendall, 2005. Page 229.

39  Pew Research Center. 2016. "America's Shrinking Middle Class: A Close Look at Changes Within Metropolitan Areas." *Pew Research Center's Social & Demographic Trends Project.* Retrieved May 23, 2017. Available at: www.pewso cialtrends.org/2016/05/11/americas-shrinking-middle-class-a-close-look-at-changes-within-metropolitan-areas/.

40  Kendall, 2005.

41  Kendall, 2005. (Page 157).

42  Butsch, Richard. 2005. "Five Decades and Three Hundred Sitcoms About Class and Gender." In G. Edgerton & B. Rose (Eds.), *Thinking Outside the Box: A Contemporary Television Genre Reader.* Lexington: University Press of Kentucky, pp. 111–135.

43  Thomas, William I. and Dorothy Swaine Thomas. 1928. *The Child in America.* New York: Knopf.

# Section 4

# Audiences

## Chapter 10

# Are We Robots?

Has *Two and a Half Men* undermined 2,500 years of Confucian values? Since at least the time of Confucius around 500 BC, Chinese society has held values emphasizing harmony, hierarchy, and collectivism. While China has gone through many political and cultural transformations during that time, many of these values still carry cultural sway. But, in recent years, with an influx of Western media, young Chinese people are encountering more music, movies, and TV shows that embody Western individualistic values rather than traditional Chinese ones. Studying Chinese college students in 2002, Yan Bing Zhang and Jake Hardwood found that those who spent more time with "imported media" were significantly less likely to endorse some types of traditional Chinese values.[1] Values that have withstood more than two millennia of social change may vanish in the face of the American sitcom.

In the U.S., there are debates about the effects of video games, cable news shout-fests, and addictive smartphones on our behavior and beliefs. In the same way that everyone thinks they are good drivers, most people believe that others are susceptible to media effects, but imagine that they themselves can resist. Like the Chinese college students, we are all shaped by mass media in some ways. The questions are how and to what extent?

As shown in chapters 2 and 6, media sociology has tended to focus on what mass media look like and how they get to be that way. The underlying assumption sociologists make is that media affect people to some extent. We wouldn't care how journalists depict social movements if we thought the framing of protests had no ramifications for how citizens think about movements. But compared with the amount of research into media production and representations, media effects research is rare within sociology. Scholars in the field of communications have conducted most of the research telling us how much mass media affect us and under what circumstances.

In this chapter, we will consider theories and research on *media effects*. The question posed in the title of this chapter—"are we robots?"—has a simple answer: no. We are not mindlessly obedient to media images; we have agency. However, to some extent, the media we encounter do have the power to persuade us, mold our thinking, and even change the physical size and shape of our brains.

## The Persuaders

There are no industries that bank on the power of media effects more than advertising and public relations (PR). Both are in the business of communicating information through various media to persuade the public in their client's favor. If the public truly was immune to media messages, professional persuaders would be out of work.

There are differences between PR and advertising. Advertisers must pay for their placement online, on TV, and in print, while PR professionals attempt to generate free media coverage for their clients. In many traditional media, although not necessarily online, advertising is required to identify its sponsor and any factual claims must be substantiated. PR is unregulated and has no such obligations. Advertising is also usually for a product, a service, or an idea, but PR can also be about shaping the public perception of a company or a person. While celebrities usually do not run advertisements simply to promote themselves, many do hire publicists to do their PR.

Despite these differences, the two forms of persuasion share a theoretical underpinning. Edward Bernays, a nephew of Sigmund Freud and the so-called "father of PR," argued such persuasion was fundamentally beneficial to society. Bernays believed that most people go through life unthinkingly, responding impulsively to whatever stimuli they happen to encounter. But, as media scholar Stuart Ewen describes it, Bernays thought that "there exist an 'intelligent few' who have been charged with the responsibility of contemplating and influencing the tide of history."[2] The "intellectual elite" must guide the masses and PR (and advertising) are the essential tools molding opinion.

Bernays himself was an unpredictable character. He created a campaign for Dixie Cups (disposable paper cups) that attempted to convince consumers that using glasses was unsanitary. He set up front groups like "Better Living Through Increased Highway Transportation" to advocate for the auto, oil, and rubber industries. He worked on behalf of Big Tobacco. But Bernays also worked on progressive causes. He organized the first convention of the National Association for the Advancement of Colored People (NAACP) and later ran anti-smoking campaigns to oppose Big Tobacco. According to Bernays, "the engineering of consent is the very essence of the democratic process."[3] When elites disagree on issues, they ought to run competing PR campaigns to settle the dispute. Whoever is most persuasive to the public wins.

Most advertising and PR professionals today would probably reject such an unabashedly elitist view of society. Their work, however, depends on the principle that most people are susceptible to media effects and that it is at least ethically acceptable, if not beneficial for society, to persuade them. For example, a substantial body of research has shown the power of children to influence their parents' spending decisions so much so that children under 14 now influence over $250 billion dollars in consumer purchases.[4] Even though parents hate it when their children nag them, nagging is one of the most effective tools for swaying parental purchases. And so commercials instruct children to nag their parents to take them to Chuckie Cheese or Disneyland, to buy Captain Crunch, or Sunny Delight.[5]

Because of children's vulnerability, many groups including the American Psychological Association (APA) have suggested significantly restricting commercial advertising to kids.[6] But children aren't alone in being affected by persuasive messaging. Political TV commercials, direct marketing emails (20% off one day sale!), and even the "Lovely day for a Guinness" sign hanging outside the pub are all highly effective in persuading adults. We know we're being sold a product, service, or an idea, but often we can't quite resist. Why?

## The Hypodermic Model

Bernays seemed to subscribe to a theory all too common in the 1930s and 1940s and still present in some public discourse today, which claims media messages are injected into the public like drugs through a hypodermic needle. The *hypodermic model* (also known as the *direct effects model*) was born in a historical moment where Hitler had effectively mobilized and garnered public support through radio addresses and propaganda films. At the same time, moral crusaders and social critics became concerned about the effect of films on children. Given their belief in a hypodermic model of media effects, it is unsurprising that they set up local censorship boards to combat "incidents of 'youths'...imitating behavior they had seen in movies, girls...learned how to kiss boys, boys how to steal."[7]

A classic myth story in this tradition concerns the first televised presidential debate between Richard Nixon and John F. Kennedy in 1960. As *Time* magazine reports,

> Nixon, pale and underweight from a recent hospitalization, appeared sickly and sweaty, while Kennedy appeared calm and confident ... those who listened to the debate on the radio thought Nixon had won. Those that watched the debate on TV thought Kennedy was the clear winner.[8]

*Figure 10.1* John F. Kennedy and Richard Nixon after Their First Televised Debate [Source: Associated Press, via Wikimedia Commons https://commons. wikimedia.org/wiki/File:Kennedy_Nixon_debate_first_Chicago_1960.jpg]

To many, it was proof positive of a hypodermic effect of TV. Except that it's not exactly true. The small sample polls used to support the claims were from different types of neighborhoods, with the radio subset being from a Republican 'stronghold.[9] Even if politicians today sometimes still apply the logic of the hypodermic model, fortunately, by the 1960s, academic researchers began to question the merit of direct effects.

## Minimal Effects

If media aren't like a shot in the arm, how might they affect us? Researchers in the *minimal effects* tradition began to recognize that while media do have effects—that is, they "do something" to us—we also have agency in choosing what to watch or read and how to make sense of it. These scholars, typically using controlled lab experiments with random assignment of participants to certain conditions, observed two patterns. First, people engage in *selective exposure*. Conservatives tend to watch Fox News and liberals tend to watch MSNBC. The readership of Reddit skews young, affluent, and male. And most of the people who follow #BlackTwitter are black.

There is also *selective retention* where we tend to absorb media messages that support our existing worldview and let the rest slide by. In a famous 1974 study, Neil Vidmar and Milton Rokeach showed teens and adults episodes of the sitcom *All in the Family*.[10] The show featured the ongoing conflicts between Archie Bunker, a conservative, bigoted, working class dad and his son, Mike, a long-haired liberal finishing up college. The researchers found that young people and those who were less prejudiced going into the experiment were more likely to see the show as critical of Archie. Older people and those with higher prejudice were more likely to see the show as critical of Mike.

If the hypodermic model were correct, the show should have produced the same effect on both groups. But it didn't. Who people were going in affected what they took away. That's not to say media have no effect on us. For an older conservative, watching *All in the Family* may strengthen their conservative convictions, while it would do just the opposite for a liberal. In fact, in recent studies of cable news viewers, we find strong evidence for selective exposure: liberals choosing MSNBC and conservatives choosing Fox. But there is still substantial evidence for media effects. Watching more Fox News *increased* conservatives' opposition to then-candidate Barack Obama in 2008 above and beyond their already unfavorable view. The inverse was also true of liberals watching coverage of John McCain on MSNBC. In this way, media do have effects, but who we are affects how media affect us.

## Uses and Gratifications

While minimal effects began to conceptualize how individual identities may moderate media effects, it still envisions a relatively passive media consumer. That vision fits with the kind of experimental design minimal effects researchers tend to use. You walk into a lab, they show you something that you didn't select and then they ask you to answer some questions or complete a quiz. But a different group of researchers in the 1970s, developing the *uses and gratifications model*, wanted to understand media users' agency more fully. For them, the most important question is "why do we use media anyway?"

Using qualitative interviews and surveys, uses and gratifications researchers explored how people select and consume media to satisfy emotional, spiritual, and intellectual needs. Current research on Facebook use, for example, tells us that users are drawn to the social networking site to keep in touch with old and new friends and to look at pictures more often than to learn about events, post social functions, or share information about themselves.[11] In the 1970s, Elihu Katz and Jay Blumer in a series of studies found that people used television in particular to satisfy a need for drama, to feel connected to real or imagined communities, and to watch authority figures, like politicians, rise and fall.[12]

Uses and gratifications help us understand that media users have agency; we make choices to fulfill needs and desires. For this reason, it represents an important corrective to early research that envisioned mindless recipients of media content. Still, it doesn't get at the heart of the question: how are

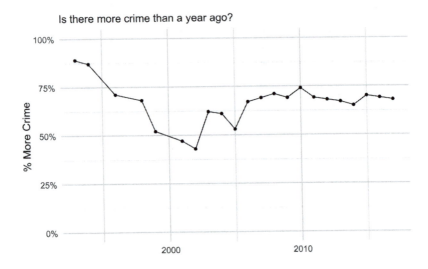

*Figure 10.2a* Public Perception vs. Reality of Crime, 1993–2017
[Source: Gallup]

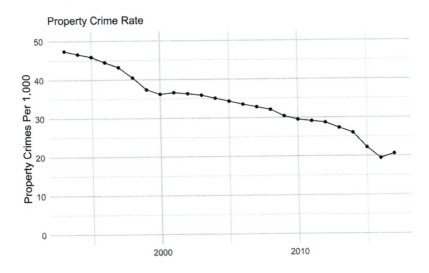

*Figure 10.2b* Public Perception vs. Reality of Crime, 1993–2017
[Source: Bureau of Justice Statistics]

we affected? After a period of research emphasizing limited effects and agency in the 1970s, the tide has turned toward theory and research suggesting stronger—if not quite hypodermic—effects once again.

## Cultivation Theory

Between 1990 and 2015, crime was cut in half. Murder and other violent crimes declined by more than 50% (see Figure 10.2). Property crime fell by 43%. The so-called "crime drop" is what Inimai Chettiar, director of New York University's Justice Program, calls "one of the most fascinating and remarkable social phenomena of our time."[13] But even as crime ticked downwards in the 2000s, the percentage of people saying that crime is getting to be more of a problem grew from 43% in 2000 to 74% in 2010. Though less than half of 1% of Americans are victims of violent crime each year, four in ten Americans feel unsafe walking home.[14] For most Americans, there really is nothing to fear but fear itself. So, why are we such nervous Nellies?

For media scholar George Gerbner and his colleagues, who developed *cultivation theory*, TV deserves the bulk of the blame. With its frequent depictions of violence and extreme overrepresentation of crime, television "cultivates" a sense of reality that is deeply distorted. Heavy television viewers develop what Gerbner called *mean world syndrome*, imagining of dangers, brutality, and constant threat. Cultivation researchers tend to use the results of surveys that ask about people's attitudes and behaviors. The findings consistently reveal a correlation between the number of hours spent watching television per week and the respondent's reported fear about the world.

However, critics of cultivation theory usually point to three issues. First, these are correlational, not causal, studies. In some samples, for example, the effect of TV on fear disappears when controlling for age. In other words, older people are more likely to watch a lot of TV and have greater fear due to their vulnerability, but it's a spurious correlation.

A second line of critique points out that the magnitude of the TV effect tends to be very small because almost all Americans watch a lot of TV and not all of us are quite so fearful. Finally, Gerbner's theory is specific to television. With an ever-widening array of items on the media menu, fewer of them are dishes served with such a heaping side of violence. Acknowledging these issues, Gerbner has pointed out that the average American still watches five hours of TV per day and noted, "just as an average temperature shift of a few degrees can lead to an ice age ... so too can a relatively small but pervasive influence make a crucial difference."[15]

## Framing and Agenda-setting

Even if Gerbner's larger empirical claim is dubious, there's a more important underlying point. Public opinion, especially regarding political issues that are difficult for us to observe directly, is formed not based on "reality" but on a social construction of reality produced by media images. For many contemporary media effects researchers, our mental map of the world is shaped by two important processes: *agenda-setting* and *framing*. Agenda-setting is the power of the media to tell the public *what* to think about, and framing is their ability to tell us *how* to think about it.[16] While that may sound a bit authoritarian, media affect us not because we lack all agency, but because they give us shortcuts we find useful.

Brains can only do so many things each day. Most of us use our limited cognitive capacity to focus on our work, family and friends, errands—mundane stuff. Even if we care about social and political issues, we're all too happy for shortcuts that help us understand the issues quickly. No offense to Denmark, but we, the authors, are usually not going to follow the Danish elections very closely. We count on the news media to tell us how much attention the Danish elections deserve and what the results mean. At any given time, we have a pre-existing *knowledge store* with both *temporary accessibility* and *chronic accessibility* portions. In our *chronic accessibility knowledge stores* are a whole bunch of ideas about Denmark: it's in Scandinavia, it's a social democratic state, the fairy tale writer Hans Christian Andersen lived in Copenhagen, etc. But we're not that tuned into their politics. If we hear a quick news segment saying that the right-wing Danish People's Party won seats in their most recent election, it will get stored in our *temporary accessibility* area and we can probably recall it later this week. However, without reinforcement through multiple news stories, it won't move to the chronic knowledge store.[17] To move into chronic accessibility, we would need repeated "activations" of information in our temporary accessibility.

In terms of agenda-setting, media gatekeepers influence what moves from people's temporary to chronic sections of their knowledge stores as they select which stories to tell, what types of people to feature, and what ideas to cover. For example, sociologist Ion Vasi and his colleagues found that communities with local screenings of the anti-hydraulic fracking documentary, *Gasland* (2010), were more likely to have more social media chatter, local news coverage, and, ultimately, more mobilization.[18] For people living in these communities, whatever their stance on fracking, the increased media attention made it something worth thinking about.

If agenda-setting is the power of media to tell us what belongs in the chronic accessibility portion of the knowledge store, media *frames* tell us what are the *salient attributes* or the most important things to remember when considering an issue. The news report on the Danish People's Party's electoral victory could use a frame suggesting that it is part of a "disturbing trend" or a frame that focuses on the happiness of citizens who voted for the party. Each frame might lead me to store different *salient attributes* of the party. The power of framing effects on public opinion has been well established in literature spanning a number of academic fields including psychology, political science, and media studies.

One of the most significant framing researchers, Shanto Iyengar, has proposed that television news reports of political issues make use of either *episodic* or *thematic* frames.[19] News stories with episodic frames focus on the actual events, often with engaging video footage, rather than the issues involved. By contrast, reports with thematic frames focus on the abstract political issues usually explained by "talking heads" and tend to cite the event primarily as an illustration. Using several content analyses and a series of field experiments, Iyengar finds that television coverage of social issues is largely episodic and that this particular type of frame leads to more individual level attributions of responsibility (in other words, hating the player, not the game). A person's stance on any given political issue is shaped by her attributions of causality and responsibility. With a thematic frame, because the reporting is more abstract and sociological, the news consumer tends to place responsibility for social problems on the collective. Whereas, with an episodic frame, which tends to deal with the specifics of an event or individual examples of a public issue, the news consumer is more likely to place both the blame for the problem and the burden of improvement on the individual. To use C. Wright Mills' language, viewers of a news story with a thematic framing see a "public issue," viewers of the episodic framing see a "personal trouble."

For example, if Congress were considering a piece of legislation to provide state relief to curb growing unemployment rates, an episodic report might focus on a specific person who had lost her job and had been unable to get work for several months. Iyengar's experimental findings suggest that the viewer of the episodic frame would conclude that the person must be lazy and that it was her/his own responsibility to get a job (and the government need not fund the legislation). By contrast, a thematic report might focus on the nature of the bill, provide statistics about the growing trend, and consider the possible effects on the national economy. In the thematic frame, the viewer can see that the problem goes far beyond the troubles of the individual and therefore would likely support the legislation.

Similarly, media effects researcher Dolf Zillman has developed *exemplification theory*, which explores the power of *examples* in shaping the public's perception of social issues. In one experiment, Zillman presented college students with a news report about carjackings that clearly stated that most carjackings do not end in even minor injury like bruising (less than 25%), let alone death (a mere 0.2%). However, some of the news stories Zillman gave participants included an anecdote about a carjacking where a person was injured or killed. Others included a less dramatic, more typical example. After a distraction, Zillman asked them to estimate the rate of carjacking injuries and fatalities. Even though all of the articles reported the actual statistics, among those students who read about an example where someone was killed, the average estimate of the fatality rate during carjackings was 15%! They estimated that 65% of carjackings result in injuries! Thus, Zillman's findings show that vivid examples used as part of frames are more readily stored as salient attributes than some dry statistics.[20]

Who we are still matters. If presented with a frame that doesn't fit with the salient attributes in our pre-existing knowledge store, we might question it. Because of selective exposure, we have some ability to select media outlets whose agenda is a good match with our own. But we only have the attention and mental energy to resist media agenda-setting and framing on issues that really matter to us. More often than not, we are the persuaded.

## The Web Brain

Media effects often occur at the sub-conscious level, such as when powerful examples prove more mentally sticky than statistics that slip through our cognitive web. Occasionally, we are consciously aware of them even as they happen. A well-executed ad featuring golden, crispy fries will get us every time, even when aware that we are falling victim to the artistry of persuasion. But there is a kind of "media effect" that is even deeper than merely sub-conscious. Forget the framings, the distorting examples, the mean world syndrome—the media we use today quite literally have the effect of changing the shape and functioning of our brains.

In 2011, journalist Nicholas Carr wrote:

> Over the past few years I've had an uncomfortable sense that someone, or something, has been tinkering with my brain, remapping the neural circuitry, reprogramming the memory. My mind isn't going—so far as I can tell—but it's changing. I'm not thinking the way I used to think. I can feel it most strongly when I'm reading. Immersing myself in a book or a lengthy article used to be easy. My mind would get caught up in the narrative or the turns of the argument, and I'd spend hours strolling through long stretches of prose. That's rarely the case anymore. Now my concentration often starts to drift after two or three pages. I get fidgety, lose the thread, begin looking for something else to do … The deep reading that used to come naturally has become a struggle.[21]

In his Pulitzer Prize-winning book, *The Shallows*, Carr links his brain's (and most of the rest of our brains') transformation to the essential nature of the medium of the web. The web with its endless offerings of entertaining distraction, interesting things to read, and dozens of forms of social interaction (texts, emails, Snapchat, Facebook messages, likes and favorites) that have the addictive powers of uncut cocaine. And he didn't know the half of it. Carr was writing most of his book in 2008, before Facebook became a juggernaut, before many of us had smartphones, and began to feel a near-constant "soul-deep throb coming from that perfectly engineered wafer of stainless steel and glass and rare earth metals in [our] pocket[s]."[22]

It's no longer debatable that mass media offers distraction from other kinds of activities. It distracts us from being fully present in social settings. It disrupts deep work flow. The smartphone is such a perfect boredom cure that it keeps us from beneficial daydreaming and reflection. But in interviewing neuroscientists, Carr finds that digital technologies not only give us a different set of activities, but change our very capabilities.

Human brains even into adulthood have great *brain plasticity*; they can change to adapt to new circumstances. Just like astronauts lose muscle in space, when you don't work a part of your brain regularly, it can change or shrink. Compared with adolescents who use the web less and engage in less gaming, teenagers who are heavy digital media users have smaller and less active pre-frontal cortexes (the thinking part of the brain) and relatively more active amygdalae, the emotional or impulsive portion of the brain.[23] As a consequence, according to communications research by Clifford Ness and his colleagues, heavy users of digital media have trouble focusing and filtering out "irrelevant information." As he notes, "They're suckers for irrelevancy. Everything distracts them."[24] Moreover, for people born after the mid-1990s, this is no preweb brain.

Who cares? The "reading brain" itself is not natural. For most of human history, people did not read. Societies with mass literacy and a culture of sustained print-based reading may have been a historical blip that occurred in wealthy western countries during the 20th century. The "digital brain" may just be the newest step in human development. Plus, web users are far more cognitively active than TV users. The web has opened up new opportunities for learning, communication, and new forms of social interaction. Digital sociologist Nathan Jurgenson argues that much of the rhetoric about current media is "digital dualism," which draws a firm line between digital life and "real life" and stigmatizes the former while refusing to acknowledge the ways it overlaps with the latter.

Still, some neuroscientists and social researchers who study media effects on the brain say that the capacity for a certain type of critical reflection is lost. As neuroscientist Maryanne Wolf says, "Deep reading ... is indistinguishable from deep thinking."[25] The kind of uninterrupted thinking we do when we read books is fundamentally different from the way your brain works when you scroll through a social media feed. Media scholar Neil Postman was long critical of electronic media like TV, arguing that print-based cultures promote seriousness that is necessary for a robust democracy.[26]

Digital communications technologies have changed the shape of brains and the patterns of blood flow through them and there are some consequences of these transformations for our ability to focus and think deeply. Whether these changes are good or bad are moral questions not easily answered by social science. Indeed, it's hard to even document the nature of the physical and social effects because empirical studies are rendered obsolete by new technological innovations before they can get published in academic journals. Like the period of modernization that spurred sociological founders Marx, Durkheim, and Weber into action, we won't understand the full and final consequences of the digital technologies revolution for some time to come.

Whether by agenda-setting, exemplification, or the medium itself, people are affected by media. But that doesn't mean that we buy a Big Mac or cast a vote for a politician every time elites instruct us to. We do have agency and, in the next chapter, we explore the ways we use it.

## Notes

1 Zhang, Yan Bing, and Jake Harwood. 2002. "Television Viewing and Perceptions of Traditional Chinese Values among Chinese College Students." *Journal of Broadcasting & Electronic Media* 46(2):245–264.
2 Ewen, Stuart. 2008. *PR!: A Social History of Spin*. New York: Basic Books, p. 9.
3 Bernays, Edward L. 1947. "The Engineering of Consent." *The Annals of the American Academy of Political and Social Science* 250:113–120.
4 Calvert, Sandra L. 2008. "Children as Consumers: Advertising and Marketing." *The Future of Children* 18(1):205–234.
5 Wilson, George, and Katie Wood. 2004. "The Influence of Children on Parental Purchases During Supermarket Shopping." *International Journal of Consumer Studies* 28(4):329–336.
6 Kunkel, Dale, et al. 2004. *Report of the APA Task Force on Advertising and Children*. Washington, DC: American Psychological Association. Available at: www.apa.org/pi/families/resources/advertising-children.pdf.
7 Butsch, Richard. 2014. "Agency, Social Interaction, and Audience Studies." In Silvio Waisbord (ed.), *Media Sociology*. Cambridge, UK: Polity Press.
8 Webley, Kayla. 2010. "How the Nixon-Kennedy Debate Changed the World." *Time*. Sept. 23. Available at: http://content.time.com/time/nation/article/0,8599,2021078,00.html.

9 Simon, Ron. 2010. "The Nixon-Kennedy Debates: A Look at the Myth." *The Paley Center for Media*. Available at: www.paleycenter.org/p-the-nixon-kennedy-debates-a-look-at-the-myth/.

10 Vidmar, Neil, and Milton Rokeach. 1974. "Archie Bunker's Bigotry: A Study in Selective Perception and Exposure." *Journal of Communication* 24(1): 36–47.

11 Raacke, John, and Jennifer Bonds-Raacke. 2008. "MySpace and Facebook: Applying the uses and Gratifications Theory to Exploring Friend-Networking Sites." *Cyberpsychology & Behavior* 11(2):169–174.

12 Blumler, Jay G. and Elihu Katz. 1974. *The Uses of Mass Communications: Current Perspectives on Gratifications Research*. Beverly Hills, CA: Sage Annual Reviews of Communication Research Volume III.

13 Chettiar, Inimai. 2015. "The Many Causes of America's Decline in Crime." *The Atlantic Monthly*. Feb 11. Available at: www.theatlantic.com/politics/arch ive/2015/02/the-many-causes-of-americas-decline-in-crime/385364/.

14 Saad, Lydia. 2011. "Most Americans Believe Crime in U.S. Is Worsening." *Gallup*. October 31. Available at: www.gallup.com/poll/150464/americans-believe-crime-worsening.aspx.

15 Gerbner, George, Larry Gross, Michael Morgan, and Nancy Signorielli. 1980. "The 'mainstreaming' of America: Violence Profile no. 11." *Journal of Communication* 30(3):10–29.

16 Terkildsen, Nayda and Frauke Schnell. 1997. "How Media Frames Move Public Opinion: An Analysis of the Women's Movement." *Political Research Quarterly* 50(4):879–900.

17 Price, Vincent and David Tewksbury. 1997. "New Values and Public Opinion: A Theoretical Account of Media Priming and Framing." In George A. Barnett and Franklin J. Boster (Eds.), *Progress in Communication Sciences: Advances in Persuasion*. New York: Ablex, Vol. 13, pp. 173–212.

18 Vasi, Ion Bogdan, Edward T. Walker, John S. Johnson, and Hui Fen Tan. 2015. "'No Fracking Way!' Documentary Film, Discursive Opportunity, and Local Opposition against Hydraulic Fracturing in the United States, 2010 to 2013." *American Sociological Review* 80(5):934–959.

19 Iyengar, Shanto. 1991. *Is Anyone Responsible?: How Television Frames Political Issues*. Chicago: University of Chicago Press.

20 Zillmann, Dolf, and Hans-Bernd Brosius. 2012. *Exemplification in Communication: The Influence of Case Reports on the Perception of Issues*. New York: Routledge.

21 Carr, Nicholas G. 2010. *The Shallows*. New York: W.W. Norton & Co.

22 McGuire, Hugh. 2015. "Why Can't we Read Anymore?" *Medium.com*. April 22. Available at: https://medium.com/@hughmcguire/why-can-t-we-read-anymore-503c38c131fe#.7o2xk7wow.

23 Choudhury, Suparna, and Kelly A. McKinney. 2013. "Digital Media, The Developing Brain and the Interpretive Plasticity of Neuroplasticity." *Transcultural Psychiatry* 50(2):192–215.

24 Gorlick, Adam. 2009. "Media Multitaskers Pay Mental Price, Stanford Study Shows." *Stanford News*. August 24. Available at: http://news.stanford.edu/news/2009/august24/multitask-research-study-082409.html.

25 Wolf, Maryanne. 2007. *Proust and the Squid*. New York: HarperCollins.

26 Postman, Neil. 2006. *Amusing Ourselves to Death: Public Discourse in the Age of Show Business*. New York: Penguin.

## Chapter 11

# Or Are We Rebels?

In 2008, just days after Barack Obama was elected president of the U.S., a group of media-savvy activists called The Yes Men (yeslab.org) created a fake copy of *The New York Times* that featured all the news they wanted to be true. Some of their headlines read: "Iraq War Ends," "After Withdrawal Peace Spreads to Conflict Zones Worldwide," "United Nations Unanimously Passes Weapons Ban," and "Maximum Wage Law Succeeds." With the help of over 1,000 volunteers, The Yes Men distributed copies throughout the streets of New York City, and they invited a documentary filmmaker to capture reactions from the public. Fittingly, the short film was later published on the video-sharing platform YouTube and spread on social media.[1] Part guerilla theater and part trademark infringement, The Yes Men's stunt sought to spark conversation and inspiration about what radical social change would actually look like, and what kinds of effort would be required to actually accomplish those goals. At the same time, it was also a satirical take on the role legacy news media outlets play in the maintenance of status quo.

The Yes Men may be one of the most striking examples of "culture jamming," but they are far from the only ones doing this work. According to communications scholar Christine Harold, the act of culture jamming might be best understood as the "artful proliferation of messages, a rhetorical process of intervention and invention, which challenges the ability of corporate discourses to make meaning in predictable ways."[2] In other words, culture jamming entails the remixing of corporate messages to subvert popular, hegemonic ideologies. As such, it has also been described as "subvertising" or "counter-propaganda."[3] The Canada-based magazine Adbusters is widely recognized for its work blurring the lines between cultural production and political activism. Its long-running reel of "spoof ads" targets numerous industries, all with an aim toward exposing the role of media and corporate advertising in shaping public consciousness. Adbusters' "environMENTAL" series includes many subvertisements that critique the media industry, in particular, including many that instruct viewers to "turn off the TV."[4]

"All the News We Hope to Print"

# The New York Times

**Special Edition**
Today, clouds part, more sunshine, recent gloom passes. Tonight, strong leftward winds. Tomorrow, a new day. Weather map throughout.

VOL. CLVIV .. No. 54,631      NEW YORK, SATURDAY, JULY 4, 2009      FREE

## Nation Sets Its Sights on Building Sane Economy

# IRAQ WAR ENDS

**True Cost Tax, Salary Caps, Trust-Busting Top List**

By T. VEBLEN

The President has called for swift passage of the Safeguards for a New Economy (S.A.N.E.) bill. The omnibus economic package includes a federal maximum wage, mandatory "True Cost Accounting," a phased withdrawal from complex financial instruments and other measures intended to improve life for ordinary Americans. (See highlights box on Page A10.) He also repeated earlier calls for passage of the "Ban on Lobbying" bill currently making its way through Congress.

Treasury Secretary Paul Krugman stressed the importance of the bill. "Markets make great servants, terrible leaders, and absurd religions," said Krugman, quoting Paul Hawken, an advocate of corporate responsibility and author of "Blessed Unrest, How the Largest Movement in the World Came into Being and Why No One Saw It Coming."

"At this point, the market is our

leader and our religion. No wonder the median standard of living has been declining so much for so long."

Krugman said that the new Treasury bill seeks to ensure the prosperity of all citizens, rather than simply supporting large corporations and the wealthy. "The market is supposed to serve us. Unfortunately, we have ended up serving the market. That's very bad."

Much as Roosevelt, after the Great Depression, put the brakes on C.E.O. wages and irresponsible banking practices, administration officials claim that today we need to rein in the industry that has caused such chaos and misery.

"The building blocks of post-World War II American middle-class prosperity have all been swept away," said House Speaker Nancy Pelosi, who initially op-

*Continued on Page A10*

### Troops to Return Immediately

By JUDE SHINBIN

WASHINGTON — Operation Iraqi Freedom and Operation Enduring Freedom were brought to an unceremonious close today with a quiet announcement by the Department of Defense that troops would be home within weeks.

"This is the best face we can put on the most unfortunate adventure in modern American history," Defense spokesman Kevin Sites said at a special joint session of Congress. "Today, we can finally enjoy peace — not the peace of the brave, perhaps, but at least peace."

As U.S. and coalition troops withdraw from Iraq and Afghanistan, the United Nations will move in to perform peacekeeping duties and aid in rebuilding. The U.N. will be responsible for keeping the two countries stable, coordinating the rebuilding of hospitals, schools, highways, and other infrastructure, and overseeing upcoming elections.

The Department of the Treasury confirmed that all U.N. dues owed by the U.S. were paid as of this morning, and that the moneys previously earmarked for the war would be sent directly to the U.N.'s Iraq Oversight Body.

The president noted that the Iraq War had resulted in the burning of many bridges. "Yet our his-

COURTESY AP/WWII

U.S. Army helicopters begin moving troops and equipment from Saddam Hussein's former Baghdad palace.

## Maximum Wage Law Succeeds

**Salary Caps Will Help Stabilize Economy**

By J.K. MALONE

WASHINGTON — After long and

## TREASURY ANNOUNCES "TRUE COST" TAX PLAN

By MARCUS S. BRIGGS

**Recruiters Train for New Life**
As a ban is imposed on recruiting minors, ex-recruiters nationwide look for new work. The Times follows one on his job-hunt odyssey through Manhattan and surround-

**USA Patriot Act Repealed**
Eight years later, a shamefaced Congress quietly repeals the much-maligned USA Patriot Act. unanimously... or almost.

BY SYBIL LUDINGTON, PAGE A8

### Ex-Secretary Apologizes for W.M.D. Scare

*Figure 11.1* The Yes Men's Satirical Version of *The New York Times* [Image by The Yes Men. Source: http://nytimes-se.com/todays-paper/NYTimes-SE.pdf Available from www.yeslab.org/museum Licensed under Creative Commons (CC BY-SA)]

But far from being a primarily professional endeavor, culture jamming has gained popularity amongst many members of the so-called "active audience." Today, culture jamming has, to an extent, gone viral. While the term "meme" was originally used to describe imitative cultural forms that are easily spread—for example, the popularizing of the "dab" far beyond the world of hip-hop dance—the concept is often used in reference to web-based images that are constantly remixed with new, humorous text.[5] The act of meme-making, and of course, meme-sharing, is almost second nature to many Internet users.

Although frequently apolitical, many memes are enabled by a kind of "meme generator" which makes it easy for Internet users to create their own without much technical knowledge. By providing users with the tools to create and spread such messages, meme generators and social media platforms illustrate a trend that applies to the examples discussed throughout this chapter: media activism is both an individual and collective endeavor. There are many rebels out there, and they can make a difference by speaking out. But, the more media activists cooperate with others who share their concerns, the more likely they are to make progress toward their goals.

Critics from across the political spectrum hold strong opinions on whether or not the media is "biased," and which direction that bias leans. As we discussed in Chapter 7, there is reason to doubt the claims of "liberal bias" despite the fact that many journalists lean liberal, because mainstream media also serve the inherently conservative function of reproducing dominant ideologies. But whatever you may think of the media, you are likely not alone. The number of Americans who trust news media reached a 40-year low in 2016,[6] and a majority think media outlets should just stick to the facts.[7] As Figure 11.2 shows, public interest in the topic of "media bias" tends to wax and wane with the seasons, peaking every four years, toward the end of each presidential election.

Whether coming from the left, right, or center, criticisms of American media are abundant. And like "the media," critiques of it are far from monolithic. Still, as this chapter and others throughout the book make clear, there are a number of clear trends in the concerns raised by media critics, including those pertaining to ownership concentration, political ideology, and representation of women and minorities. While it is true that many of these critiques, as well as the movements that often wage them, come from the political left, there are also activist groups that critique media from the right,

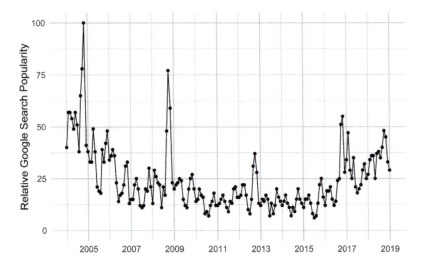

*Figure 11.2* Google Searches for "Media Bias," 2004–2019

[Source: Google Trends]

including the Media Research Center (mrc.org) and the Family Research Council (frc.org). But, at what point does media criticism become a form of activism?

Criticism is, of course, a necessary but not sufficient condition for media activism. Indeed, as we will see, media activists are a diverse bunch. Far from being robots helplessly brainwashed by an all-powerful media system, we often talk back to mass media. And while activists of all kinds use and often critique legacy media coverage on a particular issue— from race or class-based inequality to politicians and the environment— what qualifies an individual or organization as a *media activist* is a specific, if not primary, focus on issues in the media. Accordingly, this chapter provides a brief history of media reform movements and considers what tactics these rebels have used, including those battles waged in print, over the airwaves, and online.

## Dislike: A Brief History of Media Activism from the Left and Right

In *Networks of Outrage and Hope*, sociologist Manuel Castells examines the characteristics of contemporary social movements, with a particular emphasis on the role of new media and communication technologies. One common thread amongst numerous revolutionary movements from across the globe, Castells finds, is disdain for, and perceived corruption within, political and economic elites, whether they be presidents, dictators, party officials, or business tycoons. Castells argues that if conditions become dire enough, and if enough of those people are well-connected and well-educated, they are likely to organize and pursue change. The tactics they employ may differ greatly depending on the issue and context. In relatively democratic countries, organizing is more likely to focus on specific issues with an eye toward policy changes, like calling for a fairer tax code or ensuring all citizens have access to affordable health care. On the other hand, social movements spawning from more repressive countries may call for revolutionary changes like overhauling their constitution or overthrowing those in power.

While it is still far from revolutionary, the fight for media reform has a long history in the U.S. and beyond. As Robert McChesney and John Nichols describe, the debate about the role media should play in a democratic society began around the time of America's first "revolutionary" period. Shortly after the Constitution was ratified the "founding fathers" debated whether the newly formed national post office should charge a fee to deliver magazines and newspapers, or whether, as James Madison argued, it should deliver periodicals at no cost in order to encourage the free exchange of ideas and information.[8] While Madison did not get his way, his advocacy led to the creation of subsidized or discounted postage rates for commercial publications—a policy that is still in place today. This is one example of how Madison, alongside his compatriot Thomas Jefferson, played a leading role in drafting legislation to help ensure that media serve the public interest.

Over a century later, beginning in the Progressive Era (1900–1915) there was a resurgence of public concern over the commercial media system and its role in American democracy. The Broadcast Reform movement of the 1930s, made up of Americans from many sectors of society, including "education, labor, religion, the press, civic groups, and the intelligentsia" fought, unsuccessfully, against the "network-dominated, advertising-supported" model for radio.[9] Media reform efforts continued in the 1940s, driven by "grassroots activist groups, progressive policy makers," and members of the public who were concerned about the commercial nature of the media system.[10] In the 1960s, members of the budding civil rights movement took on issues of media reform, ultimately contributing to the establishment of the public broadcasting system and a more robust vetting of broadcasting license renewals.[11]

Organized efforts to reform the American media system ebbed and flowed for decades before emerging again in the 1990s. Following the passing of the Telecommunications Act of 1996, the American media market began a trend of intense consolidation that continues to draw criticism from advocates of a free press (see Chapter 4). In response, many scholars, activists, and members of the political Left began organizing to combat the trend of consolidation. As part of that response, McChesney and Nichols helped form one of the leading organizations of the media reform movement, appropriately named Free Press.

In 2003, Free Press began working with more established organizations to help galvanize public opinion about the concentration of media ownership and coordinate a campaign to pressure regulators and stop the FCC from further relaxing media ownership rules.[12] What many in the media reform movement realized was that media and communication policy were—and still are—important political issues, and if the public began to see them as such, they would be inclined to join the fight. What's more, they saw media reform as a non-partisan issue; all parties would benefit from a more diverse and democratic media system. At the same time, it quickly became clear that progressive groups stood to gain more by a diversified media market since their voices and causes had long been at odds with corporate interests.

This democratic potential is perhaps the primary reason why activists concerned about a variety of social issues become "media activists"—they see media channels as key to getting their message out there, but also as part of the problem of elite-driven politics and maintenance of the status quo. This complaint is validated by research examining the "protest paradigm," which suggests that members of radical or progressive social movements have trouble earning coverage by legacy media, and when they do, they often fail to frame coverage in ways that are friendly to their cause.[13] For example, coverage is more likely to focus on protestors' appearance, potential for violence, and lack of efficacy, rather than the issue(s) they seek to raise attention to. In other words, these stories "tend to contain extensive details about who was there, how they looked, what they did, and whether there were arrests. Often *why* the activists were motivated to act goes unmentioned."[14]

On the other hand, while media do tend to distort the messages of social movements, they also help call attention to the concerns raised by movement actors. Sociologist Todd Gitlin's famous study of media and the Anti-War protests of the Vietnam era, based largely upon qualitative analysis of historical documents, was perhaps the first to critically examine the limitations of media-centered activism.[15] One of Gitlin's most notable findings was that activists not only needed to attract media attention to spread awareness of their cause, but also to *shape* that attention. In this same vein, Sarah Sobieraj's study of election-focused political activism during the 2000, 2004, and 2008 presidential campaigns showed how legacy media pose challenges for social movements, but also how they can also be an invaluable asset. By combining participant-observation and interviews with media analysis, Sobieraj demonstrated how a diverse array of social movement organizations used similar strategies in their relations with news media. While activists often struggled to influence the gate-keeping and framing decisions of newsmakers—in other words, the battle to gain and shape media coverage, respectively—their own efforts were based on an assumption that doing so was worthwhile. For example, all but a few national organizations prioritized visibility over other strategies such as lobbying and engaging with existing membership, and then trea-ted "mainstream news media as the necessary pathway to this visibility."[16] However, when social movement actors failed to see their views reflected favorably or objectively in news reports, they often became media critics themselves.

### Meaning and Obscenity According to Interpretive Communities

The growth of media criticism is one reason media scholars increasingly see members of the media-consuming public as part of an "active audi-ence." Another, perhaps more prominent reason, is that media texts do not carry any specific meaning in and of themselves. Rather, as discussed in Chapter 2, Wendy Griswold's "cultural diamond" suggests that the meaning of cultural objects is highly contextual, based upon the complex relations between the creator of a cultural object and its receiver(s), all of which are situated within the broader social world.[17] Just like with art or religious texts, the people who consume media often read it to mean very different things. For example, while some see ABC's popular sitcom *Black-ish* as a positive discussion of race in contemporary America, others view it as a troubling attempt at humor that calls attention to stereotypes in ways that do little more than perpetuate them.[18] In this sense, media texts are said to be *polysemic*, or encoded with multiple meanings, which can only be uncovered through audience interaction.

As media scholars have long argued, meaning making is often facilitated by *interpretive communities*, which rely on a shared sense of purpose and are often driven by feelings of moral obligation.[19] Some interpretive communities are united by belief or identity (i.e., religious communities or political associations), while others may share a sense of place (i.e., neighborhood associations), circumstances (i.e., domestic violence support groups), interests (i.e., fans of a TV show), or some combination of these relations (i.e., parent-teacher associations). While some interpretive communities focus primarily on media as a form of culture, as illustrated by fans of ABC's *How to Get Away With Murder*, who frequently gush about their favorite show using the Twitter hashtag #HTGAWM,[20] others approach media texts as fodder for criticism and political mobilization.

Conservative organizations like the Media Research Center (mrc.org) claim that media content too often erodes American "family values." These organizations work to raise awareness of the alleged liberal biases in media with the goal of pressuring media companies to remove or revise the offending content, as the Parents Television Council (parentstv.org) did in response to the CBS sitcom, *$#*! My Dad Says*.[21] Similarly, in the 1980s there was a national debate over the growth of allegedly "obscene" media content, and for a time, much of the debate focused on "explicit" music lyrics. Led by Mary "Tipper" Gore, the wife of former Vice President Al Gore, the Parents Music Resource Center advocated for stricter regulation of the music industry. The result, a prominent but voluntary warning that read "Parental Advisory: Explicit Content," hit music labels in 1996. Just three years later, the "culture wars" amped up again following the infamous mass-shooting at Columbine High School in Littleton, Colorado, which many conservatives claimed was caused by the violent lyrics of Marilyn Manson. Although there is reason to doubt whether the allegations had any merit—when's the last time you committed mass murder because of a song?—and attempts to hold Manson accountable hardly got off the ground, the singer now credits the controversy with stifling his career.[22]

### Fighting for Change from Inside and Out

As Chapter 6 discussed, the process of gatekeeping allows producers to decide what news gets published based on their editorial guidelines. For the masses without access to editors' meetings, there are other, less direct mechanisms to shape the flow of news. Whereas letters to the editor provide a long-standing opportunity for members of the public to reach a broader audience, overt critiques of media rarely get through the gates and onto the page (now, screens). Tweeting at a news outlet may not be the most effective way to be heard, let alone to shape the news, but there is a growing body of evidence to suggest that members of the public can have a say in what stories make it into the news. Indeed, as John Carr found in his study of the spread of satirical news programs, Internet users' sharing of stories that were critical of major media companies helped push them to engage in "forced reflexivity" by covering events and critiques that challenged the influence of mass media.[23] For example, Stephen Colbert's roasting of political and news media elites during the 2006 White House Correspondents' Dinner, which was originally broadcast on C-SPAN and scarcely discussed in mainstream news outlets, later received coverage in many of the most-circulated American newspapers. Not only did these stories amplify Colbert's critique of mass media, but they often credited the viral sharing and online discussion of the video with making it newsworthy. Thus, what was true of the 1940s remains true today: media criticism and alternative media-making, like critical media studies, seek to "denaturalize the status quo by underscoring its contingency."[24] This is often done by calling attention to underlying ideologies and providing contrasting alternatives, which may influence the perceptions of other audience members, and perhaps play a role in shaping future coverage.

Don't worry if much of this comes as a surprise to you. How would you know? Unless you're an insider in a major media corporation or know someone who is, you're inherently reliant upon them to report on news about their own industry, and even their own organization. They rarely do. In fact, very few news organizations have a "news" or "media" beat—such topics are typically wrapped into the "business" section, and framed accordingly—and those that do rarely go beyond emphasizing the limitations of their competitors. (Think: How MSNBC or CNN report on Fox News, and vice versa.) They are even less likely to provide significant space for criticism of their own coverage.

As a consequence, media activists have long been accustomed to "watching the watchers," adapting innovative strategies to critique or expand common media frames and ownership patterns. One prominent strategy, which media scholar Axel Bruns has termed "gatewatching," entails "the republishing, publicising, contextualisation and curation of existing material" through Facebook and Twitter, blogs, and in the comment sections of news websites[25] The use of social media and popular hashtags provides a significant opportunity for members of the active audience to engage publicly and socially in acts of media criticism, and this is a form of gatewatching. For example, following NBC Nightly News anchor Brian Williams' demonstrably false statements about being in a helicopter that was shot down during the Iraq War, members of the public called on NBC to correct the record and censure Williams. While this case received more media attention than most—Williams was a celebrity, after all—it illustrates how individual and collective efforts can combine to shape the actions of media institutions.

To the extent that traditional media gatekeepers resist the frames of media activists, they often opt to engage in their own forms of media-making. Thus, while gatewatching does not require the creation of new(s) content, there is room for that strategy, too. Accordingly, Bruns coined the term "gatecrashing" to refer to the use of media to produce and disseminate original content without relying on traditional gatekeepers.[26] But gatecrashing is hardly a new phenomenon, as media activists have long created "alternative media" such as newsletters, zines, pirate radio, podcasts, blogs and vlogs. Today, social media platforms provide opportunities for the dissemination of media messages as well as the building of ties with other media activists, whether local, national, or global.

## Resist! Cultural, Legal, and Political Approaches to Reform

Media scholar danah boyd has argued that social media are powerful in part because they provide platforms for people to create their own representations, and to share them with a potentially large audience.[27] While these capabilities are important for most forms of communication, they are especially integral to activists trying to gain exposure and support for their cause. The popularity of social media platforms such as Twitter provide new opportunities for coordinated action. For example, the application Thunderclap (www.thunderclap.it) provides a platform for organizers to strategically plan social media messaging campaigns that increases their likelihood of "going viral." Inspired by the act of nature that is "sharp, loud, or sudden," the tool works in much the same way as crowdfunding and online petition sites like Kickstarter or Change.org, which allow organizers to create a petition that Internet users can support in just a few clicks.[28] But instead of donating money or a signature, Thunderclap allows supporters to lend their social media pages to the cause. The result is a grassroots mass-messaging campaign that increases the volume of a message by synchronizing many voices across multiple social media platforms.

Though they probably didn't use Thunderclap, the #OscarsSoWhite hashtag campaign succeeded at its first-order objective, which was to call attention to the lack of diversity in the Academy Awards.[29] What constitutes "success" in the context of media activism is most certainly debatable. While the #OscarsSoWhite effort was too little, too late to have a direct effect on the 2015 and 2016 awards, there was a clear shift in the diversity of nominees and award winners in 2017 and 2018.[30] Like other episodic efforts that escalate through the use of social media hashtags, #OscarsSoWhite was a reactionary, not-so-organized method of calling attention to issues of inequality in Hollywood and elsewhere in American media.[31] This spans far beyond awards ceremonies to include the roles and representations most often available to minority actors. Of course, many others have been working on this issue too, including a number of Hollywood insiders.

In her book *Reel Inequality*, sociologist Nancy Yuen documents Hollywood's role in perpetuating racial stereotypes and, through qualitative interviews with minority and non-minority actors, considers their efforts to change these trends.[32] One Japanese American actor told her director that the traditional ethnic dress her character was supposed to wear was unrealistic: "I'm running a store. I work like fourteen hours a day. I'm not going to wear those little silk kimonos." In the end, the director listened and approved the costume change "based not on its racist representation of Asians but on its implausibility as a storeowner's outfit."[33] Indeed, from negotiating costumes to revising scripts, many minority actors strive to defy stereotypes from the inside, while others turn down stereotypical roles altogether. Both of these strategies, though, are disproportionately available to more successful actors who have enough "screw-you money," as one actor put it, to turn down a role.[34] Another increasingly popular strategy, and one that is likely to attract less prominent actors, involves creating independent films or web videos that circumvent the traditional media gatekeepers.

What these two examples demonstrate, yet again, is that media-focused activism is both an individual and collective endeavor. Both strategies have an important role to play. Although collaboration is not required to engage in critique, the more coordinated the reform effort is, the more likely it is to be sustained, and therefore to achieve its goals. Whereas the individual acts of resistance and negotiation by Hollywood actors function as grassroots efforts to improve media from the inside, collective actions sparked by efforts like #OscarsSoWhite, along with other projects to educate the public on inequality in American media, play an important role in raising awareness of the issue, thus creating opportunities for change from the outside. As will be clear in the next section, the latter strategy is common amongst other media reform efforts.

## The Revolution Will (No Longer) Be Tweeted: The Fight for a Free Internet

Since the emergence of the social web there has been a healthy debate about whether or not, or to what extent, digital forms of communication such as the Internet, mobile phones and social media, afford greater opportunities for democratic participation. Within this debate, arguments fall along a spectrum ranging from those who are *optimists* about the web's role in political action to those who are *pessimists*, while more *ambivalent* or *realist* positions fall somewhere in the middle.[35]

Similarly, debates over the efficacy of so-called "slacktivism," a term used by technological pessimists to refer to Internet-focused forms of advocacy and activism that have limited or unknown influence beyond the Internet, find ample evidence in the fight for a free Internet. Communications scholars have found, on the one hand, that online forms of organizing are critically important to the eventual successes of the movement to shape Internet policy in the public interest.[36] On the other hand, there is evidence to suggest that web-centric efforts may struggle to carry over to policy debates and decisions, especially when driven by online petitions and form letters.[37]

But what happens when the public exists primarily in online spaces? In other words, how do activists for a free and open Internet organize without the Internet? This is not meant to be a riddle, but rather a practical question that many Internet activists have had to wrangle with. Of course, every person on the Internet is also a person off the Internet. And while it is possible to reach them through other means, it is hard to overlook the fact that the easiest way to reach the Internet's most passionate users—those who are most dedicated to upholding its cause—is through the Internet itself. That's exactly what organizers did when the battle to "save the internet" began in 2011. The movement was concerned with a variety of regulatory issues, including online privacy, censorship, and so-called "Net Neutrality."

As discussed in Chapter 5, Net Neutrality refers to regulatory policy that guarantees all Internet users have access to online information that is free from unnecessary throttling, censorship, or paid prioritization. After the FCC announced its plan to repeal Net Neutrality in late 2017, a coalition of pro-Internet organizations (battleforthenet.org) helped concerned citizens contact their congressional representatives and encouraged them to submit public comments to the FCC's online system. Through a related website (veizonprotests.com) and social media sites, the coalition also organized protests at Verizon stores nationwide. On December 7, 2017, thousands of protestors gathered at over 700 stores in response to the company's stance against Net Neutrality as well as their ties to FCC chairman Ajit Pai, a former Verizon lawyer.[38] Just a week after the protests, the FCC voted to overturn Net Neutrality. Nevertheless, the issue is far from settled, and is likely to remain a flashpoint of media activism for years to come.

Another subject of intense political action was the Stop Online Piracy Act (SOPA). While supporters described SOPA as an effort to protect intellectual property through copyright enforcement, critics argued that the bill gave copyright holders, which were often large media corporations, far-reaching powers to block or shut down websites or platforms that hosted or shared even a single copy of illegal content.[39] In response, activists and advocates for an open Internet began coordinating actions with ally organizations and companies, including Google, Amazon, and Facebook. Their strategies included online petitions, phone and email campaigns, online videos, websites, and viral memes. But perhaps the most extraordinary act took place on January 18, 2012, when in a symbolic "day of darkness," many popular websites were voluntarily shut down in protest. Famously, websites like Wikipedia—the fifth most popular site on the web—went dark in protest of the proposed bill.[40]

Similar actions followed in other parts of the world, including Canada, the European Union, and India. In India, the battle over Net Neutrality took a unique turn. The public was forced with a choice over whether or not to allow (non-neutral) Internet discrimination in exchange for free Internet. In the early 2010s, media companies such as Facebook partnered with cell phone service providers to provide toll-free or "zero-rating" Internet access, but the plan had some important restrictions. While supporters of this proposal argued that many low-income users could benefit from subsidized access to the Internet, critics had a different perspective. They argued that relegating some to limited web access—a so-called "walled garden" that only allowed them to access certain, provider-approved sites—was less about information equality and more about allowing media companies like Facebook to profit off of users' data and attention.

Prior to the regulatory ruling by the Telecom Regulatory Authority of India—the country's equivalent of the FCC—India's own Save the Internet Coalition (SaveTheInternet.in) facilitated a massive effort to uphold Net Neutrality by helping generate over 1 million emails to legislators.[41] Mobilizations like this eventually led to a blocking of the legislation and an end to Facebook's zero-rating efforts in India, at least temporarily. But while the coordinated effort to uphold Net Neutrality in India may have been a win for Internet activists, the country, like countless others, must

*Figure 11.3* Screenshot of Wikipedia during the Stop SOPA Blackout

[Source: Wikipedia, Pseudoanonymous at English. 2012. English Version of Wikipedia During the January 18, 2012 Blackout Licensed under Creative Commons (CC BY-SA 3.0)]

still address issues of inequality, literacy, and Internet access. Overall, this example, like others in this section, demonstrates the augmented nature of life in a digital age—what happens online invariably shapes what happens offline, and vice versa. Accordingly, efforts to regulate media, even the Internet, require a consideration of many social issues, including how various inequalities and special interests can limit individuals' access, and therefore shape their experience in profound yet invisible ways.

## Media Activism Beyond Borders

One of the defining features of a globalized society is the sharing of goods and services across state lines, often by large, transnational corporations. In the digital age, where content is hosted on networked servers and can easily be shared across the globe, it is easy to see why media reform and accountability is also a global issue. The debates over "cultural imperialism" demonstrate one reason why: what happens in one cultural context inevitably has implications for others.

*Imperialism* occurs when one nation takes control of another nation's territory. In the realm of media, however, the issue is not occupying land but influencing culture. Imagine how a traditional Chinese grandmother might feel about walking down the street she's lived on for decades to find it is now lined with billboards advertising American fast-food, clothing, and movies. Or, imagine how you might feel if you went to the movie theater and found that half of the films showing—the ones that your friends are most likely to see—are foreign. Not only are these films unlikely to have actors that look and speak like you, but they also tend to present a worldview quite different than what's considered normal in your home country. This, in a nutshell, is *cultural imperialism*.

The American film industry, which has long been atop the global market, is a classic example. Although it is difficult to measure the spread of cultural values, let alone to trace a causal chain of effects from popular Hollywood films, numerous studies have documented the prominence of American media across much of our globalized world. In 2009, Hollywood studios solely produced 13 of the 20 highest grossing films according to worldwide box office earnings, and the remaining seven were produced in collaboration with studios from other Western nations.[42] Given that global sales accounted for over 70% of American made films' box office revenue in 2016, it is clear Hollywood continues to dominate.[43]

Despite the international success of American media, there are a number of reasons to question the cultural imperialism thesis.[44] First, although film may be the most illustrative example of cultural imperialism, it is hardly representative. The most popular TV programs, for example, are far more likely to be produced locally. Second, while concerns about cultural imperialism often assume a homogenous culture being invaded by outsiders—a common trope in many science fiction films—in reality, national cultures are often quite diverse to begin with. Furthermore, the flow of media and culture in today's global marketplace is not simply one-way. On the one hand, the rapid expansion of video streaming services like Netflix, Hulu, and Amazon Prime (all American companies) provide greater opportunity to spread American media and culture across the globe, and they undoubtedly do. At the same time, they also expose American audiences to foreign media. British television series like *Sherlock* and *Black Mirror* quickly gained popularity in the U.S., as have other shows like *Shameless*, *The Office* and *House of Cards*, which were re-created for American audiences based on their success abroad. While many countries, especially those with smaller film industries, tend to import more than they export, the flow is decisively multidirectional.[45] In other words, although the channels of influence may not be equal, the point is that cultural imperialism, if we can even call it that, is increasingly a two-way street.

Third, as we have already shown, audiences are hardly passive victims of overreaching imperialism. On the contrary, they play an active role in consuming and interpreting media. Finally, as described above, media activists have long fought the spread of corporate media, and much of this resistance may be in response to the unwanted spread of media products (with their accordant cultural values) across borders. Nation-states, on the other hand, are more likely to take direct action. While the U.S. government has negotiated free trade agreements with many nations, including Australia, Canada, China, Colombia, Israel, Korea, Malaysia, South Africa, and many others, which pave the way for Hollywood films to hit box offices across the globe, these agreements often include clearly defined limits.[46] For example, China has recently limited the number of American films shown in its theaters to 34 per year, or 25% of national box office revenue, in order to protect their culture, and their economy, from too much American influence. Nevertheless, some suggest these restrictions are soon likely to be loosened significantly.[47]

The battle for control of media beyond borders is a matter of concern for the Internet as well. As former journalist and Internet freedom advocate Rebecca MacKinnon argues, the spread of media and communication technologies across the globe means that efforts to reform them must also be global in scope. One such project, which is directed by MacKinnon and supported by the non-profit think tank New America Foundation, is a corporate accountability index called Ranking Digital Rights. As a collaborative project with individuals and foundations from across the globe, Ranking Digital Rights reflects a global interest in the transparency of media companies. This is one example of how transnational organizations are working to address issues of accountability in the increasingly global media industry.

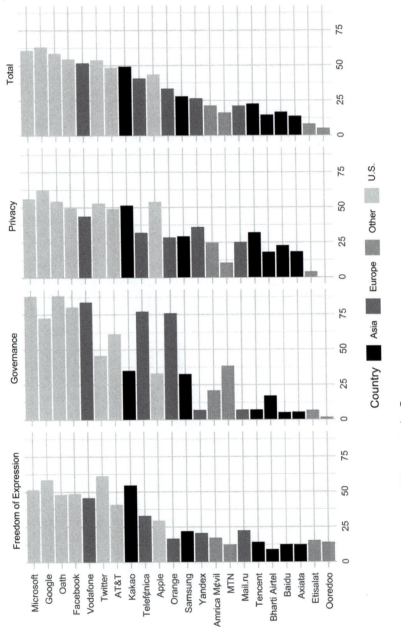

*Figure 11.4* Transparency Rankings of Companies by Category
[Source: Ranking Digital Rights, 2018]

As the title suggests, the index ranks 22 of the world's top telecommunications, Internet, and mobile companies based on their "public commitments and disclosed policies affecting users' freedom of expression and privacy."[48] While many of the companies whose headquarters are in the U.S. are ranked among the top, even the best ranking is a mere 63 out of 100, meaning that telecommunications companies across the board have a long way to go before they live up to the promise of transparency.[49] Of course, transparency is just the first step toward providing publics the information they need to make informed choices, whether as voters, consumers, or both.

### The Future of Social Media (Reform)

Despite the diversity of approaches discussed in this chapter, what each of these efforts have in common—the use of media to call attention to problems with the media—is what makes them part of the media reform movement. Most media reform efforts are "meta," in the sense that they are both *with* and *about* media. And together, these efforts form a kind of collective movement.

Of course, this chapter has shown that the methods for seeking media reform are as diverse as the goals themselves. While some emphasize the use or critique of traditional and non-digital media, others strategically employ these tools, and some do so to the near-exclusion of other forms. Accordingly, collective actions such as hashtag campaigns function as a form of gatewatching that blur the boundaries between individual and collective forms of resistance. Furthermore, the media-making and distribution practices demonstrated by Hollywood actors and citizen activists alike, which often take place on digital platforms like YouTube, demonstrate the thinning line between "makers" and "breakers" discussed in Chapter 6.

While many media critics and pop-psychologists focus on what they characterize as a terrible irony underlying the landscape of contemporary media—social media being used in seemingly anti-social ways—this chapter, like many others throughout this book, makes it clear just how crucial media are to the democratic process. But how networked publics will use them, and to what ends, remains to be seen. Still, it is abundantly clear that people are searching for ways to navigate our increasingly media-saturated society.[50] Some become avid consumers, striving to differentiate between the valuable content and everything else. Some become makers, creating their own media as a means of personal expression, social connection, and often, capital generation. Some become activists, struggling to stand out among the cacophony of voices in order to raise awareness of mass media's many inadequacies. Although each of these strategies is admirable, much of the potential for media, whether traditional or digital, depends on the political, economic, and cultural factors that span beyond any one individual, platform, or medium.

If Marshall McLuhan was correct in his famous assertion that "the medium is the message," then how media are structured matters a great deal in terms of how they are used.[51] Thus, to the extent that media will remain a platform for rebellion, rather than a mere target of it, it will be because the public and the platforms remain open channels for diverse and multidirectional communication. Such media and technological structures do not guarantee an active, participatory democracy, but in today's digital world, they play an increasingly important role in making it possible (or not). This realization begs the question underlying the final chapters of this book: Are we robots, or are we rebels?

## Notes

1  Cultures of Resistance Films. 2011. "The Yes Men: Pranksters Against War (USA)." Retrieved February 3, 2017. Available at: www.youtube.com/watch?v=AtYs6nARrHc.
2  Harold, Christine. 2004. "Pranking Rhetoric: 'Culture Jamming' as Media Activism." *Critical Studies in Media Communication* 21(3):189–211. Page 192.
3  Martin, Geoff and Erin Steuter. 2010. *Pop Culture Goes to War: Enlisting and Resisting Militarism in the War on Terror.* Lexington Books.
4  Anon. n.d. "EnvironMENTAL — Adbusters | Journal of the Mental Environment." Retrieved January 11, 2019. Available at: https://web.archive.org/web/20150612203157/http://www.adbusters.org/spoofads/environmental.
5  For example, see the Google Images search for "this is a meme": www.google.com/search?safe=active&tbm=isch&q=%22this+is+a+meme%22&cad=h.
6  Jones, Jeffrey M. 2018. "U.S. Media Trust Continues to Recover From 2016 Low." *Gallup.com*, October 12. Retrieved February 25, 2019. Available at: https://news.gallup.com/poll/243665/media-trust-continues-recover-2016-low.aspx.
7  Barthel, Michael and Jeffrey Gottfried. 2016. "Majority of U.S. Adults Think News Media Should Not Add Interpretation to the Facts." *Pew Research Center*, November 18. Retrieved March 13, 2017. Available at: www.pewre search.org/fact-tank/2016/11/18/news-media-interpretation-vs-facts/.
8  McChesney, Robert W. and John Nichols. 2005. "Creation of the Media Democracy Reform Movement." In Alan Curtis (ed.), *Patriotism, Democracy, and Common Sense: Restoring America's Promise at Home and Abroad.* Rowman and Littlefield, pp. 367–375.
9  McChesney, Robert Waterman. 1993. *Telecommunications, Mass Media, and Democracy: The Battle for the Control of U.S. Broadcasting, 1928–1935.* New York: Oxford University Press, p. 3.
10  Pickard, Victor. 2014. *America's Battle for Media Democracy: The Triumph of Corporate Libertarianism and the Future of Media Reform.* Cambridge University Press, p. 3.
11  Pickard, Victor. 2016. "Waves of Struggle: The History and Future of American Media Reform." In *Strategies for Media Reform, International Perspectives.* Fordham University Press, pp. 207–22. Retrieved April 6, 2017. Available at: www.jstor.org/stable/j.ctt1ctxqc9.20.
12  McChesney, Robert Waterman. 2007. *Communication Revolution: Critical Junctures and the Future of Media.* New Press.
13  Chan, Joseph M., and Chi-Chuan Lee. 1984. "The Journalistic Paradigm on Civil Protests: A Case Study of Hong Kong." In A. Arno and W. Dissanayake

(ed.), *The News Media in National and International Conflict*. Boulder, CO: Westview, pp. 183–202.

14 Sobieraj, Sarah. 2011. *Soundbitten: The Perils of Media-Centered Political Activism*. 5/14/11 edition. New York: NYU Press, p. 77.

15 Gitlin, Todd. 1980. *The Whole World Is Watching: Mass Media in the Making & Unmaking of the New Left*. University of California Press.

16 Sobieraj, 2011. Page 48.

17 Griswold, Wendy. 2012. *Cultures and Societies in a Changing World*. Thousand Oaks, CA: Sage.

18 Slaton, Joyce. 2014. "Black-Ish — TV Review." *Common Sense Media*. Retrieved February 16, 2018. Available at: https://www.commonsensemedia.org/tv-reviews/black-ish/user-reviews/adult.

Waters, Frances Cudjoe. 2014. "'Black-Ish': Horrible Parody of Black Family Life." *Huffington Post*. Retrieved February 16, 2018. Available at: www.huffing tonpost.com/frances-cudjoe-waters/blackish-horrible-parody-_b_5882622.html.

19 Rlindlof, Thomas. 2002. "Interpretive Community: An Approach to Media and Religion." *Journal of Media and Religion* 1(1):61–74.

20 Williams, Apryl and Vanessa Gonlin. 2017. "I Got All My Sisters with Me (on Black Twitter): Second Screening of How to Get Away with Murder as a Discourse on Black Womanhood." *Information, Communication & Society* 20(7):984–1004.

21 Abrams, Natalie. 2010. "Parents Council Protests CBS' $#*! My Dad Says." *TVGuide.Com*. Retrieved February 16, 2018. Available at: www.tvguide.com/news/parents-protests-cbs-1018806/.

22 Petridis, Alexis. 2017. "'Columbine Destroyed My Entire Career': Marilyn Manson on the Perils of Being the Lord of Darkness." *The Guardian*, September 21. Retrieved February 16, 2018. Available at: www.theguardian.com/music/2017/sep/21/columbine-destroyed-my-entire-career-marilyn-manson-on-the-perils-of-being-the-lord-of-darkness.

23 Carr, John. 2012. "No Laughing Matter: The Power of Cyberspace to Subvert Conventional Media Gatekeepers." *International Journal of Communication* 6(0):21. Page 2826.

24 Pickard, 2014. Page 2.

25 Bruns, Axel. 2014. "Gatekeeping, Gatewatching, Real-Time Feedback: New Challenges for Journalism." *Brazilian Journalism Research* 10(2 EN):224–37. Page 231.

26 Bruns, 2014.

27 boyd, danah. 2014. *It's Complicated: The Social Lives of Networked Teens*. New Haven, CT, USA: Yale University Press.

28 Anon. n.d. Retrieved March 24, 2017. Available at: www.merriam-webster.com/dictionary/thunderclap.

29 While the hashtag appears to have started in early 2015, it did not "go viral" until the 2016 Academy Award nominees were announced: https://trends.google.com/trends/explore?q=%23oscarssowhite.

30 Dockterman, Eliana. 2017. "Diversity at the 2017 Oscars: These Are the Records That Were Just Broken." *Time*, January 24. Retrieved January 11, 2019. Available at: http://time.com/4645315/oscar-nominations-2017-diversity/.

VanDerWerff, Todd. 2018. "2 Years after #OscarsSoWhite, the Academy's Diversity Efforts Seem to Be Working—Slowly." *Vox*, March 1. Retrieved January 11, 2019. Available at: www.vox.com/2018/3/1/17065160/oscars-diversity-2018.

31  Opam, Kwame. 2017. "#OscarsSoWhite Creator April Reign: 'There's Still a Lot of Work to Be Done'." *The Verge.* Retrieved March 29, 2017 Available at: www.theverge.com/2017/2/3/14490632/academy-awards-2017-oscars-so-white-april-reign-diversity-interview.

32  Yuen, Nancy Wang. 2016. *Reel Inequality: Hollywood Actors and Racism.* Rutgers University Press. Retrieved March 24, 2017. Available at: www.jstor.org/stable/j.ctt1kc6jvm.

33  Yuen, 2016. Page 108–9.

34  Yuen, 2016. Page 123.

35  Kidd, Dustin and Keith McIntosh. 2016. "Social Media and Social Movements." *Sociology Compass* 10(9):785–94.

36  Faris, Robert, Hal Roberts, Bruce Etling, Dalia Othman, and Yochai Benkler. 2016. "Net Neutrality| The Role of the Networked Public Sphere in the U.S. Net Neutrality Policy Debate." *International Journal of Communication* 10(0):26.

37  Obar, Jonathan A. 2016. "Net Neutrality| Closing the Technocratic Divide? Activist Intermediaries, Digital Form Letters, and Public Involvement in FCC Policy Making." *International Journal of Communication* 10(0):24.

38  Burns, Janet. 2017. "Thousands Braved The Cold Outside Verizon Stores Yesterday — Here's Why [PHOTOS]." *Forbes,* December 8. Retrieved February 21, 2018. Available at: www.forbes.com/sites/janetwburns/2017/12/08/thousands-braved-the-cold-outside-verizon-stores-yesterday-heres-why/.
    Free Press. 2017. "Verizon Protests Today at 700 Locations Nationwide as People Rise Up Against Ajit Pai's Plan to Undo Net Neutrality." *Free Press,* December 7. Retrieved February 22, 2018 Available at: www.freepress.net/press-release/108493/verizon-protests-today-700-locations-nationwide-people-rise-against-ajit-pais-plan.

39  Reitman, Rainey. 2016. "Electronic Frontier Foundation: Lessons from the SOPA Fight." In Freedman, Des, Jonathan Obar, Cheryl Martens, and Robert W. McChesney (eds.), *Strategies for Media Reform: International Perspectives,* 1 edition. New York: Fordham University Press, pp. 92–99.

40  Anon. n.d. "Alexa Top 500 Global Sites." Retrieved January 11, 2019 Available at: https://www.alexa.com/topsites.

41  Mukerjee, Subhayan. 2016. "Net Neutrality, Facebook, and India's Battle to #SaveTheInternet." *Communication and the Public* 1(3):356–61.

42  Crane, Diana. 2014. "Cultural Globalization and the Dominance of the American Film Industry: Cultural Policies, National Film Industries, and Transnational Film." *International Journal of Cultural Policy* 20(4):365–82.

43  "2016 Theatrical Market Statistics Report." March 2017. *Motion Picture Association of America.* Retrieved February 23, 2018. www.mpaa.org/wp-content/uploads/2017/03/MPAA-Theatrical-Market-Statistics-2016_Final-1.pdf

44  Sparks, Colin. 2012. "Media and Cultural Imperialism Reconsidered." *Chinese Journal of Communication* 5(3):281–99.

45  Crane, Diana. 2014.

46  Crane, Diana. 2014.

47  Brzeski, Patrick. 2017. "China's Quota on Hollywood Film Imports Set to Expand, State Media Says." *The Hollywood Reporter,* February 9. Retrieved February 16, 2018 Available at: www.hollywoodreporter.com/news/chinas-state-media-says-quota-hollywood-film-imports-will-expand-974224.

48  Anon. n.d. "2017 Corporate Accountability Index." *Ranking Digital Rights.* Retrieved January 11, 2019 Available at: https://rankingdigitalrights.org/index2017/.

49 Anon. n.d. "2018 Corporate Accountability Index." *Ranking Digital Rights*. Retrieved January 11, 2019 Available at: https://rankingdigitalrights.org/index2018/.

50 Gitlin, Todd. 2007. *Media Unlimited, Revised Edition: How the Torrent of Images and Sounds Overwhelms Our Lives*. Revised edition. New York: Picador.

51 McLuhan, Marshall. 1994. *Understanding Media: The Extensions of Man*. Cambridge, MA: MIT press.

# Recommended Resources for *All Media Are Social*

## Chapter 1

Brienza, Casey and Matthias Revers. 2016. "The Field of American Media Sociology: Origins, Resurrection, and Consolidation." *Sociology Compass* 10(7):539–52.

Davis, Jenny L. 2017. "Designing Emotion: How Facebook Affordances Give Us The Blues." *Cyborgology*, December 20. Available at: https://thesocietypages.org/cyborgology/2017/12/20/designing-emotion-how-facebook-affordances-give-us-the-blues/.

Jurgenson, Nathan. 2012, June 28. "The IRL Fetish." *The New Inquiry*. Retrieved February 12, 2019. Available at: https://thenewinquiry.com/the-irl-fetish/.

Nardi, Peter M. 2017, August 21. "False Balance, Binary Discourse, and Critical Thinking." *University of California Press Blog*. Retrieved January 29, 2018. Available at: www.ucpress.edu/blog/29416/false-balance-binary-discourse-and-critical-thinking/.

## Chapter 2

Askin, Noah and Michael Mauskapf. 2017. "What Makes Popular Culture Popular? Product Features and Optimal Differentiation in Music." *American Sociological Review* 82(5):910–44.

Chayko, Mary. 2014. "Techno-social Life: The Internet, Digital Technology, and Social Connectedness." *Sociology Compass* 8(7):976–91.

Eldridge, Scott A. 2018. "'Thank god for Deadspin': Interlopers, Metajournalistic Commentary, and Fake News through the Lens of 'Journalistic Realization.'" *New Media & Society*.

Podcast: "Nina Jacobson: How to Make a Hit in Hollywood." 2018, October 22. *Without Fail*. Available at: www.gimletmedia.com/without-fail/nina-jacobson-how-to-make-a-hit-in-hollywood.

Reese, Stephen D. and Pamela J. Shoemaker. 2016. "**A Media Sociology for the Networked Public Sphere: The Hierarchy of Influences Model." *Mass Communication and Society* 19(4):389–410.

## Chapter 3

Adorno, Theodor W. 1946 (2005). "The Culture Industry." In *The Culture Industry: Selected Essays on Mass Culture*. New York: Routledge.

Aelst, Peter Van, Jesper Strömbäck, Toril Aalberg, Frank Esser, Claes de Vreese, Jörg Matthes, David Hopmann, Susana Salgado, Nicolas Hubé, Agnieszka Stępińska, Stylianos Papathanassopoulos, Rosa Berganza, Guido Legnante, Carsten Reinemann, Tamir Sheafer, and James Stanyer. 2017. "Political Communication in a High-Choice Media Environment: A Challenge for Democracy?" *Annals of the International Communication Association* 41(1):3–27.

Bakker, Piet. 2012. "Aggregation, Content Farms and Huffinization." *Journalism Practice* 6(5–6):627–37.

Benson, Rodney and Matthew Powers. 2011, February. *Public Media and Political Independence: Lesson for the Future of Journalism from Around the World.* Free Press. Available at: http://rodneybenson.org/wp-content/uploads/Benson-Powers-2011-public-media-and-political-independence-1.pdf.

Jacob, Mark. 2019. *Medill Study Identifies 'Paradigm Shift' in How Local News Serves Readers.* Evanston, IL: Northwestern University. Available at: https://localnewsinitiative.north western.edu/posts/2019/02/05/northwestern-subscriber-data/index.html.

Littau, Jeremy. 2019. "Why Do All These Media Layoffs Keep Happening? A Thread." *Medium.* Retrieved February 6, 2019. Available at: https://medium.com/@jeremylit tau/why-do-all-these-media-layoffs-keep-happening-a-thread-34b4b4edbe8c.

Nixon, Brice. 2017. "The Business of News in the Attention Economy: Audience Labor and MediaNews Group's Efforts to Capitalize on News Consumption." *Journalism.* doi:10.1177/1464884917719145.

Podcast: Vedantam, Shankar, Rhaina Cohen, and Tara Boyle. 2018. "Starving The Watchdog: Who Foots The Bill When Newspapers Disappear?" *Hidden Brain | NPR*, December 10. www.npr.org/2018/12/09/675092808/starving-the-watchdog-who-foots-the-bill-when-newspapers-disappear.

Rossman, Gabriel. 2011. "Gettin' Down on 'Friday.'" *Contexts* 10(4):68–69.

Stulberg, Ariel. 2017. "In Paywall Age, Free Content Remains King for Newspaper Sites." *Columbia Journalism Review.* Retrieved January 27, 2018. Available at: www. cjr.org/business_of_news/newspaper-paywalls.php.

## Chapter 4

Bailard, Catie Snow. 2016. "Corporate Ownership and News Bias Revisited: Newspaper Coverage of the Supreme Court's Citizens United Ruling." *Political Communication* 33(4):583–604.

Benson, Rodney, Timothy Neff, and Mattias Hessérus. 2018. "Media Ownership and Public Service News: How Strong Are Institutional Logics?" *The International Journal of Press/Politics* 23(3):275–98.

Fuchs, Christian. 2018. "Propaganda 2.0: Herman and Chomsky's Propaganda Model in the Age of the Internet, Big Data and Social Media." In: Pedro-Carañana, J., Broudy, D. and Klaehn, J. (eds.). *The Propaganda Model Today: Filtering Perception and Awareness.* pp. 71–92. London: University of Westminster Press. doi:10.16997/ book27.f. License: CC-BY-NC-ND 4.0.

Gamson, Joshua and Pearl Latteier. 2004. "Do Media Monsters Devour Diversity?" *Contexts* 3(3):26–32.

Jensen, Robert. 2015. "American Journalism's Ideology: Why the 'Liberal' Media is Fundamentalist." *Resilience.* Retrieved September 17, 2018 (www.resilience.org/stor

ies/2015-06-11/american-journalism-s-ideology-why-the-liberal-media-is-funda
mentalist/).

Rohlinger, Deana and Jennifer M. Proffitt. 2017. "How Much Does Ownership
Matter? Deliberative Discourse in Local Media Coverage of the Terri Schiavo Case."
*Journalism* 18(10):1274–91.

Rossman, Gabriel. 2004. "Elites, Masses, and Media Blacklists: The Dixie Chicks
Controversy." *Social Forces* 83(1):61–79.

Video: Al Jazeera English. 2017. "Noam Chomsky – The 5 Filters of the Mass Media
Machine." Available at: www.youtube.com/watch?v=34LGPIXvU5M&t=8s.

Video: Beme News. 2018, March 28. *Fake News in Mexico.* Available at: www.youtube.
com/watch?v=gI6fE75Bnc4&feature=youtu.be.

Website: www.cjr.org/resources.

## Chapter 5

Bamford, James. 2013, August 15. "They Know Much More Than You Think."
*New York Review of Books.* Available at: www.nybooks.com/articles/2013/08/15/
nsa-they-know-much-more-you-think/.

Clayman, Steven E., John Heritage, Marc N. Elliott, and Laurie L. McDonald. 2007.
"When Does the Watchdog Bark? Conditions of Aggressive Questioning in
Presidential News Conferences." *American Sociological Review* 72(1):23–41.

MacKinnon, Rebecca. 2013. *Consent of the Networked: The Worldwide Struggle for Internet
Freedom.* New York, NY: Basic Books.

Map: "Status of Net Neutrality Around the World." Retrieved January 27, 2018. Available
at: https://dejiaccessnow.carto.com/viz/4f239c60-356f-11e5-b01c-0e853d047bba/
embed_map.

McMillan, Robert. 2014, June 23. "What Everyone Gets Wrong in the Debate Over
Net Neutrality." *WIRED.* Retrieved May 16, 2016. Available at: www.wired.com/
2014/06/net_neutrality_missing/.

Mills, Anthony, and Katharine Sarikakis 2016. "Reluctant Activists? The Impact of
Legislative and Structural Attempts of Surveillance on Investigative Journalism." *Big
Data & Society.* Available at: http://journals.sagepub.com/doi/abs/10.1177/
2053951716669381.

Pickard, Victor. 2018. "Break Facebook's Power and Renew Journalism." *The Nation,*
April 18. Retrieved February 6, 2019. Available at: www.thenation.com/article/
break-facebooks-power-and-renew-journalism/.

Video: "75 Million Americans Don't Have Internet. Here's What It's Like." 2015, January 28. *Fusion.* Retrieved January 27, 2018. Available at: www.youtube.com/
watch?v=m7I2YiobGKU.

Weissman, Cale Guthrie. 2017. "Maybe It's Time to Treat Facebook Like a Public
Utility." *Fast Company.* Retrieved January 27, 2018. Available at: www.fastcompany.
com/40414024/maybe-its-time-to-treat-facebook-like-a-public-utility.

## Chapter 6

Barnard, Stephen R. 2016. "'Tweet or Be Sacked': Twitter and the New Elements of
Journalistic Practice." *Journalism* 17(2):190–207.

Bell, Emily and Taylor Owen. 2017. "The Platform Press: How Silicon Valley Reengineered Journalism." *Columbia Journalism Review*. Retrieved June 22, 2017. Available at: www.cjr.org/tow_center_reports/platform-press-how-silicon-valley-reengineered-journalism.php.

Bielby, William T. and Denise D. Bielby. 1994. "'All Hits Are Flukes': Institutionalized Decision Making and the Rhetoric of Network Prime-Time Program Development." *American Journal of Sociology* 99(5):1287–1313.

Blanding, Michael. 2018. "Where Does Journalism End and Activism Begin?" *Nieman Reports*, August 21. Retrieved February 6, 2019. Available at: https://niemanreports.org/articles/where-does-journalism-end-and-activism-begin/.

Cline, Andrew. n.d. "Media/Political Bias." *Rhetorica.Net*. Retrieved February 7, 2019. Available at: http://rhetorica.net/bias.htm.

Inskeep, Steve. 2004. "Drummer's Book Takes Shine off Rock-Star Life." *NPR.Org*. Available at: www.npr.org/templates/story/story.php?storyId=3847612.

Krause, Monika. 2011. "Reporting and the Transformations of the Journalistic Field: US News Media, 1890–2000." *Media, Culture & Society* 33(1):89–104.

Malmelin, Nando and Mikko Villi. 2017. "Media Work in Change: Understanding the Role of Media Professionals in Times of Digital Transformation and Convergence." *Sociology Compass* 11(7):e12494.

Peiser, Jaclyn. 2019. "The Rise of the Robot Reporter." *The New York Times*, February 6. Available at: www.nytimes.com/2019/02/05/business/media/artificial-intelligence-journalism-robots.html.

Petre, Caitlin. 2015. "The Traffic Factories: Metrics at Chartbeat, Gawker Media, and The New York Times." *Columbia Journalism Review*. Retrieved June 14, 2017. Available at: www.cjr.org/tow_center_reports/the_traffic_factories_metrics_at_chartbeat_gawker_media_and_the_new_york_times.php.

Podcast: Bell, Emily and Heather Chaplin. 2019. "Can We Count On Audience Metrics?" *Tricky*, January 17. 2(5). Available at: https://journalismdesign.com/podcast/can-we-count-on-audience-metrics-2/.

Stonbely, Sarah. 2015. "The Social and Intellectual Contexts of the U.S. 'Newsroom Studies,' and the Media Sociology of Today." *Journalism Studies* 16(2):259–74.

Wiedeman, Reeves. 2015. "How The New York Times Works." *Popular Mechanics*, February 11. Retrieved February 6, 2019. Available at: www.popularmechanics.com/technology/a14030/how-the-new-york-times-works/.

Willig, Ida. 2013. "Newsroom Ethnography in a Field Perspective." *Journalism* 14(3):372–87.

# Chapter 7

Adamic, Lada A. and Natalie Glance. 2005. "The Political Blogosphere and the 2004 U.S. Election: Divided They Blog." In: *Proceedings of the 3rd International Workshop on Link Discovery, LinkKDD '05*, pp. 36–43. New York, NY: ACM.

Anderson, Janna and Lee Rainie. 2017. "The Future of Truth and Misinformation Online." *Pew Research Center: Internet, Science & Tech*. Retrieved October 19, 2017. Available at: www.pewinternet.org/2017/10/19/the-future-of-truth-and-misinformation-online/.

Barnard, Stephen R. 2018. "Tweeting #Ferguson: Mediatized Fields and the New Activist Journalist." *New Media & Society* 20(7):2252–71.

Lindner, Andrew M. 2009. "Among the Troops: Seeing the Iraq War Through Three Journalistic Vantage Points." *Social Problems* 56(1):21–48.

Robb, Amanda. 2017. "Pizzagate: Anatomy of a Fake News Scandal." *Rolling Stone.* Retrieved November 17, 2017. Available at: www.rollingstone.com/politics/news/pizzagate-anatomy-of-a-fake-news-scandal-w511904.

Roberts, David. 2017. "America is facing an epistemic crisis." *Vox.* Nov. 2. Available at: www.vox.com/policy-and-politics/2017/11/2/16588964/america-epistemic-crisis.

Rosen, Jay. 2010, November 10. "The View from Nowhere: Questions and Answers." *PressThink.* Retrieved January 28, 2018. Available at: http://pressthink.org/2010/11/the-view-from-nowhere-questions-and-answers/.

Rosen, Jay. 2011, September 15. "We Have No Idea Who's Right: Criticizing 'He Said, She Said' Journalism at NPR." *Pressthink.* Retrieved July 8, 2016. Available at: http://pressthink.org/2011/09/we-have-no-idea-whos-right-criticizing-he-said-she-said-journalism-at-npr/.

Silverman, Craig. 2017. "This is How Your Hyperpartisan Political News Gets Made." *BuzzFeed.* Retrieved December 12, 2017. Available at: www.buzzfeed.com/craigsilverman/how-the-hyperpartisan-sausage-is-made.

Video: PBS. 2018, October 29. "The Facebook Dilemma." *Frontline,* 37(4). Retrieved January 8, 2019. Available at: www.pbs.org/wgbh/frontline/film/facebook-dilemma/.

Website: Botometer: https://botometer.iuni.iu.edu/.

Website: www.worldsofjournalism.org/.

## Chapter 8

Annenberg Inclusion Initiative Available at: http://annenberg.usc.edu/research/aii and their most recent (2019) study Available at: http://assets.uscannenberg.org/docs/aii-inequality-report-2019-09-03.pdf "Inequality in 1,200 Popular Films."

Erigha, Maryann. 2015. "Race, Gender, Hollywood: Representation in Cultural Production and Digital Media's Potential for Change." *Sociology Compass* 9(1):78–89.

Google. 2017, February 17. "The Women Missing from the Silver Screen and the Technology Used to Find Them." Available at: https://about.google/main/gender-equality-films/.

McMillan Cottom, Tressie. 2015. "'Who Do You Think You Are?': When Marginality Meets Academic Microcelebrity." *Ada: A Journal of Gender, New Media, and Technology* (7). Retrieved October 12, 2017. Available at: http://adanewmedia.org/2015/04/issue7-mcmillancottom/.

Pascoe, C. J. and Sarah Diefendorf. 2019. "No Homo: Gendered Dimensions of Homophobic Epithets Online." *Sex Roles* 80(3):123–36.

Sobieraj, Sarah. 2018. "Bitch, Slut, Skank, Cunt: Patterned Resistance to Women's Visibility in Digital Publics." *Information, Communication & Society* 21(11):1700–1714.

Springer, Shira. 2019. "7 Ways to Improve Coverage of Women's Sports." *Nieman Reports,* January 7. Available at: https://niemanreports.org/articles/covering-womens-sports/.

Video: "A Brief History of Blatant Sexism on Cable News." *HuffPost.* Available at: www.huffingtonpost.com/entry/a-brief-history-of-blatant-sexism-on-cable-news_us_581285f0e4b08fac438fde92.

Video: Crenshaw, Kimberlé. 2016. *The Urgency of Intersectionality.* (www.ted.com/talks/kimberle_crenshaw_the_urgency_of_intersectionality).

Video: Smith, Stacy. 2017. The data behind Hollywood's sexism. TED Talk. Available at: www.youtube.com/watch?v=7kkRkhAXZGg.

## Chapter 9

Bjornstrom, Eileen E. S., Robert L. Kaufman, Ruth D. Peterson, and Michael D. Slater. 2010. "Race and Ethnic Representations of Lawbreakers and Victims in Crime News: A National Study of Television Coverage." *Social Problems* 57(2):269–93.

Butsch, Richard. 2003. "Ralph, Fred, Archie and Homer: Why Television Keeps Recreating the White Male Working Class Buffoon." In: Gail Dines and Jean M. Humez, eds., *Gender, Race, and Class in the Media*, pp. 575–88. Thousand Oaks, CA: Sage.

Elmasry, Mohamad Hamas and el-Nawawy. 2017. "Do Black Lives Matter?" *Journalism Practice* 11(7):857–75.

Everbach, Tracy, Meredith Clark, and Gwendelyn S. Nisbett. 2017. "#IfTheyGunnedMeDown: An Analysis of Mainstream and Social Media in the Ferguson, Missouri, Shooting of Michael Brown." *Electronic News*. doi:10.1177/1931243117697767.

Hughey, Matthew W. 2018, February 8. "Can Hollywood Separate Gold from White?" *Contexts*. Available at: https://contexts.org/blog/2018-oscars/.

Paulson, Erika L. and Thomas C. O'Guinn. 2012. "Working-Class Cast: Images of the Working Class in Advertising, 1950–2010." *The Annals of the American Academy of Political and Social Science* 644:50–69.

Schroedel, Jean Reith and Roger J. Chin. 2017. "Whose Lives Matter: The Media's Failure to Cover Police Use of Lethal Force Against Native Americans." *Race and Justice*. Advanced online publication. doi:10.1177/2153368717734614

Thakore, Bhoomi K. 2014. "Must-See TV: South Asian Characterizations in American Popular Media." *Sociology Compass* 8(2):149–56.

Video: MTV. 2018, February 7. "How Hollywood Misrepresents the Working Class Ft. Gabe Gonzalez." *Decoded*, 6(7). Retrieved March 10, 2019. Available at: www.mtv.com/episodes/ndlsid/decoded-how-hollywood-misrepresents-the-working-class-ft-gabe-gonzalez-season-6-ep-607.

## Chapter 10

Christensen, Wendy. 2012. "Torches of Freedom: Women and Smoking Propaganda – Sociological Images." *The Society Pages*, February 27. Retrieved February 5, 2019. Available at: https://thesocietypages.org/socimages/2012/02/27/torches-of-freedom-women-and-smoking-propaganda/).

Davis, Jenny L. and James B. Chouinard. 2017. "Theorizing Affordances: From Request to Refuse." *Bulletin of Science, Technology & Society*. doi:10.1177/0270467617714944.

Lewis, Paul. 2017. "'Our Minds Can Be Hijacked': The Tech Insiders Who Fear a Smartphone Dystopia." *The Guardian*, October 6. Retrieved February 6, 2019. Available at: www.theguardian.com/technology/2017/oct/05/smartphone-addiction-silicon-valley-dystopia.

Madrigal, Alexis C. 2017. "What Facebook Did to American Democracy." *The Atlantic*, October 12. Retrieved October 13, 2017. Available at: www.theatlantic.com/technology/archive/2017/10/what-facebook-did/542502/.

Oliver, Mary Beth, James P. Dillard, Keunmin Bae, and Daniel J. Tamul. 2012. "The Effect of Narrative News Format on Empathy for Stigmatized Groups." *Journalism & Mass Communication Quarterly* 89(2):205–224.

Ortiz, Michelle and Elizabeth Behm-Morawitz. 2015. "Latinos' Perceptions of Intergroup Relations in the United States." *Journal of Social Issues* 71(1):90–105.

Rothman, Lily. 2016. "Fear in America: Why We're More Afraid Than Before | Time." *Time*, January 6. Retrieved February 5, 2019. Available at: http://time.com/4158007/american-fear-history/.

Sollinger, Marc. 2017. "Full Show: Empathy and Its Consequences." *Innovation Hub | WGBH.org Blogs*. Available at: http://blogs.wgbh.org/innovation-hub/2017/8/10/full-show-empathy-and-its-consequences/.

Video: Anon. n.d. *War of the Worlds | American Experience | PBS*. Available at: www.pbs.org/wgbh/americanexperience/films/worlds/.

Video: David Hoffman. n.d. *How Americans Got Sold on Cigarettes*. Retrieved February 4, 2019. Available at: www.youtube.com/watch?v=JSdy4bdpe-E.

Video: Harris, Tristan. 2017. *How a Handful of Tech Companies Control Billions of Minds Every Day*. Retrieved January 29, 2018. Available at: www.ted.com/talks/tristan_harris_the_manipulative_tricks_tech_companies_use_to_capture_your_attention.

## Chapter 11

Amenta, Edwin, Thomas Alan Elliott, Nicole Shortt, Amber Celina Tierney, Didem Türkoğlu, and Burrel Vann. 2017. "From Bias to Coverage: What Explains How News Organizations Treat Social Movements." *Sociology Compass* 11(3):e12460.

Earl, Jennifer and Katrina Kimport. 2009. "Movement Societies and Digital Protest: Fan Activism and Other Nonpolitical Protest Online." *Sociological Theory* 27(3):220–43.

Kidd, Dustin and Keith McIntosh. 2016. "Social Media and Social Movements." *Sociology Compass* 10(9):785–94.

Löblich, Maria. 2016. "Dissent and Political Participation: The Many Faces of Communication Policy Advocacy and Activism." *Communication, Culture & Critique* 9(3):395–416.

Freedom House. 2017. "Freedom on the Net 2017: Manipulating Social Media to Undermine Democracy." *Freedom House*. Retrieved November 14, 2017. Available at: https://freedomhouse.org/report/freedom-net/freedom-net-2017.

Podcast: Ballout, Dana. 2019, February 1. "Good Morning, Kafranbel." *This American Life*. Available at: www.thisamericanlife.org/667/wartime-radio/act-two-4.

Roscigno, Vincent J. and William F. Danaher. 2001. "Media and Mobilization: The Case of Radio and Southern Textile Worker Insurgency, 1929 to 1934." *American Sociological Review* 66(1):21–48.

Shively, JoEllen. 1992. "Cowboys and Indians: Perceptions of Western Films Among American Indians and Anglos." *American Sociological Review* 57(6):725–34.

Srinivas, Lakshmi. 2002. "The Active Audience: Spectatorship, Social Relations and the Experience of Cinema in India." *Media, Culture & Society* 24(2):155–73.

Vasi, Ion Bogdan, Edward T. Walker, John S. Johnson, and Hui Fen Tan. 2015. "'No Fracking Way!' Documentary Film, Discursive Opportunity, and Local Opposition against Hydraulic Fracturing in the United States, 2010 to 2013." *American Sociological Review* 80(5):934–59.

Website: https://rsf.org/en/ranking/2018.

# Index

Note: References in *italics* are to figures, those in **bold** to tables.

21st Century Fox 56

ABC: news 47, 105; TV shows 122, 135–136, 164; *World News* 119
Abend, Gabriel 11, 23
Academy Awards 166–167
Adams, J.J. 118
Adbusters 158
Adorno, Theodor 14–15, 16, 17, 36–37
advertising 70, 146–147; and children 147; hypodermic model 147–148; online revenues *34*; product placement 39; revenue 54; social media 32–35
affordances 7
African-Americans 21–22, 106
agency 6, 79
agenda-setting 152–153
Ailes, Roger 104
Allen, Woody 16
Amazon 34, 57, 171
Amazon Prime 171
American Dream 136, 138
American News 87
American Psychological Association (APA) 147
American Sociological Association 13
anonymity-granting technology 71
Ansari, Aziz 129, 131
anti-communism 54
anti-trust laws 16, 47, 48, 57, 63
Anti-War protests 163
Apple 61, 71, 72
Arab Spring 120
*The Atlantic* 6–7, 132
AT&T 68

audience engagement 84
audiences 9, 33, 171
Austria 86
Authors United 57

Bagdikian, Ben 43, 44, 46–47
Bannon, Steve 107
Bauman, Zygmunt *et al.* 71
Baumgartner, Frank 134
BBC 38, 62
beats 82
Bechdel, Alison 113
Bechdel Test 113, 116
Beck, Glenn 103
Benkler, Yochai 16
Benson, Rodney 37–38, 78, 79
Berger, David 52–53
Berlusconi, Silvio 38
Bernays, Edward 146, 147
Berry, Jeffrey M. 104, 105
Beyoncé 119
bias 82, 164
Bielby, Denise 84
Bielby, William 84
Bigelow, Kathryn 119
*Black Panther* 4
#BlackLivesMatter 133
#BlackTwitter 148
Blumer, Jay 149
BNBC 80
Bonilla-Silva, Eduardo 126
books 8, 22, 39, 57
"bots" 109
Botwin, Nancy 117

Bourdieu, Pierre 11, 17–18, 18*f*, 23, 78, 79–80, 82
boyd, danah 166
Bradshaw, Carrie 117
brain 154–156
Breitbart, Andrew 107
Breitbart News Network 107–108
Brekhus, Wayne 131
Broadcast Reform movement 162
broadcasting licenses 64–65
Brown, Michael 132
Bruns, Axel 165, 166
Buckley, William F. 98
Bureau of Labor Statistics 134
Burkina Faso 71
*Buzzfeed* 106, 107

C-SPAN 165
cable television 29, 32, 36, 39, 40, 69, 131, 148–149
capital 79–80
capitalism 14–15, 16–17, 100
Carlin, George 68
Carr, John 165
Carr, Nicholas 154
Castells, Manuel 15–16, 161
CBS: *$#! My Dad Says* 164; Entertainment 84; news 44, 47, 80, 105
Change.org 166
Chartbeat 85
Chetiar, Inimai 151
China 70–71, 72, 145, 171
Chomsky, Noam 53, 54, 55
Christin, Angèle 86
citizen journalists 106
*Citizens United* ruling 56
civil society 80
Clark, Meredith 133
Clarke, David 94
class: and race 135; representations of 127, 128–129, 135–139; social marking 135–136
Clear Channel 45, 46, 48, 52, 64
Clinton, Bill 69
Clinton, Hillary 100, 108, 118, 131
closed systems 53
CNN 5, *83*, 165
Code of Federal Regulations 65
Colbert, Stephen 165
Columbine High School, Colorado 164
Comcast 43–44, 66
Comedy Central 69

comic books 22
common concern 15
communism 53, 54
Confucius 145
conservatism 98
constitutive choices 16
content 9, 68–70
convergence culture 84
copyright 63
Corporation for Public Broadcasting (CPB) 38, *39*, 62, 63
counter-propaganda 158
creators 13–14; cultural fields and systems 17–19; political economy 14–17
crime 135, *150*, 151
crime news 12, 21, 31, 36, 135
cultivation theory 151
cultural diamond 13, *13*; creators 13–14; cultural objects 13, 14, 19–22, 23, 163–164; receivers 13, 22–23; social world 13, 14
cultural imperialism 170–173
cultural objects 13, 14, 19–22, 23, 163–164
culture 6, 80
culture industry system 14–15, 18–19, *19*, 85
culture jamming 158–159
CW Network 36

*Deadline Hollywood* (blog) 116
DeGeneres, Ellen 122
democracy 15
Democrats 38, 51, 56, 67, 95, 98
demographic diversity 50
Department of Justice (DOJ) 48, 57, 63, 68
*Depression Quest* (video game) 117–118
deregulation 63
digital cultures 119–121
digital divide 65
digital dualism 155
digital footprints 71
digital inequalities 65–66
direct effects model 147–148
discourses 20
diversity 50–51; and media concentration 51–55; record labels 52–53
Dodd, Molly 117
Downs, Edward 117
doxa 17, 80, 82
Durkheim, Emile 11, 156

Duterte, Rodrigo 108
*Dykes to Watch Out For* (comic strip) 113

Earl, Jennifer 7
economic fundamentalism 100
economic power 53
Egypt 106, 120
El-Nawawy, Mohammed 133
Eli, Noam 48
Eliasoph, Nina 96
Ello 33
Elmasry, Mohamad 133
emergency broadcasts 45
Entman, Robert 52
Erigha, Maryann 114, 118, 127
ESPN 118
European Commission 70
European Data Protection Directive 70
Everbach, Trace 133
Ewen, Stuart 146
exemplificaion theory 153
exemplification theory 22

Facebook: diversity 51, 134; fake news
    108; "gatewatching" 165; gender 120;
    partisan media 105; revenue 32, 33,
    34–35; Stop Online Piracy 168;
    surveillance 71; use 149
fake news 54, 56, 87, 99, 108–109,
    158, *159*
false equivalency 102
Family Research Council 161
family values 164
FanDuel 44
FBI 61
Federal Communications Commission
    (FCC): access 64–67, 68; broadcasting
    licenses 64–65; content 68–70; digital
    inequalities 65–66; Fairness Doctrine
    69, 103; goals 46, 57, 62, 63–70; Net
    Neutrality 66–67, *67*, 168; ownership
    67–68, 162
Federal Trade Commission (FTC) 48, 57,
    63–70, 68
fee-based models 29–32, 36
Fejes, Fred 116, 123
feminism 21
feminist media studies 21, 23
Feministe (web site) 120
Feministing (web site) 120
Ferguson, Missouri 106, 133
field theory 17–18, *18*, 78–80

*FiveThirtyEight* 106, 107
flak 54
The Food Network 32
Foreign Intelligence Surveillance Court
    (FISA) 71
format diversity 50
Foucault, Michel 20
Fourth Amendment 71
Fox News 38, 47, 54, 56, 94, 98, 103,
    104, 105–106, 148, 149, 165
frames and framing: anti-communism
    54–55; "both sides" reporting 102; of
    class 136–138; of crime 135; episodic
    frames 153; lack of equity 128; news
    reports 152–154; of poverty 134; role
    of 130–131; thematic frames 153
Frankfurt School 14–17, 21
Franklin, Bob 86, 87
Free Press 162
*Freedom of the Press 2004 Global Survey* 38
French, David 98
Freud, Sigmund 146
FTC *see* Federal Trade Commission
fundamentalisms 100

Gallup 97
Gamergate 117, 120–121
Gamson, Joshua 50
Gannett 44
Gans, Herbert 31
*Gasland* (documentary, 2010) 152
"gatecrashing" 166
gatekeeping 18, 81, 82, 84, 85, 164–166
"gatewatching" 165
Gawker Media 85
gender and sexuality 6, 21, 113; LGBTQ
    identities in media 113, 121–123, 131;
    representing women 113, 114–121
gendertrolling 120–121
General Electric 47
Gerbner, George *et al.* 151
Germany 86
Gilens, Martin 134
Gitlin, Todd 3, 5, 37, 163
GLAAD 123
Glass, Ira 50
Glassner, Barry 135
Goffman, Erving: *Stigma* 130
Google 32, 33, 34, 40, 70, 71, 169
Gore, Mary "Tipper" 164
government 16–17
Graham, Tim 99

Gramsci, Antonio 20
Grazian, David 84
Great British Class Survey 127, 128
Grey's Anatomy 114
Griffin, Phil 104
Grindstaff, Laura 21
Griswold, Wendy 13, 19, 163–164
The Guardian 71, 121, 132
Guess, Andrew 108

Haberman, Maggie 5, 14
Habermas, Jurgen 11, 15, 16, 23, 94, 106
habitus 79–80, 82
Hachette 57
Hall, Stuart 20, 21
Hamilton, James 56
Hannity, Sean 5, 103
Hardwood, Jake 145
Harold, Christine 158
Harvard: Berkman Klein Center for
   Internet & Society 105
Hayes, Chris 104
HBO 95
hegemony 20
Herfindahl-Hirschman Index (HHI)
   48–49, **49**
Herman, Edward 53, 54, 55
Hirohito, Emperor 38
Hirsch, Paul 18–19, 19f, 85
Hispanics 21
Hitler, Adolf 147
Hollywood 114, 118–119, 122, 166–167,
   171
Homogenization Hypothesis 43, 44–47,
   52; diversity 50–51; media concentra-
   tion 47–50, 51–52
horizontal integration 44, 45
Horkheimer, Max 14
Horton, Willie 126
Hotelling-Steiner Effect 51
Hulu 171
hypodermic model 147–148

idea diversity 50
identities 21
ideology 6
#IfTheyGunnedMeDown 133, 133–134
Iñárritu, Alejandro González 118–119
inclusion 15
independence 79
India 23, 169
industry structure 19

institutional subsystem 18–19
institutions 4, 18, 96–97
intellectual property rights 16
The Intercept 107
Internet 169; access 65–67; citizen journalists 106; digital news sites 106–107;
   diversity 50; economy 16–17, 35, 40,
   62; influence 57, 74, 106; Net Neutrality 66–67, 67, 168–170; ownership
   67–68; and political action 167–171;
   Ranking Digital Rights 172, 172–173;
   regulation 65–68, 70–71; "slacktivism"
   168; Stop Online Piracy Act
   168–170, 169
Internet Service Providers (ISPs) 66
interpretive communities 164
intersectionality 118, 135
Iran 70, 71
Iraq War 47, 73, 104, 158, 165–166
isomorphism 18
Italy 38
Iyengar, Shanto 153

James, Lebron 118
Japan 37–38
Jardine, Eric 71
Jefferson, Thomas 162
Jenkins, Henry 84
Jensen, Robert 100, 101
Johnson, La David 93–94, 99, 101, 107
journalism: analytics 85–86; audience
   engagement 84; automation 86–87;
   backpack/iPhone journalists 87; conventions 82; convergence 84; data
   journalism 107; explanatory journalism
   107; the "field" 78–80; fundamentalisms 100; gatekeeping 82, 85, 164–166;
   independence 77; "junk journalism"
   87; McJournalism 86; newsrooms 84;
   norms 81–84; objectivity 79, 82, 100;
   professionalism 76–77; profit maximization 85; public service 76; purpose
   of 77–78; risk minimizatioin 84;
   routines 82
journalists: citizen journalists 106; liberal
   bias 101–103; politics of 98–101; war
   reporters 73; women 116
Jurgenson, Nathan 155

Kaniss, Phyllis 36
Katz, Elihu 149
Kelly, John 94, 99

Kendall, Diana 128–129, 135, 136
Kennedy, John F. 147–148, *148*
Kerry, John 69
Kickstarter 166
Kimport, Katrina 7
Klinenberg, Eric 44–45, 46
knowledge stores 152–153
Krugman, Paul 57

Lady Gaga 19, 119
Latteier, Pearl 50
Lauer, Matt 54
law and regulation 19
Leighton, Paul 135
Lennon, John xi
Levin, Mark 103
LGBTQ identities in media 113, 121–123, 131
liberal bias 94, 101–103
Limbaugh, Rush 69, 103
Lindner, Andrew 73
Logan, Enid 132
Lopes, Paul 53

McCain, John 131, 149
McCartney, Paul xi
McChesney, Robert 161, 162
McDonaldization 86
Macedonia 108
MacKinnon, Rebecca 172
McLuhan, Marshall 16, 17, 174
McQuail, Denis 19
Maddow, Rachel 104
Madison, James 161–162
managerial subsystem 18
manifest *vs.* latent functions 137
Manson, Marilyn 164
Mantilla, Karla 121
Marcuse, Herbert 14
market 19
market demand 31–32
market failures 63
*The Marshall Project* 106, 107
Marx, Karl 11, 14, 20, 156
mass media 9; Americans' confidence in 97, *97*; political and economic power 53; role of 3–4; social institution 6, 8; theories 11–13; *see also* cultural diamond
Mathison, Carrie 117
Matthews, Alec 71
Matthews, Chris 5, 104

mean world syndrome 151
media: defined 4; polysemic texts 164; as social institution 4; "the media" 4–5; use 3, *3*
media activism 158–161, 162–163; approaches to reform 166–170; beyond borders 170–173; fight for a free Internet 167–170; fighting for change 164–166; history 161–166; meaning and obscenity 163–164
media bias 98–103, 160, *160*
media concentration 43–44, 47–50, **49**, 51–55
media conglomerates 44
media criticism 54, 160–161; *see also* media activism
media effects 22, 145–146; agenda-setting 152–153; on the brain 154–156; cultivation theory 151; framing 152–154; hypodermic model 147–148; minimal effects 148–149; persuaders 146–147; uses and gratifications 149–151
media regulation 61
media representations 20–21
Media Research Center 100, 161, 164
Media Research Council 98
media sociology 5–8, 12–13, 80–81
media work 80–81; norms that make the news 81–84
Mediaset 38
medical dramas 114
memes 159
mental coloring 131
Merton, Robert 137
Microsoft 34
Miller *vs.* California (1973) 69
Mills, C. Wright 153
minimal effects 22, 148–149
misinformation 104
movie theaters 23, 32
movies: *Annie Hall* 16; auteur filmmakers 31; *Birdman* 119; *Breaking Bad* 36; *ET* 39; free trade agreements 171; *Get Out* 5; *Harry Potter* 19; horror movies 5; *The Hurt Locker* 119; representation of class 127, 128; representation of race 127, 128, *128*; representation of women 113, 114, *115*, 116, 118–119; *The Revenant* 119; revenue 39; *The Social Network* 32; *Star Trek* 118; *Star Wars* 29, 118; *Twilight* 113; *Zero Dark Thirty* 119; *see also* Hollywood

MSNBC 38, 54, 104–105, 148, 149, 165
Murdoch, Rupert 47, 56, 104
music industry 119, 164
Muslim cultures 120

narrowcasting 129–130
*The Nation* 103
National Association for the
  Advancement of Colored People
  (NAACP) 146
National Endowment for the Arts
  (NEA) 63
national fundamentalism 100
National Public Radio (NPR) 38, 102
*National Review* 103
National Security Agency (NSA) 71
"native advertising" 77
NBC: News 47, 54, 80, 104–105,
  165–166; "The Today Show" 43
Ness, Clifford *et al.* 154
Net Neutrality 66–67, *67*, 168–170
Netflix 34, 40, 54, 66, 171
Netherlands 86
Neveu, Erik 78
New America Foundation 171
new institutionalism 18
*New York Daily News* 35
*New York Post* 47
*The New York Times* 80, *83*, 85, 99;
  coverage 133; fake news 158, *159*; and
  gender 114, 119, 122–123; owners 56;
  and poverty 134; revenue 35–36,
  37, 77
*The New Yorker* 17, 47, 57, 117–118
News Corporation 56
Newsbusters 98, 99
NewsCorp 44
newspapers: centralization 46; circulation
  *30*, 49; content 30; ownership 55, 56;
  postage rates 161–162; representation
  of women 114, *115*, 116, 118, 119;
  representations of race 133–134; rev-
  enue 32, 35–36, 37, 40
*Newsweek* 80
Nichols, John 161, 162
Niger incident 93–94, 99, 101, 105–106,
  107, 108
Nisbett, Gwendelyn 133
Nixon, Richard 72, 147–148, *148*
non-profit status 37
North Korea 63

Norwegian Broadcasting Company
  (NRK) 38
Norwegian Media Authority (NMA) 38
NPR (National Public Radio) 38, 102
NSA (National Security Agency) 71
Nussbaum, Emily 117

Obama administration 66, 102, 107
Obama, Barack 100, 104, 118, 126, 131,
  132, 149, 158
objectivity 79, 82, 100, 101
obscenity 68, 69, 70, 164
occupational careers 19
O'Donnell, Lawrence 104
offical and elite sources 54
Okrent, Daniel 99, 122–123
Olbermann, Keith 104
open systems 53
O'Reilly, Bill 54
organization of this book 9
organization structure 19
Orwell, George: *1984* 61
#OscarsSoWhite 166–167
Our Bodies Our Blog 120
outrage rhetoric 104
owners 55–56; concentrated ownership
  43–46, 47–50, **49**, 57–58; diffused
  ownership 48; power 55; private ownership 38; profit-driven ownership 53,
  54
*Oxford English Dictionary* 4
Oxford University 108–109

Pai, Ajit 66–67, 168
Parents Music Resource Center 164
Parents Television Council 164
partisan media 54, 55, 69, 99–100,
  103–106
Patriot Act (2001) 71
payment 29; advertising-supported 32–36;
  fee-based model 29–32; media differ-
  ences 39–40; the public option 36–39
PBS (Public Broadcasting Service) 38;
  *NewsHour* 119
Peele, Jordan 5
Pelosi, Nancy 69
Pentagon 73
persuaders 146–147
Peterson, Richard A 19, 52–53
Petre, Caitlin 85
Pew Research Center 95, 99, 104, 121

Philippines 108
pirate radio stations 64–65
podcasts 85
political activism 163
political actors 72–74
political campaigns 56
political economy 14–17
political participation 96
political polarization 95, 96
political power 53
politics and social marking 131
polysemy 22–23, 164
pop music 52–53
Pope, Olivia 117
pornography 113
"post-industrial journalism" 81
post-racialism 132
postfeminism 21
Postman, Neil 156
poverty in the news 134–139
power 6, 16–17, 35, 47, 53, 55
Press, Andrea 21
press conferences 72–73
press freedom 78–79
private ownership 38
product placement 39
production of culture 9, 14, 19, 23;
    in the hands of a few 43–58;
    who pays for it? 29–40
Proffitt, Jennifer 55
profit-driven ownership 53, 54
profit maximization 85
Progressive Era 162
"propaganda model" 53–55
ProPublica 106, 107
"protest paradigm" 162–163
Public Broadcasting Service (PBS) 38, 119
public funding 37
public interest 63
"public journalism" 77
public opinion: agenda-setting 152–153;
    and fake news 87; framing 152–154;
    influences on 53, 72, 126; and Net
    Neutrality 67
public relations (PR) 146–147
public sphere 15, 94–98; political polar-
    ization 95, 96; retreat from 95, 96; TV
    politics shows 94–95
Putin, Vladimir 37
Putnam, Robert 95, 96

Quinn, Zoë 117–118, 121

race 6, 21–22, 126–127; and class 135;
    color-blind racism 126; and police
    shootings 132–133; and poverty
    134–135; representations of 127–129,
    133–134; social marking 131–135
radio 33; centralization 45–46; digital
    radio 65; FM radio 62; licenses 64–65;
    local stations 45–46; media reform 162;
    non-commercial community radio 65;
    pirate radio stations 64–65; public
    broadcasting 162; right-wing radio
    103–104; satellite radio 39; talk radio
    69; WNYC 65
Radiohead 30–31
Ranking Digital Rights 173, 171–173
rational-critical discourse 15
Reagan administration 69
receivers 13, 22–23
reception 14
record labels 52–53
Reddit.com 4, 148
reflection theory 20
regulation: access 64–67; broadcasting
    64–65; content 68–70; and the FCC
    63–70; Internet 65–68, 70–71; owner-
    ship 67–68; social media 70–71; state
    and the media 61–63, 72–74
Reiman, Jeffrey 135
Reporters Without Borders 78
representations 14; poverty in the news
    134–139; social marking 131–132; stig-
    matizing difference 130–131; see also
    class, representations of; LGBTQ iden-
    tities in media; race, representations of;
    women, representations of
Republicans 38, 51, 56, 67, 69, 95, 98,
    102–103, 104, 105
right to be forgotten 70
right to privacy 70
Rihanna 52
risk minimizatioin 84
Ritzer, George 86
Roberts, David 103
Robinov, Jeff 116
Robinson, Laura 66
Rohlinger, Deana 55
Rokeach, Milton 148–149
Romney, Mitt 99, 100, 131
Rose, Max 134
Rosen, Jay 77, 79, 84,
    101–102
Rossiya 24 37

Rossman, Gabriel 51–52
rounds 82
Rubio, Marco 99
Russia: VGTRK 37

Samberg, Andy 50
San Bernardino shooting, CA 61, 72
Sanders, Bernie 118
Sarkeesian, Anita 117
Saturday Night Live 38
Saudi Arabia 70
Sawyer, Diane 119
Scarborough, Joe 105
Schudson, Michael 35, 77–78
Scott, Ridley 61
Searls, Doc 81
selective exposure and retention
    148–149
sexual identity see LGBTQ identities in
    media
Shor, Eran 114
Silicon Valley 61
Sinclair Broadcast Group 56, 57
smartphones 6–7, 153
Smith, Stacy 117
Snowden, Edward 71
Sobieraj, Sarah 104, 105, 163
social constructions 20
social marking: and class 135–136; and
    politics 131; and poverty 134–135; and
    race 131–135
social media 4, 85, 159–160; advertising
    32–35; culture jamming 158–159;
    gatekeeping 165–166; and politicians
    73; reform 173–174; regulation of
    70–71
social movements 163
social structures 6, 14
social world 13, 14
sociology 5–8, 12, 21
Socrates 22
SOPA see Stop Online Piracy Act
Sorkin, Aaron 32
Southern Poverty Law Center 107
Spacey, Kevin 54
Spain 86
sports 36, 114, 118
Spotify 34
Sprint 68
St. Louis Post-Dispatch 133
Starr, Paul: Creation of the Media 16

"the state" 61–63; media management
    72–74; regulation and the FCC 63–70;
    surveillance 70–72
status 15
Stewart, Jon 94
Stop Online Piracy Act (SOPA)
    168–170, 169
streaming platforms 85
structure 79
subvertising 158
Sulzberger family 56
Swift, Taylor 119

technical subsystem 18
technological affordances 7
technological fundamentalism 100
technology 19
techological determinism 6–7
Telecommunications Act (1996) 46,
    55–56, 162
television: Black Entertainment Televi-
    sion (BET) 36; British television series
    171; cable TV 29, 32, 36, 39, 40, 69,
    131, 148–149; centralization 46; culti-
    vation theory 151; diversity 53; hours
    viewed 96; and LGBTQ identities 122;
    local news 51; news 100, 119; owner-
    ship 56; Parents Television Council
    164; politics shows 94–95; popular
    shows 51; representation of class
    135–139; representation of race
    128–129; representation of women
    114, 115, 116, 117, 118, 119, 121; rev-
    enue 33, 37; sports programming 36
television shows: 2 Broke Girls 137, 138;
    All in the Family 122, 137, 148–149;
    Black-ish 164; Black Mirror 171; The
    Carmichael Show 137; Chicago-themed
    series 138; The Daily Show 94; Glee
    122; Here Comes Honey Boo Boo 137;
    Homeland 117; House of Cards 95, 171;
    How to Get Away With Murder 164; The
    King of Queens 137; The L Word 122;
    The Mary Tyler Moore Show 117;
    M*A*S*H 122; Master of None 129;
    Modern Family 122, 135–136; The
    Office 171; Queer as Folk 122; Raising
    Hope 137; Roseanne 137; Scandal 95,
    117, 122; Sesame Street 40; Sex and the
    City 117; Shameless 137, 171; Sherlock
    171; The Simpsons 120, 137; Supernanny

117; *That Girl* 117; *Trading Spouses* 117; *Two and a Half Men* 145; *Veep* 95; *Weeds* 117; *The West Wing* 94–95; *Wife Swap* 117; *Will & Grace* 122
Terms of Service (TOS) agreements 34
Thakore, Boomi 130
theory 11–13, 23; the cultural diamond 13–23
Thomas, Dorothy Swaine 138
Thomas, W.I. 138
Thunderclap 166
*Time* magazine 31, 80, 147–148
Tor 71
transpartisan institutions 96–97, 98, 103, 109
Tribune Co. 44
trolls and trolling 113, 120–121
*Tropes vs. Women in Video Games* 117
Trump administration 73, 107
Trump, Donald 54, 56, 66–67, 73, 100, 108, 132; the Niger incident 93–94, 99, 101, 105–106, 107, 108
Tuchman, Gaye 80–81
Tucker, Catherine 71
Tumblr 120, 134
Tunisia 120
Twitter 32, 34, 70, 73, 113, 117, 120, 134, 164, 165
typecasting 129

United States Congress 69
United States Constitution 16, 62, 69
Univision 44

Vara, Vauhini 57
Vasi, Ion 152
verification 82
Verizon 68, 71, 168
vertical integration 44, *45*
Viacom 36
*Vice* 106, 107
video games 117–118
video streaming services 171
Vidmar, Neil 148–149
*Vox* 44, 106, 107

Waisbord, Silvio 12

Wall, Melissa 106
*Wall Street Journal (WSJ)* 5, 47, 56
Walt Disney Co. 44
War on Terror 54, 93
war reporting 73
Warner Brothers 116
*Washington Post* 4, 99, 107
web sites: gender and sexuality 113, 120–121
web users 50
Weber, Max 11, 61–62, 86, 156
Wertham, Fredic 22
White House: Correspondents' Dinner (2006) 165; press conferences 72–73
Wikipedia *169*
Williams, Brian 165–166
Williams, Serena 118
Willig, Ida 82
Wilson, Frederica S. 94, 105–106
Wilson, Woodrow 72
Wolf, Maryanne 156
women: in digital cultures 119–121; in Muslim cultures 120; online harassment 121; trolling of 120–121
women, representations of 113, 114; centrality of representation 114, 118–119; numerical representations 114–116, *115*; quality of representation 114, 116–118
Woodward, Bob 5
world 13
World Press Freedom Index 78–79
Wu, Tim 66
Wyatt, Edward 67

Yahoo 34
Yang, Alan 129
The Yes Men 158, *159*
Yorke, Thom 31
YouTube 40, 70, 117, 158
Yuen, Nancy 166

Zang, Yan Bing 145
Zillman, Dolf 153–154
Zuckerberg, Mark 32